My colleagues and I frequently liaise with people from diverse backgrounds and professions when conducting enforcement and prosecution work. Clarity and precision of language is important and a common understanding of regulatory language and principles. This book will be invaluable for assisting with cross-disciplinary discussions.

Anne Brosnan, Chief Prosecutor, Legal Services,
Environment Agency, England

There is no common doctrine, language, or reference point for regulatory professionals. It is critical that all regulatory, enforcement, and policing professionals have a shared language, this book is to regulatory professionals what *Gray's Anatomy* is to health professionals, or Blackstone's manuals are to the UK policing profession. I expect over time it will colloquially be known and referred to as 'Pink's Guide'.

Karen Dahlstrom, Director, Education Design,
Australian Institute of Police Management, Australia

Misunderstandings arising from different interpretations can compromise regulatory effort and negatively impact on achievement of regulatory outcomes. A common professional regulatory language advances regulatory culture and instils a sense of belonging to the regulatory profession.

Keith Manch, Chief Executive Officer,
Civil Aviation Authority, New Zealand

I have worked for and led regulatory 'start-ups' and new agencies formed from the merger of several previously independent regulators. If we had a book like this available to us, we could have been talking the same language from the start saving a lot of effort aligning regulatory cultures.

Rose Webb, Chair,
Australian and New Zealand School of Government (ANZSOG)
National Regulators Community of Practice (NRCoP)

D1613050

NAVIGATING
REGULATORY
LANGUAGE

An A to Z Guide

Over 500 words, terms, and concepts
to assist those working in the regulatory field

To "the Managent Team" at the office of the Scottsh Charity Regulator

Best regards

Grant Pink

Grant

23/2/23

RECAP
Consultants Pty Ltd

Published by RECAP Consultants Pty Ltd
Canberra, Australia
recapconsultants.com.au
admin@recapconsultants.com.au

First published 2021
Copyright © Grant Pink, 2021

The moral right of the author has been asserted.

 A catalogue record for this
book is available from the
National Library of Australia

ISBN: 9780645324303 (hbk)
ISBN: 9780645324310 (pbk)

Editorial Assistance by Karen Pink and Michael Tonge
Illustrations by Nathan Ashley and Alannah Jarvis
Designed and typeset by Helen Christie, Blue Wren Books
Printed by Ingram Spark

DEDICATION

This book is dedicated to the people, whether practitioners, managers, or executives, that work in regulatory and enforcement agencies.

These people:
- face challenges and complexities within an everchanging operating or *authorising environment*;
- seek to establish, hone, and master their own *regulatory practice*, and the broader *regulatory craft*; and
- make sacrifices which are in service of the *wider community* and create *public value*.

The work and efforts of these people are often:
- not fully understood;
- not fully appreciated; and
- not fully supported.

It is intended that the information and advice contained in this book honours the work of these people, and hopefully assists them in advancing their *regulatory profession*.

CONTENTS

PART 3

FOREWORD

In 1746 Dr Samuel Johnson embarked on a project to create a comprehensive dictionary of the English language. Seven years later he completed one of the most remarkable publications in the history of the language, a document that was only superseded over 170 years later by the Oxford English Dictionary (OED). This task took 27 years from its inception to its first publication and has been an ongoing project ever since. The last printed edition ran to 20 volumes.

Grant Pink's book *Navigating Regulatory Language: An A to Z Guide*, though not of the scale of Dr Johnson or the OED, is an important and original contribution to the regulatory lexicon and took considerably less time to complete than the two works described.

Regulation is an arcane field – mysterious, confusing, challenging and, to many who come to it, strange and foreign. Although many glossaries have been compiled in many regulatory books, they are only appendages to the accompanying text, often overlooked and underused, let alone understood.

In this work Grant Pink has attempted to elevate words, terms, and concepts to a central place in a regulator's toolkit. By contributing to the growth of regulatory literacy, this book plays an important part in the development of regulation as a new and independent discipline, one with its own history, language, and concepts. Like the English language itself, regulatory language grows, matures, and expands, but as with many disciplines, it is in danger of becoming arcane and obscure.

Because so many practitioners come to regulation without a background in the discipline, primarily because there are few satisfactory education or training programs in the field, Grant Pink has attempted to make regulatory language clear and accessible. Containing over 500 words, terms and concepts, this singular work provides more information about the foundations of regulation than any other comparable work.

Drawing on his more than three decades' experience as a practitioner, consultant and scholar, Grant brings an impressive breadth of knowledge to the challenging task of making sense of possibly confusing concepts. His background ensures that this work will be of practical assistance to those in the regulatory field, those affected by regulation, and those who develop regulatory policy.

If there is an antonym for the concept of 'high theory', this book is one of 'high practice'. It is one to be used as necessary rather than being read from cover to cover. However, like Dr Johnson's book and the OED, in times of need or doubt, there is no question that what might become known as 'Pink's Guide' will be an invaluable trove of information.

Arie Freiberg
Emeritus Professor
Faculty of Law, Monash University
Australia

ACKNOWLEDGEMENTS

Like any significant project or undertaking, there are many people who have assisted me along the way. In chronological order, I thank:

Karen Dahlstrom – for highlighting the need for a book of this nature, based upon the fact that regulatory practitioners lacked a common vocabulary to advance their knowledge and continuing professional development.

Karen Pink – for encouraging me to get writing again, for letting me test my thinking out loud, and for helping me to get the initial concept into shape. And perhaps above all, for reminding me throughout the writing and review process to keep the focus of the book on being a practical and useful resource.

Michael Tonge – as the first to see and fully consider the initial concept from an applied context, for immediately seeing the usefulness of the book as being of benefit for regulatory practitioners and policy makers. And for casting his 'experienced and expert' eye over numerous iterative drafts along the way.

Karen Pink – again, for reviewing the manuscript numerous times, paying particular attention to cross-referencing across words, terms, and concepts.

Arie Freiberg – for graciously agreeing to contribute to the book's foreword.

Anne Brosnan, Karen Dahlstrom, Keith Manch, and Rose Webb – for providing their testimonial comments for the book.

Nathan Ashley and Alannah Jarvis – for developing the hand drawn illustrations in the book, based upon my thoughts and extremely amateurish sketches.

Samuel Pink – for digitally converting and preparing the artists' illustrations for inclusion in the book.

Helen Christie – for typesetting and designing the layout of the book in such a way that it has made it more accessible and enjoyable for users to read.

To those above, and others who have considered aspects of the book, or politely listened as I bounced ideas off them, thank you all so very much. Your interest and support kept me motivated and focussed so that the book had the best chance of delivering what it aimed to do – and that is to assist and advance the capability, capacity, credibility, and competence of those operating in the regulatory field.

Any shortcomings are mine and mine alone.

PREFACE

The idea for this book had been developing and taking shape for many years, and I had a clear idea as to:

- '*why*' I wanted to produce the book – which was to assist with clearer regulatory communications;
- '*what*' the book would contain – which was key regulatory and enforcement words, terms, concepts, and the like;
- '*who*' would benefit from the book – which included those operating inside and outside of the regulatory profession;
- '*when*' it would most likely be used – which spanned those working in their first regulatory role; a new regulatory role; a related regulatory role; and across regulatory roles;
- '*where*' it would be used – which included in the field, office, boardroom, and study; and
- '*how*' it could be used – which includes by issue, by topic, in a linear fashion, and/or organically in any way that assisted the individual reader.

However, when it came to it, taking the first definitive step was quite difficult. It was difficult because of the:

- diversity and changing nature of the regulatory field itself; and
- varying needs and requirements of those staff now working within and across the regulatory field.

Given the diversity of the target audience, especially in terms of 'how' and 'why' they would 'want to' and/or 'need to' draw upon the book as a resource – I needed to put my mind to not only what type of book it would be, but also what its title would be.

Firstly, regarding the type of book. The book is a cross between a:

- dictionary;
- thesaurus;
- phrasebook; and
- handbook.

Secondly, regarding its title. I felt strongly and was committed that the title should accurately reflect the nature, contents, and usefulness of the book.

I went with *Navigating Regulatory Language: An A to Z Guide* – I hope it meets the self-imposed brief!

INTRODUCTION

Why regulatory literacy matters

As mentioned, the main purpose for writing this book was to provide the reader with greater clarity across various regulatory words, terms, and concepts. Specifically, words, terms, and concepts that:

- **can be so similar** – that they are frequently used interchangeably without issue – these can be referred to as **'same-same' words**;
- **appear similar on the surface, or at first pass** – but which there is a difference (sometimes a significant difference) that only appears after time – these can be referred to as **'same-but-different' words**; and
- **are so different** – that their confused and conflated use can be incredibly divisive, damaging, and deleterious to effective *regulatory delivery* and achieving *regulatory outcomes* – these can be referred to as **'completely-different' words**.

To highlight the importance of literacy as a part of a profession, it is helpful for us to look beyond the regulatory profession for a moment. When considering the medical profession, irrespective of whether the person is a nurse, general practitioner (i.e., medical doctor), surgeon, or specialist surgeon – they all learn, use, and master a common and shared literacy. This is because much of the medical professions' literacy is derived from seminal works and reference material such as the book *Gray's Anatomy*.[1]

The benefits of investing in regulatory literacy

Basic *regulatory literacy* and regulatory communications matter. They matter because they help to improve:

- *regulatory capability*;
- *regulatory capacity*;

- *regulator performance*;
- *regulatory outcomes*; and
- a range of other matters that shape *regulatory culture*.

Developing, maintaining, and advancing *regulatory literacy* is a key aspect of:
- establishing the *regulatory profession* as a profession in its own right; and
- the need for ever increasing professionalism in relation to *regulatory practice* and *regulatory delivery*.

Factors shaping a book to advance regulatory literacy

The idea for this book comes from the experiences of the author, including their:
- initial introduction and induction – into the regulatory and enforcement fields;
- performing different roles – in and across regulatory and enforcement functions;
- transitioning to different regulatory and enforcement agencies – that used various methods to implement and operationalise regulation;
- managing different regulatory functions – within and across different levels of government; and
- leading different regulatory issues – across various and intersecting tactical, operational, and strategic matters.

The author's views are based over a 30-year period and are drawn from six (6) distinct, and very different, but mutually reinforcing roles. Including as a:
- *regulatory practitioner*;
- *regulatory manager*;
- *regulatory executive*;
- regulatory scholar;
- regulatory consultant; and
- regulatory coach and mentor.

Over this 30-year period, and across all roles, the most common issue that the author saw that was preventing or limiting the successful or optimal delivery of *regulatory functions* – was an inability for *regulators* to effectively communicate with one another, due to the lack of a common and shared vocabulary.

In many cases this arose or was exacerbated due to an inability to understand and/or articulate key regulatory concepts. More specifically it was an inability to communicate clearly and concisely:
• across different *regulatory functions*;
• across different *regulatory activities*; and
• across different professions, both internal and external to what might be described as the *regulatory profession*.

In numerous situations this recurring issue would present itself in conversations, which contained similar features to the example outlined below. Namely:
• what, they said (e.g., ABC);
• what, I heard (e.g., DEF);
• what, they meant or intended to say (e.g., GHI); and
• what, I understood or interpreted them to say (e.g., JKL).

Therefore, the primary focus, aim, and intent of this book is that it be a resource for collating, clarifying, and creating information. It is in the form of a repository that will facilitate greater consistency in terms of *regulatory language*.

Domestic and international application

The author's experience covers both Australian and international contexts. Therefore, while some of the concepts are drawn from common law jurisdictions, the concepts in the book are intended to be broadly applicable internationally.

For this reason, *regulatory practitioners, managers* and *executives* have been consulted to ensure that their experiences and needs have shaped the contents of this book. This is critically important as a collective, clearer, and more consistent understanding of, and use of *regulatory language*, is central to establishing and advancing *regulatory practice* and *regulatory professionalism*.

Further exploration of regulatory literacy

The notes and in-text references and reference list provide the reader with additional resources. These resources expand upon, and enable further exploration of, the issues and topics covered in this book in greater detail.

For example, this book may direct readers to the encyclopaedic nature of Freiberg 2017. This is because, typically:

- where this book has two sentences – Freiberg has two paragraphs;
- where this book has two paragraphs – Freiberg has two pages; and
- where this book has two pages – Freiberg has ten pages, or might even dedicate an entire chapter.

The quotes in the image below operate as bookends and serve as a reminder as to the purpose of this book, that is – improving *regulatory literacy*. With improving *regulatory literacy* having flow on effects to:

- enhancing *regulatory delivery*; and
- advancing the *regulatory profession*.

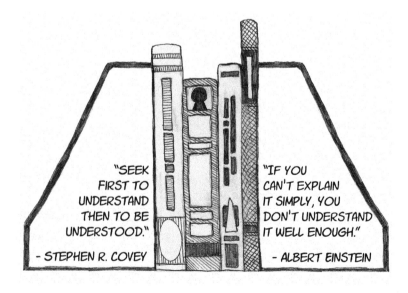

"SEEK FIRST TO UNDERSTAND THEN TO BE UNDERSTOOD."

- STEPHEN R. COVEY

"IF YOU CAN'T EXPLAIN IT SIMPLY, YOU DON'T UNDERSTAND IT WELL ENOUGH."

- ALBERT EINSTEIN

Part 1

USING THIS BOOK

KEY AND QUICK GUIDE

If you started reading this book from the beginning, you may have noticed words, terms and concepts that are italicised. In this book if something is italicised it is important enough to have its own listing.

Regulatory language – which includes and spans words, terms, concepts, phrases, and frameworks – can overlap and intermix to a large extent.

For this reason, this book contains a significant amount of cross-referencing. The table below has been developed to assist the reader.

Descriptor	Explanation and example
bold and italics	Some words, terms, and concepts that are listed under the *see also* section are in *bold and italics*: • These are expanded on in Part 3 of the book. **Extended Regulatory Spectrum** is one such example
notes	Are used as a combination of in-text referencing and to direct the reader to additional information or relevant readings
italics	Words, terms, and concepts that are in *italics* throughout this book have their own corresponding listing
see	At the top of a listing if there are words, terms, and concepts within brackets, this directs the reader to another relevant listing which contains a full description. For example: • **Frameworks** (see Regulatory Frameworks)
see also	At the bottom of a listing in brackets there are words, terms, and concepts that direct the reader to relevant similar or related listings. For example: • Regulatory Officer (see also: Authorised Officer; Inspector; Investigator; Warden)
shading	Shading is used to highlight important information

Note of Caution

Many of the words, terms, and concepts in this book are:
- based upon, intersect with, or have specific legal, operational, scientific, or technical meanings, and
  - if specialist (legal, operational, scientific, or technical) reference material is available that covers the issues in greater detail – then these resources should be explored further, after considering the information in this book; and
- used in a way which can imply a specific or slightly different meaning within a *jurisdiction*, industry, sector, or for a *regulated commodity*, and
  - if specific (jurisdictional, industry, sector, or *regulated commodity*) reference material is available that covers the issues in greater detail – then these resources should be explored further, after considering the information in this book.

Practical Tip

Given the note of caution above, to derive additional benefits from the book, readers may find it is useful to undertake the following three step process:
- Step 1 – select words or topics of interest, from listings within this book;
- Step 2 – identify and locate relevant regulatory documents (i.e., policies, procedures, and practice notes), that are also of interest to them;
- Step 3 – either manually check the hard copy documents or use the word search function on their computer to check electronic documents, to find the words or topics of interest selected in Step 1.

The important thing is to check relevant regulatory documents to see how these words, terms, and concepts:
- are used;
- relate to other corresponding/adjacent words; and
- provide additional information or insights which influence general and specific usage in your regulatory and enforcement context.

PEOPLE WHO MIGHT USE THIS BOOK

The three main groups

There are three (3) main groups of people who are likely to benefit from using this book:

Group 1 – are internal to government and have core (operational) regulatory responsibilities, functions, and interests. They include:

1. *regulatory officers*, also including auditors, standards setters, and technical advisors;
2. legal professionals, lawyers, and prosecutors; and
3. commodity (or subject matter) experts.

Group 2 – are also internal to government and have non-core (operational) regulatory responsibilities, functions, and interests. They include:

1. policy officers;
2. allied professionals (e.g., accountants, and engineers); and
3. other non-regulatory officers (both within the same *regulatory agency* and/or partner agencies).

Group 3 – are external to government and are either subject to regulations and/or are affected by or have interests in how regulation is delivered. They include:

1. *regulated entities*;
2. *stakeholders*;
3. the *wider community*; and
4. students and scholars of regulatory theory and regulatory practice.

The main group – Group 1

Group 1 are the core and target audience for this book. Therefore, the book is framed and directed towards assisting them in their daily work.

The people who are in and/or who identify with Group 1 often have very different perspectives and viewpoints, from each other, based upon:

- different practices and professional backgrounds;
- different training shaped by different professional disciplines; and
- different disciplinary languages.

Group 1 – the four main types of people and their typical backgrounds

Within Group 1 there are four (4) different types of people who are likely to benefit from using this book.

For example, if you are accessing the information in this book, it is likely that you have:

1. **recently joined the 'regulatory fold'** – and are on your own transition journey – where many of the 'regulatory' terms and phrases being used are unfamiliar to you, and you have not had time to develop an applied context, to assist embedding of their meaning;

2. **been working in the regulatory field for some time** – and are quite comfortable using 'regulatory terminology' in your own operating environment – and are already aware of how problematic different meanings and interpretations of 'regulatory' words can be when working with other *regulatory agencies* and *internal regulatory bodies* (and sometimes even in other areas of your own agency);

3. **been operating in an allied profession** – and associate with or work alongside those operating in regulatory fields, and are experiencing the challenges of communicating across disciplines due to a lack of consistent language; or

4. **found yourself having to interact with and operate alongside people who speak a 'regulatory language'** – but it is becoming clear that it is one of many 'regulatory dialects'.

Irrespective of how it is that you have come to be here, considering this book, it is likely that you already have a sense of how complicated, complex, and confusing it can be to 'speak fluent regulation!' These communication challenges:

- at best – frustrate effective *regulatory delivery*; and
- at worst – not only prevent any form of appropriate or beneficial *regulatory delivery* from occurring but reinforce or fuel the criticisms of *regulators* that they can be overly bureaucratic, insensitive to stakeholder concerns, and act as an impediment to businesses.

HOW PEOPLE MIGHT USE THIS BOOK

Given the diversity of backgrounds and professions that readers will be coming from, coupled with their different and changing operating contexts, it is anticipated that people will use this book in different ways for different reasons.

Listed on the pages that follow are four examples (or personas), which are based upon four (4) typical categories of reader that are likely to benefit from using this book.

NON-REGULATORY OFFICER	REGULATORY OFFICER
'I am new to the regulatory agency. It's almost like everyone is speaking a different language!'	'Investigations and enforcement are my bread and butter – regulation is just like enforcement, just softer.'

REGULATORY MANAGER	**REGULATORY EXECUTIVE**
'As regulators we have more in common than we have differences – this is about agency nuance.'	'I need to understand how this regulatory work supports and feeds into policy and strategy.'

Example 1: Non-Regulatory Officer
(with no previous regulatory experience)

Alicia recently joined the Media and Communications Division of a *regulatory agency*. While a trained and qualified media and communications professional with over five years' experience, this is her first exposure to regulatory work.

During her first few weeks, Alicia was involved in several meetings. In these meetings she repeatedly heard reference to the words 'advice' and 'guidance' being used separately, and the phrase '*advice and guidance*' used collectively. Often the context in which these words, and this phrase was used, was not familiar to Alicia either from a layperson's perspective or from the perspective of a media and communications professional.

Alicia would therefore use this book to look up *advice and guidance* and would consider its description. In doing so she would also see reference to other suggestions that 'general or specific *advice and guidance* might also relate to that which is intended to:
- assist a *regulated entity* to avoid instances of *non-compliance*; and
- assist a *regulated entity* to return to *compliance*.'

Alicia would also see reference to and be directed towards the *Extended Regulatory Spectrum (ERS)*. Where once again she would consider its description, and would learn of the other five phases of the *ERS*, namely:
- *Regulatory Regime Design;*
- *Licensing and Approvals;*
- *Monitoring Compliance;*
- *Enforcement;* and
- *Regulator Performance and Evaluation.*

She would also be directed to Part 3 of the book, as the **Extended Regulatory Spectrum** would appear in bold and italics in the 'see also' part of the listing.

By using this book, in this organic way, Alicia would more fully and completely understand the general and specific context of what *advice and guidance* means when used by *regulatory practitioners*, *regulatory managers*, and *regulatory executives*.

Example 2: Regulatory Officer
(from a mainstream law enforcement background)

Brian recently joined the Investigations and Enforcement Division of a *regulatory agency*. Brian's previous job saw him serve for twenty years as a police officer. As a police officer, he was trained and qualified as an *investigator*, specialising in *fraud* and other criminal matters. This however is his first role in a *regulatory agency*.

As part of conducting his first regulatory investigation Brian had cause to speak to, and take *witness statements* from, several scientific and technical staff. During the statement preparation process, it became clear to Brian that these non-regulatory staff had little or no knowledge around key investigative or evidentiary terms and processes such as:
- *burden of proof;*
- *chain of custody*; and
- *evidence* (including *expert evidence* and *opinion evidence*).

As Brian was preparing a *brief of evidence*, for a contested matter, the agency's *regulatory executives* were discussing *alternate dispute resolution* options, following receipt of a letter of negotiation from the *regulated entity's* legal representatives. The *regulatory executives* operating as the *compliance management committee* were keen to obtain Brian's views (as the lead *investigator*), on what non-criminal or non-prosecutorial options might be available.

This was foreign to Brian as all the matters he investigated in the Police were *crimes*, and if pursued always resulted in criminal prosecutions. Therefore, Brian had either never heard of, or lacked any case specific experience with:

- *civil remedies/responses/sanctions;*
- *enforceable undertakings;* and
- *injunctions.*

By using this book, Brian would more fully and completely understand the differences between:

- criminal investigations – focussing on and resulting in criminal prosecutions; and
- broader regulatory investigations – with a range of available options that can assist, advance, and enable achieving *regulatory outcomes.*

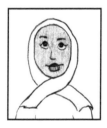

Example 3: Regulatory Manager
(with experience in other regulatory agencies)

Chandra recently joined the Compliance Monitoring Branch of a *regulatory agency.* Chandra is very experienced, with significant experience both as a *regulatory officer* and *regulatory manager.*

Chandra's regulatory background is diverse. She commenced and performed a *regulatory officer* role for five years in an economic regulator (i.e., one that regulated financial institutions), before she was promoted and moved into a *regulatory manager* role in the same agency for another five-year period. Chandra then transferred, as a *regulatory manager*, to another *regulatory agency* (i.e., one which focussed on environmental matters) for another five years.

So, Chandra comes to this her new *regulatory agency* and one that focuses on social regulation (i.e., one that regulates health benefit claims) with 15 years regulatory experience, notably 10 of which were as a *regulatory manager*.

Despite all her experience, Chandra knows that this is a different *regulatory agency* which deals with different *regulated entities*, has a different *regulatory posture*, and has responsibility for different *regulatory outcomes*. This means that she will most likely use this book in two ways:

- firstly, to calibrate her previous regulatory experiences with those required to perform her new regulatory role effectively; and
- secondly, to discuss and test the finer points of distinction and differences with her new team members and management peers.

Example 4: Regulatory Executive
(with no previous regulatory experience)

Duane is an experienced Senior Executive Service officer, having operated at this level for eight years. Duane has worked in two different agencies in three separate roles which involved policy development and service delivery.

Duane has recently been appointed to lead the Compliance and Regulatory Division. While experienced in making *administrative decisions*, this is Duane's first job where he has oversight of:

- regulatory *decisions;*
- *regulatory discretion;*
- *regulatory delivery;* and
- *regulatory outcomes.*

It is also the first time he has worked with *regulatory officers*, let alone had them reporting to him. Therefore, the following concepts are foreign to him:

- *brief of evidence;*
- *monitoring warrant* and *search warrant;*
- *prosecutorial discretion;* and
- *reasonable cause to believe* and *reasonable cause to suspect.*

By using this book, with reference to key words, terms, and concepts, as he has interactions with regulatory staff (i.e., in either broad regulatory discussions or specific case review meetings) Duane would more fully and completely understand the difference between what constitutes:

- *regulatory activities;*
- *regulatory functions;* and
- *regulatory outcomes.*

THE 6-4-3 CODE

There are three (3) concepts that appear often in this book. They provide a useful thread, and a central point of reference for the reader. They are the:

- *Extended Regulatory Spectrum*;
- *Four Key Regulatory Perspectives*; and
- *Three Levels of Operational Activity*

These key concepts are considered:

- individually and in relation to their component parts, in Part 2; and
- in their entirety, in Part 3, where three (3) additional concepts are introduced.

Three key concepts: Individual overview and usage

Given their significance it is worth providing a brief introduction here.

The **Extended Regulatory Spectrum** (ERS) is a framework that describes the six phases of regulatory activity.

Regulatory Regime Design	Advice and Guidance	Licensing and Approvals	Monitoring Compliance	Enforcement	Regulator Performance and Evaluation

(Source: Grant Pink, 2018) [2]

The first and last phases act as bookends, spanning the period from when *regulation* or a *regulatory regime/scheme* is designed, through until where the *regulator* evaluates and reports on its own performance.

The four central (shaded) phases are those *regulatory activities* that are *operational* in nature, and therefore more aligned with *regulatory practice* and *regulatory delivery*.

The **Four Key Regulatory Perspectives** (4KRP) include and reflect the four main regulatory actors: *regulator; regulated; stakeholders;* and *wider community.* The 4KRP appear in a matrix below.

Regulator	Regulated
Includes *co-* and *peer- regulators*, from regulatory and enforcement agencies (whether in the same or different level of government)	Those directly subjected to *regulation* (usually but not always by explicit *authorisation*)
Stakeholders	**Wider Community**
With clear interests and stakes in *regulation* (e.g., peak bodies representing *regulated entities*)	As the name suggests, the *wider community* (e.g., some may identify as *stakeholders*)

The **Three Levels of Operational Activity** (3LOA) within *regulatory practice* are: *tactical, operational,* and *strategic.* In this order or sequence (as outlined in the table below) the activities reflect a move from individual and specific to collective and general.

Level	Type and nature of regulatory activity
Tactical	Individual *breach* or case with a single *regulated entity*.
Operational	Group of *breaches* or cases, involving either multiple sites for the same *regulated entity*, and/or multiple (inter-related) *regulated entities*.
Strategic	System-wide/systemic *breaches*, cases or matters that involve multiple sites, *regulated entities*, regulated industries, sectors, or sub-sectors.

Three key concepts: Combined usage

As outlined above, the three key concepts are significant individually in their own right.

However, enhanced utility comes in using them in unison. This can occur by contrasting them against one another or considering them in a more systematic way.

For example, when considering a word, term, phrase, or concept it may be useful to follow the **6-4-3** code!

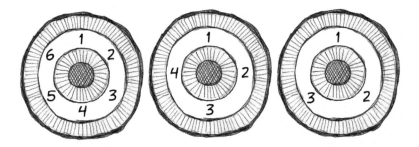

The **6-4-3** code asks …
- in which of the **6** phases …
- through which of the **4** perspectives …
- occurring within which of the **3** levels …
- … is the word, term, or concept anchored or spanning?

Part 2

REGULATORY WORDS, TERMS, AND CONCEPTS

Absolute Liability Offence

From a *regulator's* perspective, an *absolute liability offence* is an *offence* that:
- the *regulator* is only required to prove that the *physical act* (or *actus reus*) occurred;
- the *regulator* is **not** required to prove that the *accused* had any intention (or *mens rea*) to commit the *offence*; and
- the *accused* has no defence of mistaken belief (of facts) to them.

An example of an *absolute liability offence*, in a customs and border protection context, would be importation of a prohibited item (e.g., illegal drugs and weapons).

(see also: Strict Liability Offence)

Accountable/Accountability

From a *regulator's* perspective, to be *accountable* or have *accountability*, is a reference to demonstrating *compliance* with the:
- *Principles of Good Regulation*; and
- forms the **A** in the associated *PACTT* acronym.

It is important for *regulators* to consider *accountability* holistically, with:
- the *regulator* being *accountable* for its actions and decisions, with *accountability* extending to and including *co- and peer- regulators, regulated entities, stakeholders*, and the *wider community*; and
- the *regulator* being willing and able to explain, justify; and document its regulatory actions and decisions to:

- Ministers, through a *regulatory statement of intent* and lines of reporting;
- Parliament, through senate estimates or parliamentary committees (or equivalent); and
- the *executive* arm of government generally.

(see also: PACTT; Principles of Good Regulation)

Accreditation

Recognition that the party undertaking the activity has the appropriate training, qualification, competence, and systems in place to provide the products, services, or support.

For *regulators,* it is important that *accreditation* be from some authoritative body, ideally with suitability having been assessed independently and objectively to determine that the required and recognised standards are achieved or met.

(see also: Authorisation; Approval/s)

Accused

Person or *regulated entity* who has been *accused* in a court of law, either civil or criminal, of having done something wrong.

In a linear sense: *suspect, accused, defendant.*

(see also: Claimant; Defendant; Plaintiff; Suspect)

Act/s

Typically reference to an *act of parliament.* However, *act/s* can also be used interchangeably with many of the words/phrases listed under *regulation.*

(see also: Act of Parliament; Legislation; Regulation/s)

Act of Parliament

Are sometimes referred to as *primary legislation*. They are law which has been passed by the relevant legislative body within a *jurisdiction*. An *act of parliament* will often commence as a *bill*.

(see also: Act/s; Bill; Legislation)

Actus Reus [Latin]

A Latin phrase translating to 'guilty act'. A more modern term used would be the 'physical act' of a *crime* or *breach*.

Regulator's must prove or establish the *actus reus,* as an essential element of certain *offences*, to secure a conviction.

(see also: Fault Element; Mens Rea [Latin])

Administrative Appeals Tribunal (AAT)

Most *jurisdictions* have an *AAT* or equivalent body. These bodies conduct an independent *merits review* of administrative decisions made by *regulators.*

A *merits review* involves a person or body ('the reviewer'), other than the original primary decision-maker, reconsidering all the issues (whether: facts, law, or policy) associated with the original decision. The reviewer then determines what is the correct and/or preferable decision.

For example, a *regulated entity* who was refused an *authorisation* by a *regulator,* or had their *authorisation* varied, suspended, or revoked by a *regulator* through use of *administrative powers,* could appeal the matter to an *AAT* or equivalent body.

(see also: Merits Review)

Administrative Burdens

Are usually considered and discussed from the perspective of *regulated entities* and *stakeholders.* These groups tend to describe *administrative burdens* as being requirements or processes that they find unnecessary or onerous in terms of implementing their regulatory requirements. Generally, these burdens are explained as three types of costs: informational; compliance; and opportunity. For example:

- informational costs – are the costs typically associated with sourcing, providing, considering, and analysing information associated with qualifying for, entering, and participating within a *regulatory regime/scheme*;
- *compliance* costs – are the costs associated with ongoing participation in a *regulatory regime/scheme*, including:
  - the cost of acquiring new plant and equipment, training of staff, and updating internal policies, processes, and procedures; and
  - annual *licence* fees, preparing for, participating in, and responding to requests for *audits*, *inspections*, and other requests from the *regulator*; and
- opportunity costs – are the costs associated with not being able to get to the 'real' or actual business that the *regulated entity* engages in, because they are spending an inordinate amount of time on informational and *compliance* costs.

(see also: Regulatory Burden)

Administrative Case/Matter

An *administrative case/matter* involves the *regulator* operating in and making decisions in the administrative sphere of its operations.

As opposed to considering referring the matter as part of civil or criminal proceedings.

Examples of an *administrative case/matter* might include decisions and actions taken in respect to *licensing and approvals* or broader *authorisation* matters.

(see also: Civil Case/Matter; Criminal Case/Matter)

Administrative Law

Administrative law controls the activities (i.e., through procedures, *rules*, and *regulations*) of government *decision-making*.

Administrative law enables *regulatory agencies* and/or government agencies to: make *rules* about; adjudicate upon; and take regulatory actions within their regulatory remit.

Administrative law has several accountability mechanisms, including:

- *alternate dispute resolution;*
- *judicial review;* and
- *merits review.*

(see also: Administrative Appeals Tribunal; Alternate Dispute Resolution; Judicial Review; Merits Review; Natural Justice; Procedural Fairness)

Administrative Powers

Enable the administration or *enforcement* of a law. *Administrative powers* can be exercised by the different arms of government: i.e., *the executive, the legislature,* or *the judiciary.*

Administrative powers bring the *laws* into effect, with practical and discretionary application of *laws.*

For example, a *regulator* uses *administrative power* to either issue or refuse to issue an *authorisation* to a *regulated entity.* And then once issued, if need be, the *regulator* can then use *administrative powers* to vary, suspend or revoke the original (and/or relevant and related) *authorisation.*

(see also: Administrative Appeals Tribunal; Ultra Vires)

Administrative Remedy/Response/Sanction[3]

For *regulators* the terms remedy/ies, response/s, and sanction/s tend to be used interchangeably, interrelatedly, and collectively.

An *administrative remedy* tends to come in the form of or be part of a response or sanction.

An *administrative response* is a response used by a *regulator* when drawing upon the *administrative power* they have access to. Often an *administrative response* will be used either as an alternative to or in parallel with a *civil response* or a *criminal response.*

An example of when an *administrative response* is typically used is when a *regulator* establishes, or a *regulated entity* admits, a *breach* of a *licence* condition. The *regulator,* using their *administrative powers,* will initiate an *administrative response* resulting in the variation, suspension, or revocation of the *licence* (or *authorisation*) in question.

An *administrative sanction* is a penalty imposed by *regulators* itself, and under their own *authority.*[4]

For *regulators*, and depending on the *jurisdiction*, the main *administrative sanctions* typically include:

- *warnings* and *cautions*;
- *infringement notices*;[5]
- improvement notices; and
- seizure and forfeiture notices/orders.

There are other *sanctions*, depending on the *jurisdiction*, that can be defined as *administrative sanctions*.[6]

(see also: Civil Remedy/Response/Sanction; Criminal Remedy/Response/Sanction; Sanctions)

Admissibility of Evidence

There is a general rule that all irrelevant *evidence* is inadmissible, and that all relevant *evidence* is admissible.

In considering and determining whether *evidence* is admissible or not, the issues of relevance and reliability need to be considered. In terms of:

- relevance – the *evidence* must assist in proving or disproving an important or central fact in the matter,
  - if the *evidence* does not relate to a particular (important and central) fact, it will most likely be considered irrelevant and therefore most likely inadmissible; and
- reliability – refers to the source of and/or the credibility of the *evidence*,
  - this usually relates to the source of the information (e.g., a *regulator's authorisations* database) and the oral testimony of a *witness* (e.g., who attests to the integrity, maintenance, and security of the data contained within the database).

(see also: Evidence)

ADR (see Alternate Dispute Resolution)

Adverse Publicity Orders

Are a form of *regulatory response* or *sanction*. They tend to be used more in *administrative* and *civil matters*, than in *criminal matters*.

Adverse publicity orders typically direct a *regulated entity* to prepare, produce, disclose, and publish information in an advertisement (either in print or online) about their *non-compliance* or *breach*.

(see also: Name and Shame)

Advice and Guidance

Advice and guidance is a regulatory activity which involves communicating regulatory requirements to *regulated entities* (and in some instances to other *regulators; stakeholders;* and the *wider community*). The:

- purpose of *advice and guidance* is to encourage the *regulated community* to act in accordance with the *law,* by promoting the aims of the *regulation* and the *regulatory regime/scheme;* and
- aim of *advice and guidance* is to encourage and assist *regulated entities* to achieve *compliance* voluntarily.

In a linear sense, it is the second of six phases contained in the *Extended Regulatory Spectrum.*

Advice and guidance is about the setting of expectations of *compliance* and performance on *regulated entities* by the *regulator.* It includes information, which can take the form of either general or specific *advice and guidance,* relating to:

- the background, history, and general intent of the *regulations* (i.e., *regulatory regime/scheme*);
- the general nature and type of any *approvals* (or similar) that are required to operate or function within the *regulatory regime/scheme;*
- any general and/or mandatory conditions associated with any *approval;*
- any specific conditions, that may be put in place depending on a range of factors associated with any *approval;* or

- any general or specific *advice and guidance* to:
  - assist a *regulated entity* to avoid instances of *non-compliance*; and
  - assist a *regulated entity* to return to *compliance*.

(see also: **Extended Regulatory Spectrum**)

Advisory

Refers to guidance issued by and/or available from a *regulatory authority*.

(see also: Advice and Guidance)

Affidavit

Is a *written statement* confirmed by oath or affirmation, for use as *evidence* in court, or in a disputed matter.

(see also: Statutory Declaration; Witness Statement)

Agency Capture

Is a term used to suggest that an agency has been 'captured' by the very parties that it is meant to regulate. The suggestion is that a captured *regulator*, has lost its independence or objectivity and tends to act in a way that is more advantageous to the *regulated entity*.

The term is used widely in the USA, the broader and more common term would be *regulatory capture*.

(see also: Regulatory Capture; Regulatory Independence)

AGIS
(see Australian Government Investigation Standards)

Agreed Facts

Are those facts, that have been agreed to by the parties (in a *contested matter* or appeal).

The *agreed facts* are often provided in writing and are submitted to the independent arbiter/decision-maker (e.g., commissioner, judge, magistrate).

Agreed facts can be used as a basis to narrow or finalise a *contested matter*, in respect to the latter they often shape the nature of the ruling and/or penalty.

(see also: Alternate Dispute Resolution)

Agreements

Are *agreements* between parties which are often negotiated and are typically legally binding.

In a regulatory sense, *agreements* can be standalone, but often relate to or intersect with other forms of *authorisations* held by a *regulated entity*.

(see also: Authorisation)

ALARA
(see As Low As Reasonably Achievable/Allowable)

ALARP (see As Low As Reasonably Practicable)

Allegation

Is a claim or assertion that someone has done something illegal or wrong. Noting that an *allegation* can be made without proof.

For a *regulator*, it is information which suggests that a *regulated entity* has either committed a *crime* or has done something (or has omitted to do something), which puts them in *breach* of their regulatory *obligations*.

Alternate Dispute Resolution (ADR)

Includes a variety of processes that aim to assist parties to resolve (or at least focus and narrow) disputes, without the need for a *trial* or some form of *litigation*. Typical *ADR* processes include *arbitration*, mediation, and settlement conferences.

(see also: Litigation; Prosecution)

Alternate to Prosecution
(see Alternate Dispute Resolution)

Annual Operational Plans (AOPs)

Set out the priorities, objectives, and strategies that a *regulator* will focus on each year (or 12-month period) as part of:

- undertaking its *regulatory activities*;
- performing its *regulatory functions*, and
- pursuing its *regulatory outcomes*.

AOPs sit below (and provide finer levels of detail) and are complementary to a *regulator's regulatory strategy* (or equivalent). For example, *AOPs* might focus on certain:

- industries, sectors, or commodities (or sub-sets of);
- geographic locations;
- parts of a supply-chain, or transit routes;
- *offences* or legal provisions in the *legislation*; or
- risk or harm profiles.

(see also: Regulatory Operations; Regulatory Strategy; *Three Levels of Operational Activity*)

Anticipatory Regulation

Anticipatory regulation is a concept that involves *regulators* looking ahead to develop *regulation*, especially *regulation* that seeks to:

- operate in extreme and unanticipated circumstances – such as regulating the banking and financial sector during a global financial crisis, or regulating human health during a pandemic; or
- address emerging technologies – such as artificial intelligence generally, or the introduction and use of drones specifically.

The six principles of *anticipatory regulation* are:

- Inclusive and collaborative;
- Future-facing;
- Proactive;
- Iterative;
- Outcomes-based; and
- Experimental.[7]

(see also: Regulatory Posture; Regulatory Regime Design; Regulatory Statement of Intent)

Approval/s

An *approval*, in a regulatory sense, can either be:

- standalone, in that it is an *approval* by a *regulator* (or relevant body) for a *regulated entity* to carry out some activity; or
- can form part of a larger *authorisation*.

For example, a *regulated entity* may be issued with:

- a standalone *approval* in the form of a *licence* to enter a *regulatory regime/scheme,* such as customs (import and export) brokering; and
- a series of *approvals* to modify the countries, travel routes, and commodities listed and traded in the initial customs (import and export) brokering licence.

(see also: Authorisation; Licence; Permit)

Arbitration

A form of *alternate dispute resolution (ADR)* and a way to resolve disputes between parties outside of the *courts,* through an impartial and enforceable method. *Arbitration* can be either voluntary or mandatory.

The *arbitration* process is structured and involves strict *rules* and procedures, such as the giving of *evidence* and the cross-examination of *witnesses.* An independent arbitrator makes a *determination,* which is final and legally-binding on all parties.

(see also: Alternate Dispute Resolution; Determination; Litigation; Prosecution)

As Low As Reasonably Achievable/Allowable (ALARA)

Is reference to a threshold of what is:

- possible for a *regulated entity* to achieve or meet; and
- allowable (and therefore acceptable) to a *regulator.*

(see also: Compliance; Compliant)

As Low As Reasonably Practicable (ALARP)
(see As Low As Reasonably Achievable/Allowable)

Assisted Compliance

Assisted compliance is when the *regulator* provides additional information and support to those *regulated entities* who are attempting to comply, but for some reason are *non-compliant*.

Diagrammatically, it is the second of four phases contained in the *VADE Model.*

(see also: Directed Compliance; Enforced Compliance; *VADE Model*; Voluntary Compliance)

Audit/s

For *regulators,* an *audit* is an official *inspection* or examination to verify that: a *regulated entity* is *compliant* with its regulatory requirements; and/ or has put in place improvements following previous instances of *non-compliance*.

Audits are often carried out by an independent and external party, often with specialist skills (e.g., financial, technical, or scientific) as part of *compliance monitoring*.

As *audits* form part of a *regulator's compliance monitoring* program, they can be used proactively or reactively and be scheduled or random.

(see also: Certification; *Extended Regulatory Spectrum*; Verification)

Auditing (see Audit/s)

Australian Government Investigation Standards (AGIS)

The *AGIS* establish the minimum standards for Australian Government (regulatory, enforcement and policing) agencies who have responsibility for conducting *investigations*. With these standards applying to all stages of an *investigation*:

- commencing with 'receiving and recording alleged, apparent or potential breaches';[8] and
- concluding with 'quality assurance reviews of investigations'.[9]

The *AGIS* have been developed, by the Attorney-General's Department in Australia, as a means of ensuring greater consistency and quality investigative practices and outcomes.

(see also: Investigation Guidelines/Standards)

Authorisation

In a regulatory sense, *authorisation* can be a reference to both a process and an end state. For example, in terms of:
- a process – a *regulated entity* might describe that they are in the process of seeking an *authorisation* (or even renewal of an *authorisation*) of some form from the *regulator*,
  - if so, they are completing forms, having their premises inspected, and in certain circumstances would be subject to some form of 'fit and proper' test; and
- an end state – they would have received an *authorisation*, which might be temporary or permanent, and restricted or unrestricted,
  - if so, they would possess an *authorisation* (of which there are many types)[10] which provides them, as a *regulated entity*, permission to do something which would otherwise be *unlawful*.

(see also: Accreditation; Approval; Authority; Compliance History; Fit and Proper (Person) Test; Licence; Permission; Permit; Registration)

Authorised Officer (see Regulatory Officer)

Authorising Entry (to a Premises)

Regulators frequently need to enter *premises* as part of carrying out their *regulatory functions*.

While possible, it is rare that a *regulator* would be invited by *regulated entities* to enter *premises* as part of a general meeting or similar. Attending a *premise* would most often be part of a *regulator's* formal role, and therefore linked to their *statutory authority*.

Regulators, can enter *premises*:
- by *consent* – noting that *consent* needs to be given voluntarily, without threat or inducement, and *consent* should be able to be withdrawn at any time without penalty;

- by use of their *regulatory powers* – with their *regulatory powers* being clear, and that information being readily available to *regulated entities*, and *stakeholders*; and
- by use of *coercive powers* and or special instruments – typically involving a *monitoring warrant* or *search warrant*.

(see also: Coercive Powers; Consent; Monitoring Warrant; Premises; Regulatory Powers; Search Warrant)

Authorising Entry (to a Regulatory Scheme)

A broad (often all-encompassing) term/phrase relating to a range of entry controls that *regulators* have at their disposal, which authorise *regulated entities* to undertake certain activities within a regulated industry, sector, market, or scheme.

Provides permission for a *regulated entity* to undertake a particular activity, which without a specific *permission* would otherwise be *unlawful*.

(see also: Approval; Authorisation; Licence; Permit; Registration)

Authorising Environment

A *regulator's* mandate to deliver their functions is shaped by their *authorising environment*.[11]

The *authorising environment* of a *regulator* is dynamic and is subject to change. There are numerous variables that can initially shape and then subsequently alter a *regulator's authorising environment*. Variables include, but are not limited to the:

- *laws* that the *regulator* administers;
- type and profile of the sectors, industries, and commodities regulated;
- budget and resources of the *regulator*;
- level of political support provided to the *regulator*; and
- level of acceptance, support, and overall relationship with affected parties, principally:
  - peer- and *co- regulators*
  - *regulated entities*
  - *stakeholders*
  - *wider community.*

(see also: Regulatory Mandate; Regulatory Pendulum; Regulatory Posture)

Authoritative Precedent (see Binding Precedent)

Balance of Probability/ies

Is the standard of proof required in *civil cases/matters.*

The *balance of probability* standard means that a *court* (or arbiter) is satisfied on the *evidence* available that it is more likely than not to have occurred.

In percentage terms, probability that some event happens is more than 50%.

(see also: Beyond Reasonable Doubt; Burden of Proof; Civil Case/Matter; Criminal Case/Matter)

Banning Order

Is a *regulatory response* that is available to some *regulators* under certain *regulatory regimes/schemes.*

Banning orders, if available, typically form part of a *regulator's* choices/options as an *administrative response.* However, *banning orders* can also be part of a penalty or *sanction* (either *civil* or *criminal*) following the admission or finding of guilt.

Examples of *banning orders* from a liquor and/or gaming *regulator's* perspective would include an order that would prohibit:

- a *regulated entity* – from carrying out certain activities, or providing certain services, for a fixed period; and
- an individual – from entering or going near a licensed premises and/or premises where gaming/gambling can occur.

(see also: Administrative Remedy/Response/Sanction; Exclusion Order)

Behaviour Change

Behaviour change theories provide various insights as to why changes in behaviour occur in society (at an individual and group level).

From the perspective of a *regulator*, *behaviour change* involves seeking to change (or modify) the behaviour of *regulated entities*, or a regulated sector, to better or more effectively achieve a *regulatory outcome*.

This issue of *behaviour change* is important for *regulators* because:

- *Regulation* fundamentally seeks to change behaviours – or to prevent or mitigate certain undesirable behaviours; and
- *Regulation* can be considered as 'experiments'[12] – with *regulatory interventions* monitored to assess whether the *behaviour changes* being sought have been achieved or not.

(see also: Behavioural Insights; Nudge/s)

Behavioural Economics[13] (see Behavioural Insights)

Behavioural Insights

Behavioural insights assist with understanding how people (at an individual and group level) make decisions. It does so by drawing on research into *behavioural economics* and psychology.

Behavioural insights are based upon an understanding that humans do not always act rationally and will often make (or not make) decisions based on a range of seemingly unrelated factors.

For this reason, governments are seeking to incorporate and use *behavioural insights* to inform policy, improve programs (or service delivery), and increase *regulatory outcomes* as part of delivering positive results and outcomes for society.[14]

Regulators have learned that subtle changes in the way that decisions are framed, information is conveyed, and choices are offered can have significant impacts on behaviour. For this reason, *nudges* as they have become known, are increasingly being used by *regulators* as part of their expanding toolbox.

(see also: Behaviour Change; Nudge/s)

Beige Tape (also known as Grey Tape)

Is considered unnecessary and/or convoluted (or at least inefficient) processes, procedures, and reporting requirements that governments (or bureaucracies) place upon themselves, and each other (within government), when engaging in the business of governing.

Governments often try to reduce *beige tape* through internal streamlining of processes and/or administrative efficiencies.

It is often the case, and frustratingly so, that a reduction in *red tape* for *regulated entities* means an increase in *beige tape* for *regulators*.

(see also: Green Tape; Grey Tape; Red Tape; Regulatory Burden)

Bespoke Permit (see Non-Standard Permit/s)

Best-evidence Rule

Is a legal principle that the best available *evidence* to prove an issue in dispute or shed light on a matter associated with an issue should be produced.

The *best-evidence rule* primarily relates to *documentary evidence* but can equally relate to any *exhibit*.

An example of:

- best-evidence for a *regulator* for a *breach* of a *licence* condition, where they are required to prove knowledge of a specific condition, would be the original signed application form and/or signed letters which have been completed by the *accused* or *regulated entity*; and

- secondary evidence in the same example above would be photocopies of the above, noting in this instance the *regulator* would have to explain why they are unable to produce the originals, to comply with the *best-evidence rule*.

(see also: Evidence; Exhibit)

Best Practice

Reference to what is arguably current *best practice*. This means *best practice* at a moment in time, and something that relevant regulatory peers would aspire to achieve. It should be acknowledged that *best practice* is not always achievable due to a range of factors including resources, technology, training, capacity, and capability.

(see also: Better Practice; Continual Improvement; Regulatory Excellence)

Better Practice

Better practice is a relative term. It generally means practices that are better (or an improvement) on previous practices, but which do not necessarily meet what is considered *best practice*. *Better practice* therefore can be seen as part of a *regulator's* commitment to *continual improvement*.

(see also: Best Practice; Continual Improvement; Regulatory Excellence)

Beyond Compliance

Is a term used to describe a *regulated entity* who goes above and beyond, and exceeds their minimum or agreed regulatory standards, requirements, or *obligations*.

Regulated entities may be motivated to go *beyond compliance* for various reasons, including, but not limited to:
- securing a market share, or commercial advantage,
  - e.g., by having a five-star rating, or industry or *regulator* endorsement;
- impressing a third party,
  - whether: *regulator*, *stakeholder*, or *wider community*; and
- altruistic reasons, known only to themselves.

(see also: Compliance; Compliance Spectrum)

Beyond Reasonable Doubt (BRD)

Is the standard of proof required in *criminal cases/matters*.

The *beyond reasonable doubt* standard means that a *court* (judge or jury) is satisfied that every element (or essential fact) that makes up the *offence* or wrongdoing has been proven.

In percentage terms *BRD* is not 100% (i.e., beyond any doubt). Instead, it is generally accepted to be in the certainty range of 95–99% or above.

(see also: Balance of Probabilities; Burden of Proof; Civil Case/Matter; Criminal Case/ Matter)

Bill

Is a draft piece of *legislation* that is introduced into parliament which proposes to either make a new *law* or to amend an existing *act*.

(see also: Act/s; Act of Parliament; Legislation)

Binding Precedent
(also known as Authoritative Precedent)

A *binding precedent* is one that must be followed in latter cases of a similar nature.

This is especially so for *judicial officers* in court cases when the binding decision comes from a higher *court*. But *binding precedents* are equally useful for regulatory decision-makers, as a source of information to help inform decisions they take in terms of commencing, continuing, and concluding various regulatory matters.

For a *precedent* to be binding, on a latter case or regulatory matter:
- the material facts of the case or matter – must be similar; and
- the original decision – must come from a higher (authority) *court.*

(see also: Non-Binding Precedent; Precedent)

Breach/es

Is an act of breaking a *law, regulation,* guideline, or *agreement.*

At its broadest, a *breach* is when a *regulated entity* fails to comply with one or more of their regulatory *obligations.*

Breaches may be administrative, civil, or criminal in nature.

(see also: Administrative Case/Matter; Civil Case/Matter; Criminal Case/Matter; Non-Compliance; Offence/s; Violation/s)

Brief of Evidence

A *brief of evidence* is all relevant evidentiary material that the *prosecuting authority* will produce and rely upon as part of prosecuting a matter.

A *brief of evidence* is the collection of documents including *affidavits/ statements,* photographs, and other *documentary evidence* that the *prosecuting authority* will rely upon as the basis of its *evidence* during proceedings.

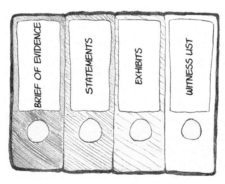

The actual makeup of a *brief of evidence,* in terms of mandatory, desirable, and discretionary inclusions will be based upon the requirements of the:
- *court* or *tribunal* hearing the matter;
- *prosecuting authority* (e.g., Director of Public Prosecutions, or equivalent);

- lead and instructing *regulatory agency*; and
- nature of the *breach*, or alleged wrongdoing.

(see also: Litigation; Prosecution)

Burden of Proof (also referred to as Standard of Proof)

Burden of proof can define the duty placed upon a party to prove or disprove a disputed fact, or it can define which party bears this burden.

In *criminal cases*, the *burden of proof* is placed on the *prosecution*, who must demonstrate that the *defendant* is guilty before a jury may convict him or her.

But in some *jurisdictions*, the *defendant* has the burden of establishing the existence of certain facts that give rise to a defence, such as the insanity plea. In *civil cases*, the *plaintiff* is normally charged with the *burden of proof*, but the *defendant* can be required to establish certain defences.

(see also: Balance of Probability/ies; Beyond Reasonable Doubt)

CAC Regulation (see Command and Control)

CAP (see Compliance Assessment Plan)

C&E

Abbreviation for *compliance* and *enforcement*.

(see also: CME; Compliance; Enforcement)

Cancellation (of Authorisation)

Is when a *regulator* cancels (sometimes referred to as *revokes*) an *authorisation,* that allows a *regulatory entity* to operate within certain *regulatory regimes/schemes* and/or conduct certain activities.

Cancellation, if available, typically forms part of a *regulator's* choices/options as an *administrative response.* However, *cancellation* can also be part of a penalty or *sanction* (either civilly or criminally) following the admission or finding of guilt.

Often a *regulator,* depending on the circumstance, prior to moving to outright *cancellation* may vary or suspend the *authorisation* to provide the *regulated entity* the opportunity to return to *compliance.*

(see also: Administrative Remedy/Response/Sanction; Suspend/Suspension (of Authorisation); Vary/Variation (of Authorisation))

Capture (see Regulatory Capture)

Case Decision Record (CDR)

A *case decision record* is a written record of the decisions made during an *investigation* or inquiry into matters of alleged *non-compliance*.

A *case decision record* is typically used to formally record critical decisions that are made, modified, or ratified during an *investigation* or inquiry.

As part of accountability, governance and transparency, *case decision records* are usually prepared as a standalone template or their content is incorporated into a broader briefing paper, which is then considered and endorsed by a *regulatory manager* or *regulatory executive*. *Case decision records* are increasingly being considered by *internal regulatory bodies*.

It is important that *regulators* see a *case decision record* as a supplement and not a substitute for the numerous decisions that are made by an *authorised officer* and/or *non-authorised officer* surrounding a case or matter throughout its life. Those decisions are made and are typically recorded in the *authorised officer's* notebook, case notes, or investigation diary (or some form of case management system).

(see also: Accountability; Decision/s; Decision-Making; Decision-Review; Record of Decision)

Case Law

Is the collection of *law* that contains past decisions by *courts* and tribunals.

Case law from previous cases, accumulates and is then used to assist in deciding and resolving current cases or disputes.

(see also: Binding Precedent; Common Law; Jurisprudence; Non-Binding Precedent; Precedent)

Case Management Committee
(see Internal Regulatory Body/ies)

Caution (see Warnings and Cautions)

Cease-and-desist Letter

A *cease-and-desist letter* **asks** that a *regulated entity* stop a certain activity or practice which is or is likely to put them in *breach* of a regulatory *obligation*.

A *cease-and-desist letter* would usually be written by a delegated decision-maker within the *regulatory agency*, or the agency's legal area. It might even be written by a private legal firm or *prosecuting authority*, acting on behalf of the *regulator*.

In addition to asking the *regulated entity* to stop the activity, *cease-and-desist letters* will usually:

- **request** the *regulated entity* for a response, as part of *natural justice* and *procedural fairness*; and
- advise that failure to stop **may** subject them to escalated *enforcement* action, and possibly initiation of legal proceedings.

A *cease-and-desist letter* can be a precursor to a *cease-and-desist order*.

(see also: Cease-and-desist Order)

Cease-and-desist Order

A *cease-and-desist order* **requires** that a *regulated entity* stop a certain activity or practice which is or is likely to put them in *breach* of a regulatory *obligation*.

A *cease-and-desist order* may be written by *a regulator* or their representative (as per the *cease-and-desist letter* above) or by a *court* (or issuing body).

In addition to requiring the *regulated entity* to stop the activity, *cease and desist orders* will usually:

- **require** the *regulated entity* to respond, and that response should be directed to the *regulator* or the *court* (or issuing body); and
- advise that failure to stop **will** subject them to escalated *enforcement* action and/or initiation of legal proceedings, as continuing the activity or practice is prohibited.

A *cease-and-desist order* may be preceded by a *cease-and-desist letter*.

(see also: Cease-and-desist Letter)

Certification
(as part of authorising entry to a regulated scheme)

A *certification* can be a reference to one of the many types of *authorisations* that allow a *person* or *regulated entity* to engage in *regulated activities*. For example, an electrician may hold a *certification* to install a certain class of power boards.

(see also: Authorisation)

Certification (as proof of a process or occurrence)

Certification can be a reference to a *person* or *regulated entity* having independent *verification* that they have achieved a certain level of expertise by:
- having gone through a process;
- conforming to a *standard*; and/or
- been admitted into a certain industry or *peak body*.

This example could relate to an accountant who has gone through a training or continual professional development process, met the requisite *standard*, and applied for and been accepted into a body like the Association of Certified Practicing Accountants (or similar).

(see also: Industry Representative Organisation; Verification)

Certifier/s

Is a *person* or body that provides *verification* and *certification*.

A *certifier* may be engaged by the *regulator*, the *regulated entity*; a *stakeholder*; or *wider community* (usually in the form of interest groups).

For example, a licensed building certifier would inspect and verify certain aspects of a building's construction at different stages.

(see also: Audit; Independence)

Chain of Custody

A *chain of custody* documents (by electronic or paper trail) who has custody and control of a physical or electronic item.

For a *regulator,* a *chain of custody* should be maintained:

- from the moment the item is seized or received;
- for any transfer of the item, resulting in a change in storage location or change in custody/control of the item;
- for any testing or analysis of the item; and
- up until the item is either returned or destroyed.

A *chain of custody* **might** be considered *best practice* for a range of regulatory activities.

A *chain of custody* **is** important for matters that are, or are likely, to be subject to *prosecution* or proceedings. Especially for items which the *regulator* seeks to present as legally admissible *evidence.*

Chain of custody has much in common with *chain of evidence* and is often used interchangeably. The primary difference is that a *chain of custody* has a broader application, whereas a *chain of evidence* relates more narrowly to an *exhibit* and *evidence.*

(see also: Chain of Evidence)

Chain of Evidence

A *chain of evidence* establishes continuity of an item (usually referred to as an *exhibit*) from the moment it is seized or received, up until it is produced in *court* or as part of proceedings.

It is called a *chain of evidence,* as the *evidence* should appear like an unbroken chain.

Chain of evidence has much in common with *chain of custody* and is often used interchangeably. The primary difference is that a *chain of evidence* relates to an *exhibit* and *evidence,* whereas a *chain of custody* has broader application.

(see also: Chain of Custody; Evidence; Exhibit)

Charge Bargaining/Negotiating

Occurs when the *accused* agrees to plead guilty (or does not contest a matter) based on some agreement and concessions made by the *regulator*, or *prosecuting authority*.

Charge bargaining usually or typically occurs by:

- substitution – of a less serious charge, than the *accused* was originally charged with,
  - an example might be industrial homicide to industrial manslaughter;
- agreement – that a lesser penalty will be sought, or that certain penalties will not be sought,
  - an example might be that the *prosecuting authority* agrees not to seek a custodial sentence, in preference to a larger monetary *fine* to be directed to site remediation and/or initiation of a Work Safety Compliance Program;
- modification – of the basis of the facts which are put to the court or tribunal
  - an example might be that the *prosecuting authority* would proceed, based on what is considered *agreed facts*, in that it might:
    › frame its submissions (e.g., from being deliberate to indifferent, or indifferent to reckless) in a certain way, or
    › will not challenge, either at all, or vigorously, the submissions of the other side.

(see also: Agreed Facts)

Chief Regulatory Advisor

A *chief regulatory advisor* position would typically sit at the whole of government level.

Such a position could operate along much the same lines of the Chief Scientific Advisor, or Chief Medical Advisor positions.

The New Zealand Productivity Commission indicated that, if pursued, a *chief regulatory advisor* position could be responsible for:

- 'disseminating information on the latest developments in regulatory theory and practice;

- coordinating the development of professional development pathways and accredited qualifications;
- working with chief executives of regulatory bodies to identify common capability gaps and strategies for filling these gaps across the system;
- working with research organisations to investigate regulatory issues of importance to New Zealand agencies;
- developing and maintaining good practice guidance;
- promoting a common "professional language" throughout New Zealand regulatory agencies;
- coordinate study tours and visits by international experts and leading academics in the field of regulatory studies; and
- leading and managing professional forums of regulators'.[15]

It is important for *regulators* that they establish, maintain, and invest in positions such as chief *regulatory advisors* – as positions such as these are critical in developing an appropriate *regulatory culture* and supporting the *regulatory profession*.

(see also: Chief Regulatory Officer; Regulatory Culture)

Chief Regulatory Officer

A *chief regulatory officer* position would typically sit at the whole of *regulatory agency* level.

Such a position could operate along much the same lines of the Chief Financial Officer, or Chief Operating Officer positions.

The aim and benefit of a *chief regulatory officer* position would be that it would provide for increased institutional stability across matters including, but not limited to:
- *regulatory capability*;
- *regulatory capacity*;
- *regulatory competence*; and
- *regulatory culture*.

It is important for *regulators* that they establish, maintain, and invest in positions such as a *chief regulatory officer* – as positions such as these are critical in developing an appropriate *regulatory culture* and *regulatory posture*. They would also provide additional support to *regulatory executives* and *regulatory boards*, and overall advance the *regulatory profession*.

(see also: Chief Regulatory Advisor; Regulatory Culture)

Citizen Suit (see Third Party Action)

Civil Case/Matter

A *civil case/matter* involves the *regulator* operating in, making decisions, and involving others in civil proceedings.

As opposed to the *regulator* operating in and making decisions in the administrative sphere of its operations, and/or referring the matter as part of criminal proceedings.

Examples of a *civil case/matter* might include decisions and actions taken in respect to seeking *enforceable undertakings* and *injunctions*.

(see also: Administrative Case/Matter; Criminal Case/Matter)

Civil Penalty

A *civil penalty* is a penalty that is imposed as part of civil proceedings.

Civil penalty provisions are separate to criminal prosecution, conviction, and sentence.

(see also: Civil Remedy/Response/Sanction; Sanctions)

Civil Remedy/Response/Sanction[16]

For *regulators* the terms remedy/ies, response/s, and sanction/s tend to be used interchangeably, interrelatedly, and collectively.

A *civil remedy* tends to come in the form of or be part of a response or *sanction*.

A *civil response* is a response that is available to a *regulator* when drawing upon the civil power they have access to. Often a *civil response* will be used either as an alternative to or in parallel with an *administrative response* or a *criminal response*.

An example of a *civil response* is when a *regulator* establishes, or a *regulated entity* admits, a *breach* of a *licence* condition. If the breach is of such gravity that the *regulator*, using their *civil powers*, will initiate a *civil response* through the appropriate *court* or body within their *jurisdiction*.

Regulators will do so when the outcome or remedy is not one which is available to them either as an *administrative response* or *criminal response*. Payment of monies to remediate damage caused is an example of a *civil response*.

A *civil sanction*, although standalone, is often viewed by *regulators* as a hybrid. This is because *civil sanctions* tend to offer:

- more options than what a *regulator* can do itself (administratively); and
- more and different options than what a *court* can direct in its criminal capacity.

Non-compliance with *civil sanctions* can be very serious, as *non-compliance* can potentially reconstitute the original *offence* (that may have been negotiated as part of an *ADR* or negotiated settlement) or it can attract *contempt of court* penalties, which are themselves criminal in nature.

For *regulators*, and depending on the *jurisdiction*, the main *civil sanctions* typically are:

- civil monetary penalties;
- *enforceable undertakings*;
- *injunctions*; and
- remediation orders.

There are other *sanctions*, depending on the *jurisdiction*, that can be defined as *civil sanctions*.[17]

(see also: Administrative Remedy/Response/Sanction; Criminal Remedy/Response/Sanction)

Claimant

The *person* (or entity) that is seeking to or is making a claim.

A term used for a *person* (or entity) seeking some form of legal relief, especially in *civil matters*.

Once proceedings have commenced the *claimant* will then be referred to as the *plaintiff*.

(see also: Accused; Defendant; Plaintiff)

CME

Abbreviation for *compliance, monitoring* and *enforcement*.

(see also: C&E; Compliance; Enforcement; Monitoring)

Code/s

Is a set of *rules, laws,* principles, or similar that describe how something should be done.

Codes often underpin *co-regulation*. For example, where mandatory *compliance* with the *code* is set by government, but the technical content of the *code* is derived by the industry/sector itself.

For some *regulators, code/s* might be a relevant consideration and form part of assessing the suitability of an entity to enter a *regulatory regime/scheme*. For example, it may be a mandatory condition of entry for financial auditors that they show (usually through membership of the national or international professional body) that they understand, can assess, and report against the national accounting standards.

For *regulators,* reference to *code/s* can sometimes be found in different forms of *authorisations*. For example, in a *permit* or *approval* to carry out works for a licenced electrician, it might have an additional overarching clause or condition requiring they conform with the relevant national wiring *codes*.

(see also: Co-regulation; Law/s; Regulation; Rules; Standards)

Code/s of Practice

Provide a practical guide on how to comply.

For *regulators,* a *code of practice* might be standalone (and more like *codes* above), or they might supplement other forms of *advice and guidance* about the regulatory *obligations* of a *regulated* entity.

Codes of practice are published and are often actively endorsed or supported by *regulators,* peak professional associations or bodies, industries or sectors, and *stakeholders.*

Codes of practice tend to be either voluntary or mandatory in nature.

(see also: Accreditation; Authorisation; Code/s)

Coercive Powers

Coercive powers are those powers that:
- involve the use of force or threats, as part of influencing a *person* or *regulated entity* to do something, and
- have *sanctions* attached to them for *non-compliance.*

Perhaps the most common, or well known, examples of *coercive powers* being used by a *regulator* involve:
- use of a *search warrant* to forcibly enter a *premise,* where *consent* or *permission* has been refused; or
- compelling a *person* to answer a question, in circumstances which would normally infringe upon their right to not self-incriminate themselves.

Regulators tend to use *coercive powers* judiciously and with appropriate governance and oversight mechanisms in place. This is because *regulators* have been granted *coercive powers* for use in limited situations and contexts, as they often impinge on a *person's* or entity's rights and freedoms more than usual.

An example of a *coercive power*:

- for an individual person – might involve being served with a notice, in the form of a 'notice to attend' a *regulators* office for the purpose of being interviewed about an alleged *offence*,
  - and further, during that interview being directed to answer specific questions; and
- for a *regulated entity* – might be to provide certain business records,
  - an example being a finance director of a company being served a notice, in the form of a 'notice to produce', requesting all records relating to staff wages, in a case of alleged underpayment of wages and allowances.

It is important that *regulators* note that in some *jurisdictions* there are *coercive powers* that operate across multiple *acts*, while for others access to *coercive powers* are *act* specific.

(see also: Internal Regulatory Body; Regulatory Powers)

Command and Control (C2)

Command and control, as a term and general approach (to *decision-making*, resource allocation, and implementation), has military history and usage, where it is referred to as *C2*.

In the military context – command is having the *authority* to direct, and control is about the ability to control and co-ordinate resources and functions. And then combining them in pursuit of accomplishing a mission.

From the description above, it is easy to see how *command and control* can have some attractive elements for policing, *enforcement*, and *regulatory agencies*.

Command and Control Regulation (CAC Regulation)

CAC regulation is a particular style of *regulation*, and *regulatory approach*, that involves *rules* or *laws* that are enforced (or are capable of being enforced) with *sanctions*.

Regulatory practitioners tend to like *CAC regulation* due to its somewhat linear and binary nature, which flows onto *decision-making*. For example:

- is the activity *in-system* or *out-of-system*?;
- is the regulated activity legal or illegal/right or wrong?;
- is the *regulated entity* either *compliant* or *non-compliant*?; and
- is a *sanction* appropriate and justifiable or not?

For the reasons above, *CAC regulation* has been criticised as being too prescriptive and lacking nuance. It is for this reason that many *regulated entities* do not like *CAC regulation*.[18] Instead, they prefer to be subjected to *principles-* or *performance- based regulation*, where *regulatory responses* are considered less-prescriptive and formulaic.

(see also: In-System (Regulation); Out-of-System (Regulation); Regulation; Types of Regulation)

Common Law

Common law is *law* that:

- is based upon general custom and usage; and
- has been recognised by the courts, and which is enforced by the courts.

Common law is derived from the traditional law of England as developed by judicial precedents, interpretation, expansion, and modification. As such, *common law* is sometimes referred to as *judge made law* as distinct from *statute* law.

(see also: Case Law; Law; Statute)

Community/ies of Practice (CoP)

A *community of practice* is a reference to:

- a group of people who share a concern or a passion for something they do; and

- a mechanism through which they learn how to do it better, as they interact regularly.

There are three elements to a *community of practice*: [19]
- domain – which provides and defines the shared domain of interest;
- community – which identifies the component part of the shared domain within which participants interact, engage and share; and
- practice – which requires that participants be practitioners (that is to be engaged in practice) and that interactions develop over time.

For example, for *regulators*:
- domain – might relate to *regulatory reform/regulatory regime design*, or *regulatory delivery*;
- community – might relate to functional activities like *audit*, *inspection*, *investigation*, or *litigation*; and
- practice – might relate to focussing on policies, procedures, or practices.

Organisations, including *regulatory agencies,* are increasingly looking to *communities of practice* (as a way) to improve their performance. With *communities of practice* often operating under and within *networks*.

It is important that *regulators* and *regulatory executives* note that by their nature, *communities of practice* are quite organic and transitory. Therefore, if *regulatory agencies* overly formalise the *community of practice* to the extent that they hardwire them as part of 'business as usual', they can lose some of their attraction, which impacts negatively on actual and potential benefits.

(see also: Network/s; **Working Together**)

Community Order/Community Service Order

Is a *regulatory tool* that is available to some *regulators* under certain *regulatory regimes/schemes.*

Community orders, if available, typically form part of a *regulator's* choices/options as a *criminal response. Community orders* are typically part of a penalty or *sanction,* following the admission or finding of guilt, and have clear benefits for the community.

An example of a *community order* from an environmental *regulator's* perspective, is for a bulldozer/JCB driver who carried out illegal clearance of native or protected vegetation, might include an order that:

- requires that they perform 100 hours of work with a land care group that plants and maintains trees in public greenspaces.

(see also: Criminal Remedy/Response/Sanction; Sanction; Suspended Sentence)

Competent Authority

Term widely used in Europe to describe what would be called a *regulatory agency* in other countries.

It is also a reference to those agencies/bodies with a mandate to respond on matters of international *law* (international *treaties*). For example, the *competent authority* to respond to *contraventions* of the:

- MARPOL Convention[20] in New Zealand, is Maritime New Zealand; and
- Ramsar Convention[21] in Canada, is the Canadian Wildlife Service.

(see also: Lead Agency; Regulatory Agency/ies)

Complainant

Complainant has two main meanings for regulators.

Firstly, in a legal sense, is the *person* (or entity) that makes the initial *complaint* or *allegation* of a *crime*, *breach*, or some form of wrongdoing.

In civil proceedings the *complainant* may be referred to as the *plaintiff*.

Secondly, in a customer service sense, is the *person* (or entity) that complains.

The *person* (or entity) that makes a *complaint* or is dissatisfied, in a service delivery/client sense.

(see also: Complaint; Complaint handling; Defendant; Plaintiff; Witness)

Complaint

The word *complaint* can have multiple meanings for a *regulator*.

For example, a *complaint* can be considered as:

- some initial and general information that is received (especially if it is anonymous);

- the initiating step in *litigation* or proceedings, when someone (usually a victim, *witness*, or concerned party) comes forward;
- a process (often framed as 'the laying of the complaint') involving a *judicial officer*; or
- a formal legal document used in the lower courts (e.g., Magistrates and Local Court) that contains sufficient facts, information, and reasons as to why the *accused person* is suspected of having committed a *crime*, *breach*, or some form of wrongdoing.

(see also: Information; Litigation; Proceedings)

Complaint Handling

The process of handling *complaints*, from receipt through to conclusion or outcome.

Complaint handling processes may vary, from agency to agency, but typically involve the following key stages:

- *complaint* – received;
- *complaint* – recorded;
- *complaint* – acknowledged; and
- *complaint* – assessed.

If it is deemed that the *complaint* warrants or requires an *investigation*, then:

- *complaint* – investigated;
- *complainant* updated – this may occur several times if the *investigation* is complex or protracted; and
- *complaint* finalised – the outcome has been determined, and any follow up options detailed.

For *regulators,* it is important to be clear about the difference between processes that relate to dealing with and responding to:

- a *complaint* – in terms of someone (i.e., a *regulated entity*, *stakeholder*, concerned citizen, or other) expressing dissatisfaction, with a *regulatory*: activity, decision, *process*, or *outcome*; and
- an *allegation* – of *non-compliance*.

It is important for *regulators* to be clear about differences between a *complaint* and an *allegation*.

The differences can be exacerbated due to differences in expectations and perceptions around whether the *complainant* is a:

- *customer* (i.e., receiving a service or goods with the associated genuine choice); or
- is a *regulated entity* (i.e., subject to duties and *obligations*).

(see also: Allegation)

Compliance

Compliance is a term that is used frequently when *regulators* come together, especially when discussing *regulatory practice* and *regulatory delivery*.

The word *compliance* can be used on its own or in combination with other words.

Firstly, when used on its own, it tends to be used in two main contexts. For example, it can reflect that a *regulated entity* has or did comply. More specifically:

- in a linear (and ongoing) process **is** deemed to be complying with necessary (statutory) requirements; or
- in terms of an end-state was found to be complying with necessary (statutory) requirements.

Secondly, when used in combination, it can have multiple meanings in different contexts. For example, it can be used as:

- a point of comparison, e.g., *regulatory* vs *compliance* vs *enforcement* activities; or
- a way to give greater clarity and context to another word, e.g., *compliance assistance*, *compliance monitoring*, or any number of other examples.

(see also: Compliant)

Compliance and Enforcement Policy

A *compliance and enforcement policy* is a published and publicly available document.

The purpose of a *compliance and enforcement policy* is to provide simple and clear information about how a *regulator* will go about performing their mandated *regulatory role* and *regulatory functions*.

The *compliance and enforcement policy* of a *regulator* will typically set out the *framework*, principles, approaches, and responses it will use to achieve *compliance* within the *regulatory regime/scheme* it administers.

A *compliance and enforcement policy* may provide examples of how the *regulator* intends to work with *co-* and *peer- regulators, regulated entities, stakeholders*, and the *wider community*.

A *compliance and enforcement policy* will typically be mentioned and cross-referenced in other key regulatory documents, including but not limited to *annual operational plans, regulatory statements of intent, regulatory strategy*, and *prosecution policy*.

(see also: Compliance Policy; Enforcement Policy; Prosecution Policy; Regulatory Policy)

Compliance and Enforcement Principles

Are the principles that a *regulator* articulates, publicises, and then uses to underpin their *regulatory functions* and activities.

The specific principles that a *regulator* lists, and endeavours to adhere to, will often be based on:

- principles that might be considered generic and universal to all *regulators*, e.g., fair, firm, and approachable, or
- principles that are specific to certain types of *regulators*, whether economic, environmental, or social, e.g., financially responsible, sustainable, and equitable respectively, or
- principles that are specific to certain industries, sectors, commodities, or *jurisdictions*, e.g., innovative, flexible, responsive, and progressive respectively, or
- a combination of any of the above.

(see also: PACTT, Principles of Good Regulation)

Compliance Assessment Plan

A *compliance assessment plan* (CAP) is used to monitor *compliance*. A CAP:
- ensures that within a defined time frame that *compliance* against all relevant regulatory requirements are checked; and
- can be developed at an individual *premise*/site level or at sector or industry level.

(see also: Audit; Compliance Monitoring)

Compliance Assistance

Compliance assistance is assistance that helps *regulated entities* to comply with their regulatory *obligations*.

Compliance assistance can:
- be proactive or reactive;
- be led by the *regulator*, or a *third party*;
- be *ad hoc* or part of a formal *compliance assistance* program; and
- can occur anywhere within the four central phases of the *Extended Regulatory Spectrum*, noting that *regulators* tend to direct most of their:
  - proactive *compliance assistance* in the *advice and guidance* and *licencing and approval* phases; and
  - reactive or responsive *compliance assistance* in the *monitoring compliance* and *enforcement* phases.

(see also: Compliance Promotion; ***Extended Regulatory Spectrum***)

Compliance Assurance

Compliance assurance refers to various means by which it can be determined if a *regulated entity* is *compliant*, or in *compliance*.

Compliance assurance methods or activities typically include:
- *audits* or *inspections*;
- monitoring;
- record keeping;
- reporting; and
- sampling and testing.

(see also: Compliance; Non-compliance)

Compliance Assurance Indicators

Compliance assurance indicators are a result of research and analysis conducted by the Organisation for Economic Co-operation and Development (OECD)[22] in relation to the design and implementation of quantitatively measurable indicators. These indicators are to assist *regulators* to measure the effectiveness of their *compliance* efforts.[23]

The catalyst for the research was an increasing demand and expectation for *regulators* to be able to demonstrate their results-oriented work.

The research established four categories of *compliance assurance indicators*,[24] namely:

- inputs – typically measured in terms of resources, e.g., the number of *inspectors* on staff;
- outputs – typically measured in terms of activities, e.g., numbers of *inspections* or *audits* conducted;
- intermediate outcomes – typically measured in terms of the level of knowledge and behaviour of the *regulated* community, e.g., reflected in increased *voluntary compliance* rates; and
- final outcomes – typically measured in terms of the outcomes achieved, e.g., the *regulatory outcomes* themselves and/or reflected through successful programmatic activities.

(see also: Regulatory Outcomes)

Compliance History

A record that indicates the *compliance history* of a *regulated entity*.

For a *regulator* the *compliance history* of a *regulated entity* might be recorded in:

- specific terms – against each **individual** *regulatory regime/scheme* that the *regulated entity* participates in; or
- grouped terms – against each **group or similar type** of *regulatory regime/scheme* the *regulated entity* participates in (e.g., economic, environmental, social); or
- in collective/aggregated terms – across **all** the *regulatory regimes/ schemes* that the *regulated entity* participates in.

Regulators tend to use *compliance history* as one of the indicators to determine:

- whether a *regulated entity* is permitted to **enter** a *regulatory regime/scheme*;
- whether a *regulated entity* is permitted to **remain within** a *regulatory regime/scheme*; or
- what frequency, nature, and extent of *monitoring* the *regulated entity* will be subjected to, across any and/or all *regulatory regimes/schemes* that they participate in.

(see also: Compliance Posture; Earned Autonomy/Recognition; Fit and Proper (Person) Test)

Compliance Management

Compliance management is the act or process of ensuring that a *regulated entity*, and the staff operating within it, are complying with all necessary regulatory *obligations*.

Compliance management broadly involves a *regulated entity* documenting, training, and monitoring itself and its staff. To assist, a *regulated entity* will use policies, procedures, and practices directed towards achieving and demonstrating *compliance*.

Regulated entities, especially large and multinational ones, will often appoint a dedicated internal *compliance officer* to oversee *compliance management*. Their roles and functions are often expansive and can include:

- proactive work – around education, prevention, and liaising internally with management and externally with *regulators, stakeholders,* and the *wider community*;
- reactive work – responding to, managing, reporting, and following up on instances of *non-compliance* (including 'near-misses'); and
- responsive work – providing or co-ordinating requests for *information* or status updates from the *regulator* in relation to the findings of *audits, inspections,* and *investigations* (or other *regulatory activities*).

(see also: Compliance; Compliance History; Compliance Officer (in Regulated Entity/ies)).

Compliance Management Committee
(see Internal Regulatory Body/ies)

Compliance Monitoring

Monitoring carried out to ensure that a *regulated entity* is meeting (complying) with its regulatory *obligations*.

Compliance monitoring can be initiated by:
- the *regulated entity* itself;
- the *regulator*; or
- a third party.

Compliance monitoring can involve a range of activities or methods which are usually carried out by *authorised officers* (usually *auditors* or *inspectors*) or authorised or contracted third parties. However, some *compliance monitoring* might take the form of tracking data on spreadsheets and look more like *quality assurance* and quality control, which could be performed by non-authorised officers (usually commodity or technical experts).

For further information/detail see those monitoring activities listed under *monitoring compliance*.

(see also: CME; Compliance; **Extended Regulatory Spectrum**; Monitoring; Monitoring Compliance).

Compliance Officer (in Regulatory Agency/ies)

A *compliance officer* is either an *authorised officer*, or someone who has a role in monitoring a *regulated entity's* state or level of *compliance*.

Compliance officers in *regulatory agencies* are outward facing, as they are checking whether *regulated entities* are complying with requirements.

(see also: Auditor; Authorised Officer; Inspector; Investigator; Ranger; Regulatory Officer; Warden)

Compliance Officer (in Regulated Entity/ies)

Inside some *regulated entities* there is an internal position of *compliance officer* (sometimes called a *regulatory compliance* officer).

Compliance officers in *regulated entities* are inward facing, as they are checking whether the business/enterprise is legally *compliant* with a myriad of legal/regulatory responsibilities, including but not limited to: anti-money laundering requirements; staff employment conditions; immigration and visa status of workers; tax/revenue matters; and work health and safety requirements.

(see also: Compliance Management; Regulated Entity/ies)

Compliance Policy
(see Compliance and Enforcement Policy)

If a *regulator* does not have a combined *compliance and enforcement policy*, it is likely that they will have a *compliance policy* and then a separate, but complementary, *enforcement policy* and/or *prosecution policy*.

(see also: Compliance and Enforcement Policy, Enforcement Policy, Prosecution Policy; Regulatory Policy)

Compliance Posture

Compliance posture is the approach or stance that a *person* or *regulated entity* adopts towards being regulated.

Compliance posture involves the *person* or *regulated entity* balancing primary tensions between:
- their intent or willingness to comply; and
- their capability and capacity to comply.

There are indicators and signs of the *compliance posture* that a *person* or *regulated entity* might take, which can be seen or reflected by:
- their level of engagement and candour with the *regulator*;
- the nature of their responses and communications with the *regulator*;
- the level of responsiveness to requests from the *regulator*; and
- their *compliance history*.

The above combine to reflect the behaviours of the *person* or *regulated entity* in terms of their willingness to comply with their regulatory requirements. This, in turn contributes towards the achievement of the *regulatory outcomes* sought by the *regulator*.

It is important for *regulators* to keep the *compliance posture* of a *person* or *regulated entity* under review, as it may require the *regulator* to adjust its own *regulatory posture*.

The continual monitoring and adjusting of a *regulatory posture* will assist the *regulator* to ensure its *regulatory responses* are proportionate to the demonstrated behaviours of the regulated community, when compared against the *regulatory risks* it seeks to manage and the *regulatory outcomes* it seeks to advance or achieve.

(see also: Compliance History; Regulatory Posture)

Compliance Promotion

Compliance promotion are activities that encourage *voluntary compliance* amongst *regulated entities*.

Compliance promotion activities can vary greatly and will be informed by the industry, sector, commodities, and *jurisdiction* that the *regulated entity* operates in.

From a *regulator's* perspective, *compliance promotion* forms part of an overall strategy of integrated *regulatory activities* that can culminate in *enforcement*.

(see also: Compliance Assistance; Compliance Pyramid/Triangle; Voluntary Compliance)

Compliance Pyramid/Triangle

Is a diagrammatic representation of the *responsive regulation* theory.

For *regulators, compliance pyramid/triangle* diagrams tend to be arranged in a hierarchy from most co-operative or facilitative (or least intrusive) at the base or bottom – through to more directive (or most intrusive) at the peak or top.

From bottom to top the layers/levels tend to reflect:
• *Voluntary compliance* and persuasion;
• *Warnings and cautions*;
• *Sanctions* (civil and criminal); and
• *Suspension* and *revocation*.

Given the above, the *compliance pyramid/triangle* has become a popular way for *regulators* to visually communicate aspects of their *regulatory approaches* and *regulatory posture*. For this reason, contextualised and customised versions of the *compliance pyramid/triangle* often appear in a *compliance and enforcement policy, regulatory strategy* or equivalent.

(see also: Compliance and Enforcement Policy; Regulatory Strategy; Responsive Regulation; *VADE Model*)

Compliance Spectrum

The *Compliance Spectrum* allocates six descriptors to the behaviours and attributes of different types of *regulated entity*.[25]

For example:

1. Criminal – are actively and deliberately non-compliant;
2. Chancer – push boundaries, test the system, compliant when forced;
3. Careless – conscious and subconscious factors lead to non-compliance;
4. Confused – try to do the right thing, often need additional assistance;
5. Compliant – understand the requirements and comply voluntarily; and
6. Champion – go beyond compliance, are often sector leaders.

These descriptors align well with the *VADE Model*. For example, the behaviours and attributes in:
- 5 and 6 are in **V**oluntary;
- 4 and 3 are in **A**ssisted;
- 2 are in **D**irected; and
- 1 is in **E**nforced.

(See also: *VADE Model*)

Compliance Strategy

A *compliance strategy* is concerned with those strategies that assist with achieving and maintaining *compliance*.

Compliance strategies tend to be based on time frames that range from three to five years, and which are renewed on a rolling annual basis.

Compliance strategies can be focussed and directed inwards or outwards. For example:

- *regulated entities* – tend to have inward focussed strategies that assist them to adhere to and demonstrate their *compliance* with regulatory *obligations*; and
- *regulators* – tend to have outward focussed strategies that assist them to both:
  - enable and support *regulated entities* to meet their regulatory *obligations*; and
  - detail how they will undertake (including: identifying, prioritising, resourcing, implementing, and evaluating) their *regulatory activities* as part of delivering the *regulatory outcomes* they have been charged with.

(See also: Annual Operational Plans; Compliance and Enforcement Policy; Regulatory Policy)

Compliance Triangle/Pyramid
(see Compliance Pyramid/Triangle)

Compliant

State of *compliance*, reflecting that a *regulated entity* is complying with necessary (statutory) requirements

(see also: Compliance; Non-Compliant)

Consent

Is having or being given permission to do something.

If a *regulator* lacks *statutory authority* or a *regulatory power* to do something – they may seek *consent*, from a *regulated entity* or their representative.

Even if a *regulator* does have the *statutory authority* or a *regulatory power* to do something – they may still seek *consent*. Seeking permission to enter a *premise* is a situation where *consent* is frequently sought.

The reason for seeking *consent* is two-fold:

- it is a less adversarial approach, and assists the *regulator* in maintaining an appropriate relationship with the *regulated entity*; and/or
- it provides the *regulated entity* with the ability to demonstrate that they co-operated fully with a *regulator*, which may be taken into consideration (as a mitigating factor) in any subsequent penalty.

It is important for *regulators* to note that *consent* needs to be given voluntarily, without threat or inducement, and *consent* should be able to be withdrawn at any time without penalty.

(see also: Authorising Entry (to a Premises); Regulatory Powers)

Consistent/Consistency

From a *regulator's* perspective, means their actions and responses should be repeatable when considering circumstances with the same or similar facts. Being *consistent* or acting with *consistency* demonstrates *compliance* with the:

- *Principles of Good Regulation*; and
- forms the **C** in the associated *PACTT* acronym.

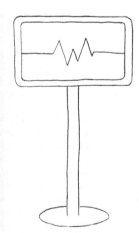

It is important for *regulators* that *consistency* is not interpreted as needing to treat every similar instance of *non-compliance* in the same (formulaic) way.

Regulatory practice and effective *regulatory delivery* require a level of considered and customised delivery.

Therefore, and instead of seeing *consistency* as a formulaic process, *regulators* should: prepare for; be able to explain and justify; and document – when they act or respond in what might be considered an in-consistent way.

(see also PACTT; Principles of Good Regulation; Problem-Solving approach to regulation)

Contempt of Court

What constitutes *contempt of court* varies between *jurisdictions* and the type and nature of the *court*.

For the purposes of this book, and to assist *regulators,* there are two main circumstances where a *regulator* and its staff may become involved in issues associated with a *contempt of court.*

The first relates to *regulatory officers* and their attendance and demeanour during *court* proceedings. For example, *regulatory officers* (and non-regulatory officers for that matter) may find themselves in *contempt of court* for not displaying and maintaining a respectful attitude towards the *court* and its proceedings. Typically, staff would be at risk of being in *contempt of court* for:

- failing to attend court in response to a summons or subpoena, for the purpose of giving *evidence* or assisting with proceedings;
- failing to remain silent, when asked to do so;
- failing to answer a question, when asked;
- being deliberately evasive, and repeatedly avoiding a question; and/or
- generally showing disrespect for the *court* proceedings.

The second relates to the *regulator* and *regulated entities* (or any party subject to the proceedings for that matter) and their behaviour and *compliance* with court orders following *court* proceedings. For example, if either the *prosecution* (i.e., applicant/*claimant* in *civil matters*), defence (i.e., *respondent* in *civil matters*), or party to proceedings (i.e., a *witness*) are at risk of being in *contempt of court* for:

- disobeying outright a *court* order;
- failing to comply with a *court* order; and/or
- breaching a formal undertaking, e.g., an *enforceable undertaking.*

It is important for *regulators,* especially those whose work intersects and spans *administrative, civil,* and *criminal matters,* to be aware of the potential resource implications and impacts of *contempt of court* proceedings. Because *non-compliance* with civil orders by an (*in-system*) *person* or *regulated entity* or an (*out-of-system*) *person* or entity can constitute *contempt of court*. As a result, the *regulator* may find itself back in *court* as part of *contempt of court* proceedings and be seeking further *enforcement* action.

(see also: Contested Hearing/Matter/Case; Court/s)

Contested Hearing/Matter/Case

A *contested hearing* is when the *court* (or tribunal) hears *evidence* from both the *prosecution* and defence, to determine whether the *prosecution* has made the case to the requisite *burden of proof*.

A *contested hearing* occurs if the *accused* party pleads not guilty, or the matter cannot be resolved by negotiation and/or following an *ADR* process.

(see also: Litigation; Prosecution; Trial)

Continual/Continuous Improvement

Is the philosophy and practice of constantly re-examining and improving processes, practices, and performance.

Regulators can come across references to *continual improvement* as it is one of the seven principles of a Quality Management System (QMS), which can form part of third-party *audits* or *assessments*.

(see also: Best Practice; Better Practice)

Continuing Professional Development (CPD)

Continuing professional development is a commitment by practitioners to maintain and improve their professional skills and knowledge, as part of increasing their professional expertise and competence.

CPD activities include, but are not limited to:
- 'seminars, workshops, lectures and conferences;
- in-house seminars or discussion groups;
- participation in a multimedia or web-based program; and
- private study of audio/visual material'.[26]

CPD **activities** assist professionals, on an individual level, to:
- 'build the knowledge and skills needed to succeed in a competitive professional environment;
- achieve personal development and career goals;
- excel in their role, creating value for the organisation and its clients or customers;
- enhance their transferable skills, thereby increasing employability; and
- engage with the profession and the wider community'.[27]

On a broader level, *CPD* **requirements**:
- 'allow governing bodies to ensure high standards of performance and up-to-date knowledge are maintained within the profession;
- instil greater consumer and client confidence in the work of professionals; and
- build a sense of ownership and a strive for high-performance within a profession or industry'.[28]

It is important for *regulatory executives* and *regulatory managers* to acknowledge the role that *CPD* plays in an emerging profession like the *regulatory profession* – and enable and support *regulatory practitioners* to undertake and participate in relevant *CPD* activities.

(see also: Regulatory Profession; Regulatory Professional; Training)

Contravention

A *regulator* tends to consider a *contravention* as an act or action by a *regulated entity* that breaks a *law, rule, code* or similar.

A *court* will consider a *contravention* as an act or action where a party to proceedings fails to comply with a ruling or order, that forms part of settling a matter (whether by agreement, negotiation, penalty, or *sentencing*).

(see also: Breach; Crime; Offence)

Convention

An agreement between nation states on matters of common interest or concern.

Regulators, especially those that deal with regulatory, *enforcement,* or policing matters that cross national and international borders, will be familiar with *conventions* that take the form of *international agreements* and *treaties.* These *treaties* enable, co-ordinate, and facilitate development and delivery of international *law.*

CoP (see Community/ies of Practice)

CPD (see Continuing Professional Development)

Co-regulation

A particular style or type of *regulation.*

Co-regulation typically occurs when an industry or sector (either alone or with an *industry representative organisation; stakeholders;* or government) develops and administers its own regulatory arrangements.

Government, through *regulators* then develop and put in place the necessary underpinning *laws* to enforce it.

Co-regulation involves various methods, including *certification, codes, schemes,* and *standards.* Examples of *co-regulation* include:

- the *regulation* of radio and television content in Australia;[29] and
- the *regulation* of marine safety in ports and harbours in New Zealand.[30]

(see also: Regulation; Types of Regulation)

Co-regulator

A *co-regulator* is a *regulator* whose *regulatory activities* and interests span or overlap with another *regulator,* either in terms of the *regulatory domain,* sector, or commodity.

For example, for *regulators* that regulate food safety and hygiene in commercial restaurants, their *co-regulators* would typically include:

- labour/wage inspectorate – relating to wages and worker entitlements;
- liquor inspectorate – relating to responsible service of alcohol; and
- workplace health and safety – relating to the safety of staff and patrons.

Whereas a *peer-regulator* is a *regulator* that regulates the same matters and issues in another *jurisdiction*.

For example, all *regulators* that regulate food safety and hygiene in commercial restaurants, irrespective of whether at the local, state/provincial, or federal/central level of government, would be *peer-regulators* of one another.

Co-regulators are included as *regulators* as one of the four main groups that provide key regulatory perspectives, the others are: *regulated*; *stakeholders* and *wider-community*.

(see also: Jurisdiction; **Four Key Regulatory Perspectives**; Peer-regulator)

Corroboration

Information that confirms or supports something else.

Regulators seek to corroborate many things as they go about conducting their *regulatory activities*, including but not limited to facts, observations, opinions, statements, and theories.

However, *regulators* mostly discuss *corroboration* in terms of corroborating *evidence*. This is because *prosecuting authorities* will often ask *regulators* for additional forms of *corroboration* to be contained within *affidavits, statements,* and *briefs of evidence*, especially if the matter is likely to be subject to a *contested hearing* or some form of legal proceedings.

(see also: Brief of Evidence; Burden of Proof; Evidence)

Corruption

Is dishonest or fraudulent conduct for personal benefit or gain, by those in a position of trusted authority or power.

The opportunity for, and the nature of, *corruption* will vary from *regulator* to *regulator*. Factors affecting *corruption* can include the industry, sector, commodities, and *jurisdictions* that the *regulated entity* operates within and across.

Corruption is typically associated with receiving cash bribes, but it can also include receiving other items of value, reciprocal favours, or protection.

(see also: Noble Cause Corruption; Regulatory Capture)

Court/s

A body established to administer justice.

Courts have authority (*jurisdiction*) to hear and adjudicate on legal disputes, whether administrative, civil, or criminal in nature.

Courts are most often presided over by a judge, judges, or magistrate.

Court proceedings may occur in front of a judge and/or jury.

(see also: Alternate Dispute Resolution; Contested Matter; Judicial Officer; (The) Judiciary; Trial)

Crime/s

An act or omission (i.e., a failure to act) that it punishable by law.

Crimes consist of two elements:
- *actus reus* [Latin] – meaning the physical act; and
- *mens rea* [Latin] – meaning the mental act.

Regulators see and consider *crimes* in both a narrow and broader context. For example:

- *crime* narrowly – are matters that satisfy the criminal definition, and are dealt with by the criminal courts (or criminal justice system in their *jurisdiction*); or
- *crime* broadly – are matters that are seen more as *offences*, punishable by the *regulator* as an instrument of the State, which can be dealt with in the administrative, civil, or criminal justice systems in their *jurisdiction*.

(see also: Balance of Probabilities; Beyond Reasonable Doubt; Breach/es; Burden of Proof; Offence/s; Violation/s)

Criminal Case/Matter

A *criminal case/matter* involves the *regulator* operating in, making decisions, and involving others in criminal proceedings.

As opposed to the *regulator* operating in and making decisions in the administrative sphere of its operations, and/or referring the matter as part of civil proceedings.

Examples of a *criminal case/matter* might include decisions and actions taken in respect to seeking *imprisonment* or *community service orders*.

(see also: Administrative Case/Matter; Civil Case/Matter)

Criminal Remedy/Response/Sanction[31]

For *regulators* the terms remedy/ies, response/s, and sanction/s tend to be used interchangeably, interrelatedly, and collectively. However, it should be noted that *criminal remedy/ies* are more aligned with punishment, while *civil remedy/ies* may also be designed to incorporate aspects of compensation.

A *criminal remedy* tends to come in the form of or be part of a response or sanction.

A *criminal response* is a response that is available to a *regulator* when drawing upon the *criminal power* they have access to. Often a *criminal response* will be used either as an alternative to or in parallel with an *administrative response* or a *civil response*.

An example of a *criminal* response is when a *regulator* establishes, or a *regulated entity* admits to, a *breach* of a *licence* condition. The *regulator* may either:

- initiate a *criminal response* themselves through the appropriate *court* or body within their *jurisdiction*, if they have the capability, capacity, and the necessary arrangements in place; or
- refer the matter to the relevant *prosecuting authority* within their *jurisdiction*.

Regulators generally initiate a *criminal response* when the *criminal sanctions* are appropriate given the circumstances of the offending or *breach*. The recording of a criminal conviction, *fines*, and *imprisonment* are examples of some of the outcomes of a *criminal response*.

Criminal sanctions are penalties or other means of *enforcement* which are used to provide incentives for obedience (*compliance*) with the *law*, and/or relevant *rules* or *regulations*.

Given their link with *crime* and criminality, *criminal sanctions* traditionally tend to be viewed as a reflection of society's strong moral condemnation for the illegal behaviour.

For *regulators*, and depending on the *jurisdiction*, the three main *criminal sanctions* that typically apply are:

- *imprisonment* (served or suspended);
- *fines*; and
- *community service order/s*.

There are other sanctions, depending on the *jurisdiction*, that can be defined as *criminal sanctions*.[32]

(see also: Administrative Remedy/Response/Sanction; Civil Remedy/Response/Sanction)

Criteria

Is a standard by which something can be judged, decided, or dealt with.

When *regulators* use the word *criteria*, they tend to be discussing it in terms of the *criteria* being used to inform:

- their *risk profiles* or settings – as contained in their *risk matrix* (or equivalent);
- their approach to initial assessment and allocation of *cases* – as contained in their *triaging* procedures (or equivalent); and/or
- their approach to escalating or de-escalating a *regulatory response* – in accordance with their *compliance and enforcement policy* (or equivalent).

(see also: Risk Criteria; Risk Matrix; Risk Profile; Risk Ratings)

Customer/s

Regulators **do not** have *customers*. Therefore, the word *customer* should not be used.

There are several reasons why the term *customer* is at worst wrong, or at best extremely problematic. The two main reasons include the fact that:

- *regulated entities* do not have the right of choice. They cannot choose which agency regulates them – and the issue of choice (i.e., the ability to vote with your feet if you like) is central to the customer vs service provider relationship; and
- *regulators* do not provide services (in the traditional sense). Instead, if anything, *regulators* impose duties and *obligations* on *regulated entities*[33] – and therefore are not a service provider.

It is important for *regulators* to note that *regulated entities* 'can never be considered customers in the ordinary sense of the word. Regulation is ultimately the exercise of the coercive power of the state'.[34]

(see also: Regulated Entities; Regulator)

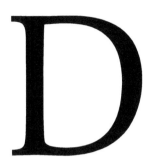

Decision/s (see Statutory Decisions)

Decision-Making

Making a choice (or choices) to determine the best or most appropriate course of action, from a range of possible options, by accessing and using the best *information* available.

The *decisions* that *regulators* make in respect to regulatory matters[35] tend to occur in three typical contexts:

- initial regulatory *decisions* – are *decisions* that *authorised officers* make (either in the field or at their desk), which often involve the use of *regulatory powers/statutory authority*,
  - these *decisions* often involve the *authorised officer* using their general *discretion*;
- subsequent regulatory *decisions* – where the above-mentioned *decisions* are then fed into or inform a broader set/range of *decisions*,
  - these *decisions* may be made by another *authorised officer*, or a *regulatory manager* or *regulatory executive* who may or may not be an *authorised officer*; and
- delegated regulatory *decisions* – are *decisions* made by the decision-maker utilising their formal/designated *delegation*,
  - *delegations* tend to be used for more important *decisions*, or *decisions* that can have serious or broader implications, for example accessing *coercive powers* or initiating *litigation*.

(see also: Binding Precedent; Decision/s; Decision-Review; Delegation; Discretion; Internal Regulatory Bodies; Non-Binding Precedent; Precedent/s)

Decision-Review

The process of reviewing a *decision* to establish whether the appropriate *decision* was made. And/or if this is not possible, determining whether the proper *decision-making* processes were followed, and that relevant factors were considered.

Decisions can be reviewed internally or externally, with:

- internal reviews – usually conducted by a senior officer, who was not involved (or had any vested interest) in the original *decision/s*; and
- external reviews – can be made by any number of bodies, if *independence* and *transparency* can be demonstrated.

Decisions can be reviewed informally or formally. With the choice being triggered or informed by:

- fixed factors – such as legislative, policy, or procedural requirements; and
- variable factors – such as the nature of the original *decision*; who made the original *decision*; and the impact and ramifications of the *decision*.

While a *decision-review* might be related (directly or indirectly) to a *complaint* or *allegation*, efforts should be made not to conflate it with *decisions* made relating to a *complaint* or *allegation*.

(see also: Binding Precedent; Decision/s; Decision-Making; Delegation; Discretion; Internal Regulatory Bodies; Merits Review; Non-Binding Precedent; Precedent/s)

Defendant

Person or *regulated entity* who has been *accused* in a court of law, either civil or criminal, of having done something wrong.

In a linear sense: *suspect, accused, defendant.*

(see also: Accused; Claimant; Defendant; Plaintiff; Suspect).

Delegated Legislation (see Secondary Legislation)

Delegation

Granting formal authority and responsibility for functions or *decisions*.

For *regulators*, and in reference to *decision-making* purposes, *delegation* typically relates to the devolution of statutory powers or *regulatory functions* from one authority ('the delegator') to another authority ('the delegate').

A *delegation* takes the form of a written document ('the instrument') which details specifically, or by class (or group), the statutory powers that have been delegated.

(see also: Decision-Making; Discretion)

De-regulation

De-regulation refers to the removal, lessening, or streamlining of *regulations* or restrictions on *regulated entities* (whether individuals or companies).

De-regulation and associated de-regulatory activities can be directed towards:

- **all forms** of regulation – irrespective of the *regulatory regime/scheme,*
  - an example might be the 'one in one out rule' which means that for every new *regulation* or *rule* introduced, one existing *regulation* or *rule* needs to be repealed or removed;
- **certain types** of *regulation* – either economic, environmental, or social,
  - an example in environmental *regulation* might be that specific *permits*, for activities (or classes or prescribed activities) that sit beneath an overarching *approval*, are no longer required for environmental (land clearance) activities;
- **sub-sets** of *regulated entities* – either by industry, sector, or geographic location,
  - an example might be reducing the scheme-entry requirements for *regulated entities* operating as customs brokers, because the government wants to streamline supply chain movement to speed up the economic recovery; and/or

- **certain aspects** of *regulation* – in terms of specific *regulatory functions*,
  - an example might be reducing the number of *inspections* a regulated *premise* is subjected to in a year from four to two, by changing *inspections* from every three months (quarterly) to every six months (biannually).

(see also: Red Tape; Regulatory Burden; Stock, Flow and Effectiveness (of regulation))

Deter, Detect, Disrupt (as a mantra and approach)

Reference to a multi-layered approach that a *regulator* might use as part of its proactive and preventative measures. For example:

- *regulators* might initially direct efforts to **deter** wrongdoing, through a range of activities including use of media and communications strategies,
  - rationale: prevention is better and cheaper than needing to intervene;
- *regulators* might also have established processes, mechanisms, systems, and arrangements in place to assist them to **detect** wrongdoing, this often includes use of data and *information* held by other regulatory, enforcement, or policing bodies,
  - rationale: if prevention is not possible let's make sure we have a chance to detect wrongdoing, otherwise we will always be responding reactively; and
- *regulators* might also attempt to **disrupt** wrongdoing, through use of various arrangements, systems, and processes,
  - rationale: if prevention and detection is not possible let's make it more difficult for wrongdoing to occur.

(see also: Engage, Educate, and Enforce (as a mantra and approach))

Determination

A *determination* has various meanings, the main ones that impact on the work of *regulators* include:

- a type of *legislative instrument*;
- a decision made by an impartial third party, such as a *judicial officer* (judge or magistrate); or

- where an *authorised officer* makes a judgement call as to whether an *act* or *regulations* have not been complied with by a *regulated entity*.

(see also: Burden of Proof; Legislative Instrument)

Deterrence

Deterrence is the act of preventing something from occurring.

Deterrence has a long history and is frequently discussed in regulatory, enforcement, and policing agencies, in relation to its effectiveness in administrative, civil, and/or criminal contexts.

Deterrence can be specific or general, for example:

- specific *deterrence* – might involve a *regulator* actively pursuing an individual *person* or *regulated entity* to drive home the point that *non-compliance* will not be tolerated; or
- general *deterrence* – might involve a *regulator* increasing its *inspection* frequency and intensity, which has impacts on a broader group of *regulated entities* operating in the same industry or sector that a *breach* or instance of specific *deterrence* highlighted.

Deterrence in the regulatory context, is founded on the *deterrence* theory, which is based upon the threat that punishment will deter *regulated entities* from committing *crimes* or failing to comply with their regulatory *obligations*. However, for *deterrence* to be effective it is said that four factors need to exist. Namely that:

- there is a likelihood of being detected;
- that once detected there is a reasonable chance of being apprehended;
- that having been apprehended there is a likelihood of being punished; and
- that the punishment exceeds the benefit of the wrongdoing.

The problem with the *deterrence* theory is that it assumes that individuals (that lead and/or work within *regulated entities*) are rational actors. This is not always the case and is not consistent with the experiences of *regulators*, who can cite numerous examples of what led to an *offence*, *breach*, or instance of *non-compliance* not being based on rational thought, choice, or actions.[36]

(see also: Deter, Detect, Disrupt (as a mantra and approach); Regulatory Approach)

Direct Government Regulation

Direct government regulation is the most used form of *regulation* and involves *regulation* that is underpinned by *primary legislation* and *subordinate legislation.*

(see also: Primary Legislation; Subordinate Legislation)

Directed Compliance

Directed compliance is when the *regulator* becomes more directive with those *regulated entities* who have shown that they are not able or willing to comply, even after they have been offered assistance, or have demonstrated a propensity for *non-compliance.*

Diagrammatically, it is the third of four phases contained in the *VADE Model.*

(see also: Assisted Compliance; Enforced Compliance; Voluntary Compliance; *VADE Model*)

Directive

An official instruction, direction, or order, issued by someone in authority.

In a regulatory context, *directive* can have several meanings or interpretations, including when:

- *regulators* are accused of being *directive* – it can indicate that they are (or are perceived as being) over reliant on *rules* based and prescriptive *regulation*;
- *regulators* utilise *directive* approaches – it can indicate that voluntary, and assisted approaches to bring an entity back into *compliance* have been unsuccessful and that *enforced compliance* approaches might be necessary (see the *VADE Model*).

(see also: Regulation; *VADE Model*)

Discretion

Discretion relates to the ability or choice to decide what should be done in a particular situation.

For *regulators,* it is important that the *discretion* they use is:
- confined to the *authorising environment* that they are operating in;
- within their overall *regulatory mandate*; and
- consistent with their *regulatory powers.*[37]

Ironically, *discretion* is most often used by *regulators* as the basis not to do something or to modify a course of action that is underway. For example:
- *regulatory practitioners* (in the field) – especially in *authorised officer* roles may conduct an *inspection* of a regulated *premise* and detect four separate *breaches* of a *permit,*
  - using their **individual** *discretion*, they decide to issue three notices, as they form the opinion that the three notices adequately reflect the nature of the *breach*;
- *regulatory managers* (in the field, but most likely office) – especially in supervisory/*quality assurance* roles, may check or vet the three notices in the example above,
  - using their **management** *discretion*, they decide to withdraw one of the notices, as they form the opinion that pursuing the two remaining notices adequately reflects the nature of the *breach*, given the current *regulatory posture* the *regulator* is projecting/maintaining in the *regulated sector* that the *breaches* occurred; and
- *regulatory executives* (in the office) – especially in governance and oversight roles, may consider the two notices in the example above as part of an *internal regulatory body,*
  - using their **senior executive management** *discretion*, they refer the two remaining notices to their *prosecuting authority* for advice on suspending the notices and initiating *litigation*. As they believe a recent shift in the *authorising environment* and the collective behaviour of the *regulated sector* means that *litigation* might be more appropriate and be consistent with their *regulatory strategy*; and
- *prosecuting authorities* – when exercising their own *discretion*, in the form of *prosecutorial discretion*.

It is important for *regulators* to note that *discretion* cannot be fettered, i.e., a statutory decision-maker with legal *discretion* cannot be ordered to decide a specific outcome.

(see also: Intra Vires; Ultra Vires; Prosecutorial Discretion)

Diversion

For *regulators*, *diversion* tends to be used in two main contexts:

- generally – relating to diverting from the current course or activity to another, for example diverting some, or all, of their resources or regulatory focus from A to B; or
- specifically – referring to the process of *diversion* which moves an *accused*, *offender*, or *regulated entity* from one process to another, for example moving them out of the criminal justice system and into an alternate (non-prosecutorial) process or program.

(see also: Alternate Dispute Resolution)

Documentary Evidence

Is *evidence* that is in written form, as opposed to spoken (i.e., *oral evidence*).

For a *regulator*, an example of *documentary evidence* might be:

- the provision of a *written statement* or *affidavit* as part of proceedings; or
- an application for a *licence* or *permit* (that has been filled in by hand, lodged on-line, or at least signed by the applicant) taking the form of an exhibit in proceedings.

(see also: Evidence; Oral Evidence)

Duty Holder/s (see Regulated)

Earned Autonomy/Recognition

Earned autonomy is based on the principle that well or higher performing entities are subjected to less control than bad or poor performing entities.

In practice, *earned autonomy* for:

- *regulated entities* – means being subjected to less controls, most usually in the form of less frequent and intense *inspections* or *audits* and might even result in lower *licensing* or *registration* fees (see OPRA); and

- *regulators* – means assessing and determining the level of *regulatory risk* for a *regulated entity* or *regulatory sector*, with due consideration and recognition of the way in which the *regulated entity* is addressing (i.e., identifying, managing, and responding) *regulatory risk* and their rates of *compliance*.

(see also: Compliance History; Regulated Self-Assurance; Regulatory Posture; Regulatory Sandbox/es; Responsive Regulation; Risk-based Prioritisation)

Educate (see Engage, Educate, and Enforce)

Note: often used in conjunction with *engage* and *enforce*.

Enforce (see Engage, Educate, and Enforce)

Note: often used in conjunction with *engage* and *educate*.

Enforceable

Reference to a *law, rule,* or *obligation* that can be imposed, so that it must be complied with, and which if not complied with has an expectation that it can and will be enforced.

(see also: Enforcement; Engage, Educate, and Enforce (as a mantra and approach))

Enforceable Order

Is an order issued by a *court* which demands that a *person* or *regulated entity* comply with a *regulation* or *law.*

Non-compliance with an *enforceable order*, in some *jurisdictions*, might result in a penalty being issued (e.g., in circumstances where there has been a *contempt of court*).

(see also: Contempt of Court)

Enforceable Regulation[38]

Means *regulations* that are written in such a way that they can be enforced.

Key elements that assist in making *regulation* enforceable include that the:

- *regulated entities* or sector subject to the *obligations* are clearly defined;
- *obligations* on *regulated entities* are unambiguous, understandable, and achievable;
- *obligations* are communicated clearly and consistently; and
- *enforcement* responses and options available to the *regulator,* and the circumstances in which they will generally be deployed, are disclosed to *regulated entities* (e.g., by way of a *compliance and enforcement policy*).

(see also: Compliance and Enforcement Policy; Enforcement; Prosecution Policy)

Enforceable Undertaking[39]

An *enforceable undertaking* (EU) is a written and legally binding undertaking given by a *person* or *regulated entity,* to the *regulator,* as a remedy for *non-compliance* or a *breach* of *legislation.* EUs can appear very contract-like in their construction.

EUs are usually used as an alternative to criminal *litigation,* and are typically used to fix a problem or issue to prevent it from occurring again. As such *EUs* tend to incorporate elements of *restorative justice.*

For example, an *EU* might require a *person* or *regulated entity* to:

- improve or put new systems in place;
- improve or put new processes and procedures in place;
- provide additional training to staff and contractors; and
- provide funds to third parties to rehabilitate impacted sites.

(see also: Regulatory Response; Restorative Justice; Sanction)

Enforced Compliance

Enforced compliance is when a *regulator* uses *enforcement* (*litigation* and *prosecution*) mechanisms to access regulatory *sanctions* that either force *regulated entities* into *compliance* or remove them from a *regulatory regime/scheme.*

Diagrammatically, it is the fourth and narrowest of four phases contained in the *VADE Model.*

(see also: Assisted Compliance; Directed Compliance; **VADE Model**; Voluntary Compliance)

Enforcement

Enforcement is a *regulatory activity* which involves the *regulator* initiating or taking action against *regulated entities* who are in *breach* of regulatory requirements (i.e., *non-compliant*). It also involves the *regulator* using their *regulatory powers* and the force of the *law* to return *regulated entities* to *compliance* and/or *sanction* them as a deterrent.

Enforcement activities actively progress in a tangible way from the preliminary observations, suspicions and findings that occur in the *monitoring compliance* phase. It includes a specific focus on:

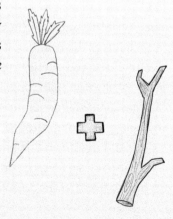

- escalated use of the *regulator's powers* – whether individually or in partnership with *co-* and *peer-regulators*; and
- engagement in *litigation* – whether administrative; civil; or criminal.

In a linear sense, it is the fifth of six phases contained in the *Extended Regulatory Spectrum*.

REGULATORY REGIME DESIGN	ADVICE AND GUIDANCE	LICENSING AND APPROVALS	MONITORING COMPLIANCE	ENFORCEMENT	REGULATOR PERFORMANCE AND EVALUATION

Enforcement activities include, but are not limited to:

- *fines*;
- *injunctions*;
- *prosecutions*; and
- revoking an *authorisation* so the *regulated entity* cannot legally participate in the relevant *regulatory regime/scheme* (market).

(see also: Deterrence, *Extended Regulatory Spectrum*; *VADE Model*)

Enforcement Committee
(see Internal Regulatory Bodies)

Enforcement Criteria

Are the criteria used by *regulators* in determining whether they initiate escalated *enforcement* action or not.

The number, nature, and extent of the *enforcement criteria* used by *regulators* are many and varied – and in some instances run into several dozen criteria and sub-criteria.

Whatever the number, it is usual for the *enforcement criteria* to be documented and detailed in the *regulator's compliance and enforcement policy*; *enforcement policy*; or *prosecution policy* (or equivalent).

Regulators will generally base their *enforcement criteria* on factors including, but not limited to, the:

- *acts* and *regulations* that are administered;
- industries, sectors, or commodities *regulated*;
- *jurisdictions* that the *regulator* is operating in and across; and

- parliamentary, public, and governmental expectations in terms of holding *regulated entities* to account.

The way in which *enforcement criteria* is used, along with the number of criteria used, can vary from one regulator to another. For example:
- two criteria[40] –
  - impact – e.g., serious, major, moderate, minor, or low, and
  - culpability – e.g., serious, moderate, or low; and
- three criteria[41] –
  - extent of detriment – which unpack into a further ten sub-criteria,
  - seriousness of conduct – which unpack into a further six sub-criteria, and
  - public interest – which unpack into a further seven sub-criteria

It is therefore important that all criteria and their related and interrelated factors are fully considered.

(see also: Enforcement Policy; Enforcement Principles; Enforcement Priorities; Statement of Expectations)

Enforcement Networks (see Networks)

Enforcement Policy

The policy developed by a *regulator* detailing how it will approach *enforcement* of the *acts* and *regulations* it administers.

A standalone *enforcement policy* is not common, as the *enforcement* elements of a policy are usually combined as part of either a *compliance and enforcement policy*, or a *prosecutions policy*.

If standalone, the *enforcement* elements of a *policy* tend to be brought together as a nested set with an education policy, and engagement policy.

(see also: Compliance and Enforcement Policy; Compliance Policy; Prosecution Policy; Regulatory Policy)

Enforcement Principles
(see Compliance and Enforcement Principles)

Enforcement Priorities (see Enforcement Criteria)

Enforcement Pyramid/Triangle
(see Compliance Pyramid/Triangle)

The *enforcement pyramid/triangle* is like the *compliance pyramid/triangle* but with a focus on the access to or use of *enforcement* tools, approaches, and *sanctions*.

(see also: Compliance Pyramid/Triangle; Enforced Compliance; Responsive Regulation; **VADE Model**)

Enforcement Strategies

Are the strategies that *regulators* develop and use as part of their *enforcement* activities.

Enforcement strategies can be:
- fixed and ongoing – in that they are enduring and are in place to address a (*strategic*) priority issue contained within the current *regulatory strategy* (or similar);
- fixed and non-ongoing – in that they might be used to address an emerging (*strategic* or *operational*) issue or risk that is not catered for in the current *regulatory strategy* (or similar), but will likely be included as an enduring priority in the next update; or
- flexible and non-ongoing – in that they might be used to address an emerging (*strategic, operational, or tactical*) issue or risk that is not catered for in the current *regulatory strategy* (or similar).

Enforcement strategies can be used:
- individually or in combination;
- within one or more of the four central phases of the *Extended Regulatory Spectrum*;
- deployed proactively or reactively; and
- with a preventative or punitive intent.

(see also: Enforcement; **Extended Regulatory Spectrum**; Regulatory Strategy; **Three Levels of Operational Activity**; **VADE Model**)

Engage (see Engage, Educate, and Enforce)

Note – often used in conjunction with *educate* and *enforce*.

Engage, Educate, and Enforce[42]
(as a mantra and approach)

Is a three-step approach that a *regulator* might use as part of its proactive and responsive regulatory activities, as well as representing escalating levels of government intervention. For example:

- *engage* – involves the *regulator* identifying and then working primarily with *regulated entities* (but can include *stakeholders* and the *wider community*), about what the *regulator* is attempting to achieve, and how they can (or more easily) comply with their regulatory requirements,
  - rationale: engagement assists in increasing rates of *voluntary compliance* and identifies those more likely to require *assisted compliance*;
- *educate* – involves the *regulator* providing or making information available to *regulated entities* about their rights and responsibilities, and how they can (or more easily) comply with their regulatory requirements,
  - rationale: education assists in increasing rates of *voluntary compliance*; and
- *enforce* – involves the *regulator* identifying *regulated entities* that are *non-compliant* (and who usually have not responded to assistance and direction (see *VADE Model*)) and using a range of *enforcement* options to bring the *regulated entity* back into *compliance* with their regulatory requirements,
  - rationale: *enforcement* assists in increasing rates of *directed compliance* because of the *deterrence* affect.

(see also: Deter, Detect, Disrupt (as a mantra and approach); *VADE Model*)

Ethical Business Practice (EBP)

Is a concept which has both a *regulator* and *regulated entity* dimension.

Ethical business practice requires regulated entities to be able to demonstrate that they are engaged in *ethical business practices*.

99

Ethical business practice occurs or exists in:

> '[a]n organisation in which the leaders consciously and consistently strive to create an effective ethical culture where employees do the right thing, based upon ethical values and supported by cultural norms and formal institutions. EBP requires people who can recognise ethical dilemmas, challenge constructively, speak up if they know or suspect unethical behaviour, and who use mistakes and wrongdoing as an opportunity to learn and improve. Engagement with [Ethical Business Regulation] EBR then requires the organisation to be open with its regulators and provide evidence of EBP'.[43]

(see also: Ethical Business Regulation)

Ethical Business Regulation (EBR)

Is a concept which has both a *regulator* and *regulated entity* dimension.

Ethical business regulation requires *regulators* to be able to demonstrate that they are engaged in *ethical business regulation*.

Ethical business regulation can be seen when there is a:

> '… relationship between a business [*regulated entity*], or a group of businesses [*regulated entities*], and a regulator, or group of regulators, in which the business [*regulated entity*] produces evidence of its ongoing commitment to [*Ethical Business Practice*] EBP and the regulator recognises and encourages that commitment'.[44]

(see also: Ethical Business Practice)

Evidence

Evidence is usually any document, testimony, or *exhibit* that is presented to and introduced to the independent arbiter (usually a judge or a jury), to prove or add weight to a point or element of a *contested matter.*

(see also: Best-evidence Rule; Documentary Evidence; Expert Evidence; Opinion Evidence; Oral Evidence; Secondary Evidence)

Evidence (process of giving evidence)

From time to time, *witnesses* are required to give *evidence* in proceedings, especially in *contested matters*.

There are various legal principles, conventions, and *rules* relating to what may or may not be admissible as *evidence* as part of a *contested matter*. These are influenced by *jurisdictional* issues and should be clarified with a lawyer or the *prosecuting authority*.[45]

The *evidence* that a *witness* can give is generally limited to those things that they have perceived through one or more of their five senses (i.e., sight, hearing; touch, taste, and smell).

Giving *evidence* in *court* and/or proceedings is a formal process, and usually involves formal notification of attendance through a witness request or subpoena.

Prior to giving *evidence* – a *witness* for the prosecution would usually have:

- produced or supplied a *statement* or *affidavit* about their involvement in a matter;
- had the opportunity to speak with (or be 'briefed' by) the lawyer or *prosecutor* representing the *prosecuting authority*; and
- had the opportunity to refresh their memory by reading their *statement* or *affidavit*.

Process of giving *evidence* – for a *witness* usually involves:

- examination in chief – this involves the *prosecutor* asking the *witness* a series of questions to enable the *witness* to detail their observations and account;
- cross-examination – this involves the defence (attorney/lawyer) asking the *witness* a series of questions which are intended to test and challenge (with the intention of discrediting) the voracity of the observations and account of the *witness*; and
- re-examination – this involves the *prosecutor* asking the *witness* some additional questions, from matters that have arisen during cross-examination, to clarify any aspects of the *evidence* the *witness* has given which is either unclear or might be misinterpreted.

(see also: Best-evidence Rule; Documentary Evidence; Expert Evidence; Opinion Evidence; Oral Evidence; Secondary Evidence; Witness; Witness Statement)

Ex-ante Regulation

Ex-ante is Latin for 'before the event', so *ex-ante* activities are based on forecasts rather than actual results.

Therefore, most regulation is *ex-ante regulation*.

Ex-ante regulation seeks to identify problems beforehand and then shape *stakeholder* behaviour and responses through *regulatory intervention*.

Ex-ante regulation therefore occurs when government action is taken prior to the bad or offending behaviour by a *person* or *regulated entity* (or sector), as a form of anticipatory government intervention.

(see also: Ex-post Regulation)

Exclusion Order

Is a *regulatory response* that is available to some *regulators* under certain *regulatory regimes/schemes*.

Exclusion orders, if available, typically form part of a *regulator's* choices/options as an *administrative response*. However, *exclusion orders* can also be part of a penalty or *sanction* (either civilly or criminally) following the admission or finding of guilt.

Examples of *exclusion orders* from a liquor and/or gaming *regulator's* perspective would include an order that would prohibit:

- an individual – from entering or going near a licensed premises and/or premises where alcohol is sold or consumed.
- an individual – from entering or going near a licensed premises and/or premises where gaming/gambling can occur.

Exclusion orders can share similarities with *banning orders*, as they have a protective element, often protecting the person from themselves.

(see also: Administrative Remedy/Response/Sanction; Banning Order)

(The) Executive

The *executive* is one of the three branches of government in a Westminster System of government.

Executive powers are one of three powers subject to separation under the Westminster System of government. The other two are judicial and legislative powers.

For *regulators*, the role of the *executive* is associated with executing and enforcing *law*. *Regulators* usually report to and are accountable to the *executive*, typically in the form of a government minister. While *regulators* are often given statutory *discretion* in day-to-day operational *decision-making*, the *executive* branch of government are increasingly making their broader expectations of the *regulator* known, through mechanisms such as a *statement of expectations* or equivalent.

(see also: (The) Judiciary; (The) Legislature)

Exhibit

An *exhibit* is a physical object or document that can be produced and/or identified in *court* (or proceedings) for use as *evidence*.

An *exhibit* is usually produced and explained by a *witness* in *court*, but they can equally be referred to in a *statement* or *affidavit* prepared by a *witness*.

(see also: Affidavit; Best-evidence Rule; Chain of Custody; Secondary Evidence; Statement)

Ex-officio [Latin]

Is Latin for 'from the office' or 'by right of office'.

Ex-officio appointments relate to a position and not an individual person.

Some *acts* have a clause which states that a certain type or class of position holder is or may be appointed *ex-officio*. For example, section 397 of the *Environment Protection and Biodiversity Conservation Act* 1999 (Cwth./AU) provides for a range of *ex-officio* appointments for *inspectors*, including:

- each member or special member of the Australian Federal Police;[46]
- each member of the police force of an external Territory;[47]
- each officer of Customs;[48]
- each quarantine officer;[49] and
- officers or employees of the Public Service of the State or Territory, or of an authority of the State or Territory (including a local government body).

(see also: Authorised Officer; Inspector; Ranger; Warden)

Expert Evidence

Expert evidence is *evidence* that is given by a *person*:
- whose opinion is based upon (a combination of) education, training, certification, skills, or experience; and
- is accepted by the judge (or tribunal) as an expert.

An *expert witness* has a duty to assist the *court* in areas within their field of expertise. This duty to the *court* is independent of, and overrides, any instruction they are taking from the party they are representing, employed by, or taking payment from.

(see also: Evidence; Opinion Evidence)

Expert Model, of regulation

The *expert model of regulation* focusses on *risks*, as the overarching *framework* for *regulatory activities* and operations.[50]

(see also: Legal Model, of regulation)

Ex-post regulation

Ex-post is Latin for 'after the event', so *ex-post* activities are based on actual results rather than predictions or forecasts.

Ex-post regulation seeks to address problems after the event and then shape *stakeholder* behaviour and responses through *regulatory intervention*.

Ex-post regulation therefore occurs when government action is taken post the bad or offending behaviour by a *regulated entity* (or sector), as a form of remedial government intervention.

(see also: Ex-ante Regulation)

Extended Regulatory Spectrum

REGULATORY REGIME DESIGN	ADVICE AND GUIDANCE	LICENSING AND APPROVALS	MONITORING COMPLIANCE	ENFORCEMENT	REGULATOR PERFORMANCE AND EVALUATION

The six phases of the *Extended Regulatory Spectrum*[51] provide a framework of activities for holistic *regulatory practice*. They are (in a linear sense, from left to right):

- *Regulatory Regime Design;*
- *Advice and Guidance;*
- *Licensing and Approvals;*
- *Monitoring Compliance;*
- *Enforcement;* and
- *Regulator Performance and Evaluation.*

(see also: **Extended Regulatory Spectrum**)

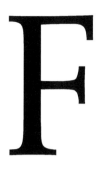

Fault Element

Fault elements (also known as *mental elements*) are those elements that a *regulator* needs to cover or prove for *offences* where a *mental element* or *fault element* needs to be established.

Fault elements include intention, knowledge, recklessness, and negligence.[52]

(see also: Actus Reus [Latin]; Mental Element)

Fine/s

Is a *regulatory response* that is available to some *regulators* under certain *regulatory regimes/schemes*.

Fines, if available, typically form part of a *regulator's* choices/options as a *criminal response*. However, *fines* can also be part of a penalty or *sanction* (either administrative or civil) following the admission or finding of guilt.

Fines are a monetary penalty. The amount of the *fine* is in the currency of the *jurisdiction* in which the *breach* or offending occurred, and penalty is issued. The amount of the *fine* is either a defined and prescribed amount, or it may fall within a pre-determined range.

(see also: Administrative Remedy/Response/Sanction; Civil Remedy/Response/Sanction; Criminal Remedy/Response/Sanction; Sanction)

Fit and Proper (Person) Test

The purpose of a *fit and proper (person) test* is to determine whether an applicant is suitable for entry into a restricted scheme.

Fit and proper (person) tests therefore form part of the pre-entry assessment and approval process.

The nature and extent of the *fit and proper (person) test* will vary from one *regulator* to another, and potentially between one *regulatory regime/ scheme* and another. Even if the test is administered by the same *regulator* or *regulatory body*.

Despite differences, an aspect of *fit and proper (person) tests* is usually a questionnaire and associated declaration, which typically include questions relating to the applicant (and in some instances their associates or business partners) in terms of:

- previous criminal history, especially relating to dishonesty *offences* or matters relating to integrity and ethics;
- any pending *court* proceeding or disciplinary matters;
- financial history, in terms of viability, including debts, and previous insolvency; and
- whether they have previously been disqualified from holding directorships of companies.

There can be significant penalties for providing false or misleading information in a *fit and proper (person) test*.

Although, *fit and proper (person) tests* are primarily undertaken as part of the initial pre-entry assessment and approval process, they may also be:

- an ongoing *obligation* for the applicant, if something changes in their personal or professional circumstances, to inform or make a disclosure to the authorising body; and
- required if circumstances such as several instances of *non-compliance* or proven *breaches* occur, which may trigger a re-assessment/ re-disclosure.

This is an important tool for *regulators* – as many *regulators* have regretted not undertaking this process or not undertaking it comprehensively enough. It is often easier to prevent a person or *regulated entity* from entering a *regulatory regime/scheme* than it is to establish the grounds necessary to remove them.

(see also: Authorisation; Earned Autonomy/Recognition; Compliance History)

Fixed Penalty Notice
(colloquially an 'On-the-spot-fine')

Is a *regulatory response* that is available to some *regulators* under certain *regulatory regimes/schemes.*

A *fixed penalty notice* is a subset of the broader *fines* listing.

Fixed penalty notices, if available, typically form part of a *regulator's* choices/options as an *administrative response.*

Fixed penalty notices are only able to be issued to a *person* or *regulated entity* for certain (prescribed) *offences.*

A key feature of a *fixed penalty notice* is that a *person* or *regulated entity* pay the prescribed amount of money (attached to the respective notice) without an admission of guilt.

(see also: Fine/s, Infringement Notice; On-the-spot-fine; Infringement Notice)

Four Key Regulatory Perspectives (4KRP)

The *Four Key Regulatory Perspectives (4KRP)* include and reflect the four main regulatory actors, and the respective lenses that they consider regulatory matters through. The *4KRP* are:

- *regulator* – includes *co-* and *peer-* regulators, from *regulatory* and *enforcement agencies* (whether in the same or different level of government);
- *regulated* – those directly subjected to *regulation* (usually but not always by explicit *authorisation*);

- *stakeholders* – with clear interests and stakes in *regulation* (e.g., *peak bodies,* representing *regulated entities*); and
- *wider community* – as the name suggests, are those individuals who do not identify as being a *regulator, regulated,* or belonging to a specific *stakeholder* group.

(see also: **Four Key Regulatory Perspectives**)

REGULATOR	REGULATED
STAKEHOLDER	WIDER COMMUNITY

Frameworks (see Regulatory Frameworks)

Fraud

Fraud is a *crime* for which there are criminal penalties.

Fraud occurs when intentional deception is used to secure an unfair or *unlawful* benefit.

Fraud generally involves a *person* or *regulated entity*:

- receiving some form of advantage or benefit (whether financial or non-financial); or
- avoiding an *obligation* or cost.

Fraud can intersect with *regulatory* and *enforcement* work in several ways. Examples of fraud might include a *person* or *regulated entity*:

- using counterfeit certificates or counterfeit *permits* to facilitate the trade in endangered species;[53]
- falsifying records ahead of an *audit* conducted by the *regulator;* and
- securing a benefit that one is not entitled to; or using another person's identity to secure a benefit or avoid an *obligation*.

Fraud is an important issue for *regulators* to be aware of – particularly so for those *regulators* whose *regulatory regimes/schemes* intersect with programs and incentives.

(see also: Crime)

Functional approach, to regulation

Involves clustering or grouping *regulatory activities* into functional (or like groups).

For example, the core and non-core *regulatory functions* within a *regulatory agency* might be arranged by:

- primary approach – e.g., education; engagement; and *enforcement*;
- process descriptors – e.g., *approvals* and assessment; *audit* and *inspection*; *investigation* and *prosecution*;
- job descriptions – e.g., assessor; auditor; *inspector*; *investigator*; lawyer; *prosecutor*; or
- regulated domain – e.g., industry; sector; site.

The *functional approach to regulation* is popular with *regulators* as they often see it as:

- a way to recognise and support the expertise that exists, within and across these functions; and
- a means to preserve and develop such expertise.

(see also: Regulatory Activity/ies; Regulatory Delivery; Regulatory Practice)

Gaming Behaviour/Gaming the System

These terms refer to the deliberate manipulation or exploitation of the *rules*, processes, procedures, or broad requirements that are designed to regulate and control a given system. *Regulated entities* engage in such behaviour, in an attempt to gain some form of advantage over other users.[54]

In a regulatory context, these are activities undertaken by, or behaviours displayed by *regulated entities* to circumvent or frustrate a *regulatory regime/scheme*.

A *regulated entity* may attempt to manipulate aspects (especially weaknesses) of a *regulatory regime/scheme* for maximum benefit.

Examples might include a *person* or *regulated entity*:

- engaging in practices and/or establishing company structures, to evade tax;
- breaking financial transactions down, to ensure bank transfers are less than the reporting threshold for anti-money laundering *regulation*;
- exploiting (by manipulating and deliberately misinterpreting) a legal loophole intended to only be used in exceptional circumstances; or
- contriving to report figures that sit just beneath a threshold that would trigger other regulatory *obligations*.

A *regulated entity* who uses *gaming behaviour* or is *gaming the system*, may give the outward appearance of *compliance* and co-operation. However, this will often not be reflected by tangible or demonstrable *compliance*. As such, *regulated entities* operating in this way will often come across to *authorised officers* as not being genuine.

(see also: Non-compliance)

General Preventative Duty (GPD)

A *general preventative duty*, as the name suggests, moves the focus to prevention and in turn transfers greater responsibility to the *person* or *regulated entity* to ensure they are complying with their regulatory *obligations* and/or legislative requirements.

From the perspective of the *regulator* a *GPD*:

- can impact upon their *authorising environment* and *regulatory practices* because it generally reflects a move away from a prescriptive and responsive approach, towards one that is more principles and outcomes based and preventative.

From the perspective of *regulated entities*, a *GPD*:

- might first be socialised with them as part of *regulatory regime design* consultations;
- may require different types and levels of detail in terms of the *advice and guidance* material produced and made available by *regulators*;
- will most likely be first observable in terms of changes to their *authorisation* (or broader *licensing and approvals*);

- will then be observable in changes to the *monitoring compliance* activities they are subjected to by the *regulator*; and
- will be especially apparent in relation to the *burden of proof* required to establish and prove *breaches* or instances of *non-compliance,* for the *enforcement* activities a *regulated entity* becomes involved in.

(see also: Authorising Environment; Regulatory Practices)

GPD (see General Preventative Duty)

Green Tape

Green tape relates to processes or requirements that are associated with environmental protection, including natural resource management and/or heritage matters.

Green tape is considered, to be any unnecessary and/or convoluted (or at least inefficient) processes, procedures, and reporting requirements that governments (or bureaucracies) place upon *regulated entities,* that are attempting to engage in environmental, natural resource management or heritage approvals and works, or similar.

Green tape is an additional layer of regulatory complexity, distinguishable from *red tape.*

(see also: Beige Tape; Grey Tape; Red Tape; Regulatory Burden)

Grey Tape (see Beige Tape)

Guilty Knowledge (see *Mens Rea*)

Hampton Principles

(see also: Hampton Review; PACTT; Principles of Good Regulation)

Hampton Review

The *Hampton Review* was a review that occurred in the United Kingdom in 2005, under the auspice of the HM Treasury.

The focus of the *Hampton Review* was on effective regulatory *inspection* and *enforcement*.

The core principles (sometimes referred to as the *Hampton Principles*) that came out of that review were summarised as: *Proportionality, Accountability, Consistency, Transparency, and Targeting (or PACTT)* and which when considered in combination inform the *Principles of Good Regulation.*

The complete set of principles of *inspection* and *enforcement* include that:

- 'regulators, and the regulatory system as a whole, should use comprehensive risk assessment to concentrate resources on the areas that need them most;
- regulators should be accountable for the efficiency and effectiveness of their activities, while remaining independent in the decisions they take;
- all regulations should be written so that they are easily understood, easily implemented, and easily enforced, and all interested parties should be consulted when they are being drafted;
- no inspection should take place without a reason;

- businesses should not have to give unnecessary information, nor give the same piece of information twice;
- the few businesses that persistently break regulations should be identified quickly, and face proportionate and meaningful sanctions;
- regulators should provide authoritative, accessible advice easily and cheaply;
- when new policies are being developed, explicit consideration should be given to how they can be enforced using existing systems and data to minimise the administrative burden imposed;
- regulators should be of the right size and scope, and no new regulator should be created where an existing one can do the work; and
- regulators should recognise that a key element of their activity will be to allow, or even encourage, economic progress and only to intervene when there is a clear case for protection'.[55]

The principles of *inspection* and *enforcement* are important for *regulators* given that *inspection* and *enforcement* activities are central activities to *regulatory practice* and *regulatory delivery*. The nature, style, frequency and intensity of *inspection* and *enforcement* activities strongly reflect and impact upon a regulator's *regulatory posture*, and influences their overall regulatory credibility among *co-regulators, regulated entities, stakeholders,* and the *wider community*.

The way that any *sanctions* arising from *inspection* and *enforcement* activities are approached is also important, this is addressed in the *Macrory Review*.

(see also: Macrory Review; PACTT; Principles of Good Regulation; Regulatory Posture)

Harms-based Regulation

Harms-based regulation involves a *regulator* targeting or directing regulatory resources and activities towards the most serious harms they are asked to control.

For example, the seriousness of harms may include and be measured in terms of deaths, workplace injuries, and hospitalisations associated with food poisoning – for road safety, work health and safety, and food safety *regulators* respectively.

Harms often present as complex and multi-dimensional problems that come about because of a range of factors. If *regulators* aspire to follow a harms-based approach then the harms[56] need to be well understood and analysed – especially before any interventions are designed, developed, and deployed. This is because the more specific the targeting of interventions are the greater the likelihood of nullifying or at least reducing the harm/s.

Harms-based regulation therefore involves using the following methods:
- *risk management*;
- systematic harm identification; and
- the *problem-solving approach to regulation*.

Harms-based regulation sees *regulators*:
- directing efforts towards the management of harms which are at a scale, and which can or have the ability, to impact on the delivery of *regulatory outcomes*;
- prioritising and co-ordinating response efforts, within their *regulatory agency* and in conjunction with their *co-* and *peer- regulators*, *stakeholders*, and in some instances the *wider community*; and
- developing more customised and effective responses, instead of trying to treat an unusual or unique harm with a conventional *regulatory response*.

Harms-based regulation tends to have multiple meanings which can then be interpreted differently, especially in an applied sense of implementation. It is therefore critical that *regulators* be:
- very clear and precise about what class/es of harm they are attempting to address; and
- purposeful and transparent about and clearly communicate their reasons for selecting and prioritising any particular or specific harms.

(see also: Risk-based Regulation; Problem-Solving approach to regulation; Types of Regulation)

Identification Card (see Identity Card)

Identity Card

Identity cards are cards issued to *authorised officers* or *authorised persons*.

Identity cards vary between *jurisdictions* and can have different requirements due the *act* or *regulations* that they cover. However, they tend to have several standard features, which include:

- a photograph of the person named on the card (the card holder);
- reference to the *act/s* or *regulation/s* that the card holder is appointed under;
- the agency or body that the card holder is either employed by or acting on behalf of; and
- any limitations or restrictions to specific powers or authority.

Identity cards are critically important for *regulators*. This is because in some instances, possessing and producing (showing) an *identity card* is a pre-requisite for exercising certain *regulatory powers*, e.g., as an *authorised officer* seeking to enter a *premise*.

For this reason, *regulators* need to demonstrate due diligence across all aspects associated with the issuing of *identity cards*. With the key aspects including, but not limited to, that:

- applicants hold the requisite minimum and mandatory qualifications for initial and ongoing appointment;
- there are policies and procedures in place for the initial and ongoing appointment of *authorised officers*;
- the person officially appointing the *authorised officer* holds the appropriate *delegation*, and delegations are up to date;
- *identity cards* and relevant written instruments or statutory appointments are correctly constructed and valid, including any limitations or restrictions associated with the appointment; and
- there is adequate governance and quality control over initial appointments and re-appointments of *authorised officers*.

(see also: Warrant Card)

Impact Analysis

Impact analysis, when discussed by *regulators* tends to be a shorthand reference to *regulatory impact analysis* (RIA[a]).

Impact analysis is an *ex-ante* analysis of the impacts new *regulation* is expected to have on *regulated entities*.

(see also: Impact Assessment; Impact Statement; Regulatory Impact Analysis)

Impact Assessment

Impact assessment, when discussed by *regulators* tends to be a shorthand reference to *regulatory impact assessment* (RIA[b]).

(see also: Impact Analysis; Impact Statement; Regulatory Impact Assessment)

Impact Statement

Impact statement, when discussed by *regulators* tends to be a shorthand reference to *regulation impact statement (RIS)*.

However, it can also be a reference to the impact a *crime* or *breach* has had on:

- a human victim – which is then referred to as a *victim impact statement*; or
- a non-human victim (usually the natural environment) – which then forms part of the broader impact, harm and associated factors in sentencing submissions or negotiations around penalty, restitution, and remediation.

(see also: Impact Analysis; Impact Assessment; Regulation Impact Statement; Victim Impact Statement)

Implementation

Implementation, when discussed by *regulators* tends to be a shorthand reference to actively implementing or executing:

- *regulatory policy;*
- *regulatory activities;* or
- *regulatory strategies*, operations, and tactics.

Implementation reflects a move beyond policy development and planning – and instead involves the *operational* (four central) phases of the *Extended Regulatory Spectrum*.

(see also: ***Extended Regulatory Spectrum***; Regulatory Delivery)

Imprisonment

Is a *regulatory response* that is available to some *regulators* under certain *regulatory regimes/schemes*.

Imprisonment is part of a *regulator's* choices/options as a *criminal response* and relies on a criminal conviction, following the admission or finding of guilt.

It is the top of the *compliance pyramid/triangle* and, outside of mainstream *law enforcement*, is typically used as a last resort in responding to *breaches* or *non-compliance* with *regulatory regimes/schemes*.

Terms of *imprisonment* can be:

- served completely – i.e., a custodial sentence, served in a correctional facility;
- served intermittently – i.e., a custodial sentence, served during weekends;
- served conditionally – i.e., a custodial sentence, in the form of house arrest; or
- suspended – i.e., a non-custodial sentence, but subject to probation conditions.

(see also: Civil Remedy/Response/Sanction; Criminal Remedy/Response/Sanction; Sanction; Suspended Sentence)

Independence

Independence when discussed by *regulators* tends to have several usual meanings, including reference to the *independence* of:

- the *regulator* itself – from undue external influence,[57] usually of or from government.[58] For example, allowing a *regulator* to issue or revoke an *authorisation*; and perform the day-to-day *operational* oversight (and *decision-making*) of a *regulator*;
- the *regulated* themselves – to conduct their activities without (undue) interference from the *regulator*, especially under *principles-based regulation* or *performance-based regulation*; and
- *third parties* – who undertake activities for either the *regulator* or *regulated*, with *audit* and *certification* being two examples.

(see also: Regulator Independence)

Indictable Offence

An *indictable offence* is a type or classification of *offence*, and one where the *defendant* has the right to elect to have a trial by jury.

Each *jurisdiction* has its own threshold for what constitutes an *indictable offence*.

Indictable offences are usually the more serious types of *offences* (against people, property, and society) and which attract longer terms of *imprisonment* or higher maximum *fines* than *summary offences*.

There are two categories of *indictable offences*:
- minor *indictable offences* – these can be heard in lower courts (e.g., Magistrates Court) where there is no jury, or the *defendant* can elect (or choose) to have the matter heard in a higher court (e.g., District or Supreme Court); and
- major *indictable offences* – which must be heard in the District or Supreme Court, which will be heard before a judge and jury, unless the *defendant* elects (or chooses) to have the matter heard before a judge alone.

The classification of *offences* is an important issue for *regulators* to be aware of – as it can affect a range of *regulatory activities*, including:
- how they might be required to collect *evidence* (usually the format of interviews);
- how they might be able to share *information* and *intelligence* with other *law enforcement* and *regulatory agencies*; and
- how these *offences* might meet or satisfy definitions such as 'serious crimes' which form part of a number of international *treaties* and *conventions*.[59]

(see also: Summary Offence/s)

Industry Representative Organisation

Refers to a body that represents (directly and indirectly) members or entities within a specified industry, sector, profession, or trade.

Examples that might intersect with *regulatory activities* include:
- Association of Civil Engineers – acting on behalf of an engineer whose work or advice has become part of an *investigation* being led by building and construction *inspectors*; or
- Society of Certified Practicing Accountants – acting on behalf of an accountant whose work, advice, or records have relevance to a *fraud* matter being led by tax/inland revenue auditors.

(see also: Stakeholder/s)

Information

The word *information* can have multiple meanings for a *regulator*.

For example, *information* can be considered as:

- some initial and general *information* that is received (especially if it is anonymous);
- the initiating step in *litigation* or proceedings, when someone (usually a victim, *witness*, or concerned party) comes forward;
- a process (often framed as 'the laying of an information') involving a *judicial officer*; or
- a formal legal document used in the higher courts (e.g., District or Supreme Court) that contains sufficient facts, *information*, and reasons as to why the *accused person* is suspected of having committed a *crime, breach*, or some form of wrongdoing.

(see also: Complaint; Litigation; Proceedings)

Information (sharing of, for law enforcement purposes)

Noting here that *information* relates to *information* that is held by, in the control of, or accessible by a third party, usually a government body.

Society has valid expectations that governments will only collect, hold, maintain, disclose, and use personal *information* and property consistent with their lawful *authority*.

It is for this reason, that most *jurisdictions* have:

- specific *legislation* and guidelines that govern matters relating to the collection and use of personal *information*; and
- oversight bodies such as an *information* or privacy commissioner or equivalent.

Sharing *information* within and across *regulatory, enforcement,* and policing agencies is a legitimate activity, and plays an important role in preventing, detecting, and establishing that *crimes* and/or *breaches* have been committed.

Generally, *information* can lawfully be shared with a *regulatory agency* for *law enforcement* purposes, or to ensure an *act, regulation* or regulatory provisions have or are being complied with.

(see also: Intelligence; Investigation)

Infringement Notice (see Fixed Penalty Notice)

Initial investigation

Regulators tend to use the term *initial investigation* and *preliminary investigation* interchangeably.

Regulators tend to conduct an *initial investigation,* to make an assessment of the known facts and *information* that is already or readily available to them, to determine if:

- the matter can be closed, as it may be a *vexatious complaint,* or it is simply not possible to substantiate it (even if a complete and thorough *investigation* was to be conducted);
- a *prima facie* case has been established; or
- sufficient *information* exists to escalate a matter to a more detailed *investigation.*

Initial investigation may be described within different agencies or *jurisdictions* as a detailed *investigation;* formal *investigation;* in-depth *investigation.* All typically involve the development of an *investigation* plan and access to additional resources beyond the lead investigator themselves.

(see also: Protracted Investigation)

Injunction

A *court order* directing a *person* (or *regulated entity*) to either:

- do a specific thing; or
- (more commonly) not to do, or continue to do, a specific thing.

Is a *regulatory response* that is available to some *regulators* under certain *regulatory regimes/schemes.*

Injunctions, if available, typically form part of a *regulator's* choices/options as an *administrative response or civil response.* However, *injunctions* can also be part of a penalty or *sanction* (either administratively, civilly, or criminally) following the admission or finding of guilt.

Examples of *injunctions,* from an environmental *regulator's* perspective, to:

- **do a specific thing** – could include ordering a *regulated entity* to engage an independent and certified waste removal transporter to remove stockpiled contaminated waste, that exceeds their *licence condition,* from the site; and
- **not do a specific thing** – could include ordering a *regulated entity* to stop removing contaminated waste from the site, unless performed by an independent and certified waste removal transporter.

(see also: Administrative Remedy/Response/Sanction; Civil Remedy/Response/Sanction; Criminal Remedy/Response/Sanction; Exclusion Order)

Inspection/s

The common meaning of *inspection*/s is to subject something to careful examination or scrutiny.

From a *regulator's* perspective an *inspection* generally involves the *regulator,* either directly through its staff (usually in the form of an *authorised officer*), or a contracted *third party,* physically attending or looking at a regulated thing to determine whether a *law* or *regulation* has been, is being, or will be complied with.

Examples from different types of *regulatory agencies* include:

- building and construction *regulators* – inspecting a building site while under construction;
- food health *regulators* – inspecting a commercial kitchen for food hygiene during food preparation activities; and
- work health and safety *regulators* – attending a factory to check safety measures while the production line is operational.

The OECD consider that:

- 'inspections are the most visible and important among regulatory enforcement activities';[60] and
- 'inspections are one of the most important ways to enforce regulations and to ensure regulatory compliance.'[61]

Inspections are relevant for most, if not all, regulated sectors, industries, or commodities. Therefore, the term *inspections* can be used synonymously with other terms including:

- *audits* and *investigations;*
- *compliance* checks; and
- examinations.

Given their various applications and usage, *inspections* can occur using single or multiple methods in combination. Methods include:
- desktop;
- physical;
- remote monitoring; and
- self-monitoring and reporting.

Inspections can be directed towards *regulatory activities* and *regulatory strategies* at the *Three Levels of Operational Activity*, which are:
- *strategic;*
- *operational;*
- *tactical;* or
- a combination.

For all the reasons above, *inspections* may be:
- part of a proactive or reactive response;
- scheduled or random; and/or
- announced or unannounced.

Inspections are critically important for *regulators* as they form a central part of a *regulator's monitoring* and *compliance* activities. *Inspections* reinforce, check, and verify in a tangible way that a *person* or *regulated entity* is complying with *laws* and their regulatory *obligations*.

　Inspections often cause several challenges for *regulators* across a range of *regulatory activities*, including:
- who to inspect;
- what to inspect;
- where to inspect;
- when to inspect;
- why to inspect; and
- how to inspect.

These issues often come together in the form of regulatory outputs.

(see also: Audit; Investigation; Monitoring Compliance)

Inspection numbers

Refer to the amount or number of *inspections* that a *regulator* conducts in any given period.

Inspection numbers are frequently the topic of discussion and debate, especially:

- during annual, periodic, or extraordinary reporting by the *regulator*;
- during public hearings or inquiries;
- in response to queries or complaints from the *regulated*, *stakeholders*, or the *wider community*; and
- when the *regulator* is reallocating resources in response to changes in its *authorising environment*.

The OECD list *inspections* as 'outputs', which are one of four categories of *compliance assurance indicators*.[62]

(see also: Audit; Compliance Assurance Indicators; Inspection/s; Investigation; Monitoring Compliance; Regulatory Pendulum; Targeted/Targeting)

Inspector (see Authorised Officer)

In-System (Regulation)

Means a *regulated entity* is operating within the confines of a *regulatory regime/scheme* and/or is subject to some form of *authorisation*.

In-system regulatory regimes/schemes see the *regulator* playing both a gatekeeper and monitoring role.

As a gatekeeper – *regulators* support government policy objectives by denying entry to applicants who are assessed as not meeting the necessary (*regulatory* or *fit and proper (person) test*) requirements.

By monitoring – *regulators* help maintain the integrity of the system by *monitoring* those within the *regulatory regime/scheme* to ensure they are *compliant* with its conditions.

For example, a licensed panel beater operating in a commercial workshop as part of a national chain, will most-likely be operating *in-system*, whereas an unlicensed panel beater (a 'backyard' operator) will most-likely be operating *out-of-system*.

(see also: Out-of-System (Regulation))

Intelligence

From a *regulator's* perspective, *intelligence* is a term that relates to the collection, collation, analysis, and dissemination of *information* to assist with *decision-making*.

Regulators primarily use *intelligence* to support decision-makers as they determine *regulatory intervention* priorities whether *strategic, operational,* or *tactical* in nature.

Aligned with the *Three Levels of Operational Activity*, the three levels of *intelligence* are:

- *strategic intelligence* – which supports strategic, policy and long-term capability development;
- *operational intelligence* – which supports *operational* (beneath strategic but above tactical) activity, and medium-term capability development; and
- *tactical intelligence* – which supports immediate tactical activity at the front-line, and short-term capability development.

Intelligence is an important issue for *regulators* to understand – and an important capability for *regulators* to develop and deploy – because *regulatory* staff often conflate *information, intelligence,* and *evidence*.

To clarify:

- *information* is not *intelligence*;
- *intelligence* is *information* which has been value-added to (by being subjected to the intelligence process, by going through the *intelligence cycle*); and
- *intelligence* is not *evidence*.

Therefore, not all *information* becomes *intelligence*, and not all *intelligence* becomes or should be referred to as *evidence* – although interrelated they are three uniquely different things.

(see also: Evidence; Information; Intelligence Cycle; Regulatory Intelligence)

Intelligence-Based/Intelligence-Led

Some *regulators* describe their *regulatory approach* as being *intelligence-based* or *intelligence-led*.

This means that they:

- see *intelligence* as a core element of their *regulatory approach*, and
- use *intelligence* to inform *decision-making* about how to manage key *compliance* risks.

(see also: Intelligence; Intelligence Cycle; Regulatory Approach/es; Regulatory Intelligence)

Intelligence Cycle

Is a cycle that depicts how *intelligence* products are conceived of and developed.

The *intelligence cycle* is a process, which when captured diagrammatically usually includes between five or six stages (depending on how the steps within the stages are grouped).

For example:

- five stage models usually include – direction, collation, analysis, dissemination, and feedback and review;[63] and
- six stage models usually include – direction and planning, information collection, collation evaluation and storage, intelligence analysis, production dissemination, and feedback and review.[64]

At its core, the basic *intelligence cycle* consists of five stages:

- Direction – is the first and crucial stage where the *intelligence* task is defined;
- Collation – is the collecting, compiling, and collating of relevant *information* from various and often disparate sources;
- Analysis – involves subjecting the *information*/data collected to interrogation often with analytical tools (predominantly software based);
- Dissemination – the *intelligence* product/s are disseminated to the client/s to inform *decision-making*; and
- Feedback and review – this stage considers the utility of the products and as an iterative process either informs the next iteration of the product (the direction stage) or informs a refinement of similar products in the future.

(see also: Information; Intelligence)

Intent

Generally, refers to the mental desire behind an action which influences how a *person* acts or does not act in a certain way.

Intent sits higher than *recklessness* which in turn sits higher than *negligence*.

Therefore, the *intent* of a *person* or *regulated entity* (whether an *accused* or an *offender*) is a factor that influences a *regulator's decision-making* at critical times, including:

- initially – as part of the initial *triaging* process, to determine the priority of response to a *breach* or *allegation* of *non-compliance*;
- ongoing – throughout various *compliance* activities, but especially *audits*, *inspections*, and *investigations*; and
- finally – as part of determining the nature and quantum of penalty submissions.

(see also: Burden of Proof; Mens Rea [Latin]; Recklessness)

Internal Regulatory Body/ies

Internal regulatory bodies within *regulatory agencies* perform several roles, including:

- value-adding – by bringing together various and disparate professions, skillsets, and knowledge; and
- governance – by overseeing and making recommendations and/or endorsing decisions relating to progressing regulatory matters, and/or pursuing *regulatory outcomes.*

Internal regulatory bodies are known by several names, several of which are listed below:

- Enforcement Committee – focus usually limited to *enforcement* matters, typically those requiring the use/application of escalated or *coercive powers;*
- Compliance Management Committee – focus on broader *compliance* matters, including those still within the preliminary stages of *investigation;*
- Case Management Committee – focus on *compliance* cases, typically those that have progressed through preliminary stages of *investigation;* and
- Regulatory Advice Panel – focus on regulatory matters, including those that may or may not require an escalated *compliance* or *enforcement* response.

(see also: Decision-Making; Delegation; Discretion)

International Agreements (see Convention)

Intra Vires [Latin]

A Latin phrase which translates to 'inside' or 'within the powers'.

Regulators (and *regulatory officers*) must always be able to explain and demonstrate how they are operating within and/or consistent with their *regulatory powers* and *authority* – it is central to demonstrating that they are acting with *accountability* and *transparency.*

(see also: Accountability; Transparency; Ultra Vires)

Investigation

In general usage, an *investigation* describes the act of investigating something or someone, through a formal or systematic examination or research.

Amongst *regulators* (especially those involved in *enforcement, serious non-compliance, investigation,* and *prosecution* roles) an *investigation* tends to be seen more as a formal inquiry, the aim of which is to discover the truth. This definition aligns more with what is used in traditional and mainstream *law enforcement.* Therefore, formal *investigations* are often governed by set guidelines, protocols, or standards specific to the *jurisdiction.*

The definition below comes from the *Australian Government Investigations Standards* (AGIS):

> 'An investigation is a process of seeking information relevant to an alleged, apparent or potential breach of the law, involving possible judicial proceedings. The primary purpose of an investigation is to gather admissible evidence for any subsequent action, whether under criminal, civil penalty, civil, disciplinary or administrative sanctions'.[65]

Regulators need to be clear on what the official or working definition of an *investigation* is within their *jurisdiction,* portfolio, or agency. Clarity around a definition for what constitutes an *investigation* enables the *regulator* to be clear about a range of factors, including what:

- priority – the *investigation* has been allocated;
- purpose or aim – the *investigation* seeks to deliver or achieve;
- process – the *investigation* involves; and
- powers – the *investigation* has access to.

The issues listed above are often of extreme interest to the:

- *regulators* (whether *co-,* or *peer- regulators*);
- *regulated;*
- *stakeholders;* and
- *wider community.*

(see also: Initial Investigation; Protracted Investigation; Statute of Limitations)

Investigation Guidelines/Standards

Are the guidelines and/or (minimum) standards that *regulatory agencies* and their *regulatory staff* should follow and satisfy when conducting or are involved in an *investigation*.

As guidelines and standards, if there is ever a conflict (or potential conflict) between the guidelines and standards themselves and a *law* or *regulation* – the legislative requirements take precedence.

The *Australian Government Investigations Standards* (AGIS), for example, is a comprehensive document that runs to 29 pages, and breaks an *investigation* down into 15 component parts, these are:

- Investigation management;
- Investigation commencement;
- Planning phase;
- Risk management;
- Implementation phase;
- Activity recording;
- Situation reporting;
- Supervisor's review of investigations;
- File and information management;
- Critical decisions;
- Operational orders or tactical plans;
- Investigation closure;
- Brief (of Evidence) preparation;
- Finalising investigations; and
- Quality assurance review of investigations.[66]

Having and adhering to *investigation guidelines/standards* is a vitally important issue for *regulators* – it enables their *investigations* to withstand scrutiny, whether judicial, parliamentary, or in the 'court of public opinion'.

(see also: Australian Government Investigation Standards)

Investigation Warrant

An *investigation warrant* is a tool which enables the *investigation* powers of a *regulator* to be accessed in certain circumstances.[67]

An *investigation warrant* is used to gather material that relates to the contravention of an *offence* or *breach* of the provisions of an *act* or *authorisation*. This means there **is a** need to suspect that a specific *offence* or *breach* has been, is being, or is about to be committed – which is not the case for obtaining a *monitoring warrant*.

The process for obtaining an *investigation warrant* usually involves an authorised *person* or *authorised officer* providing information (on oath or affirmation) to a *judicial officer,* who is satisfied that the *regulator* should be given access to certain *premises* for the purpose of determining whether there is currently, or soon to be (evidential) material on the *premises*.

If issued, the *investigation warrant* then provides the *regulator* with access to their usual *regulatory powers*.

(see also: Offence-related Warrant; Regulatory Powers; Search Warrant; Warrant)

Investigator

A person who conducts a formal inquiry or an *investigation,* to discover the truth.

In a *regulatory agency* an *investigator's* role is to undertake the more formal and complex *investigations*.

(see also: Authorised Officer; Inspector; Ranger; Regulatory Officer; Warden)

Judge Made Law (see Common Law)

Judges' Rules Caution

The *judges' rules caution* serves to protect *suspects* or *accused persons* against self-incrimination.

The *judges' rules caution* is usually administered to *suspects/accused persons* (not *complainants* or *witnesses*) when an *authorised officer* has the requisite belief (usually *believes on reasonable grounds*) that the *person* has committed an *offence* or *breach*.

The importance of the *judges' rules caution* for *regulators*, and putting the *admissibility of evidence* aside, is that the comments made and/or statements given by a *suspect* or *accused person* who is said to be 'under caution' are more likely to be admissible in *evidence* or proceedings.

(see also: Accused; Admissibility of Evidence; Suspect)

Judicial Officer/s

A *judicial officer* has responsibilities and powers to make decisions and provide directions, on matters relating to the application of the *law*.

The titles or name of *judicial officers* vary, but typically include:

- Judges;
- Magistrates; and
- Justices of the Peace.

The powers of *judicial officers* also vary and are usually confined to a *jurisdiction*.

(see also: Jurisdiction)

Judicial Review

A *judicial review* is a mechanism that is specified in some *jurisdictions* for the review of decisions made by government, by the *judiciary*.

For *regulators* this might involve the *judiciary* reviewing individual decisions made by the *regulator* as to their lawfulness. *Judicial review* holds public officials accountable for the lawful use of their powers.

(The) Judiciary

The *judiciary* is one of the three branches of government in a Westminster System of government.

Judicial powers are one of three powers subject to separation under the Westminster System of government. The other two are *executive* and legislative powers.

For *regulators* the role of the *judiciary* is to provide an independent courts system where *decisions* are made by judges and magistrates. The *judiciary* interpret the *law* as made by the *legislature*.

(see also: (The) Executive; (The) Legislature)

Jurisdiction

For *regulators*, *jurisdiction* is the scope and range of the practical *authority* granted to them to administer and deal with *regulatory* and/or legal matters within a defined area of responsibility.

Jurisdiction is a multifaceted issue for *regulators* and might refer to their:

- domain – i.e., operating within a certain (economic, environmental, or social) domain,
  - e.g., on a joint *inspection* involving the tax/revenue, environmental, and health and safety *regulators*, they would see their

jurisdiction as relating to economic, environmental, and social matters respectively;

- geographic area – i.e., operating within a defined geographic location,
  - e.g., within a defined local council, state/territory, national, or regional area;
- tier of government – i.e., operating within and across tiers,
  - e.g., local, sub-national, national, regional, or international; and
- *court* or body – they are required to refer matters to,
  - e.g., to deal with summary, minor indictable or major indictable matters.

The multifaceted and overlapping contexts listed above tend to combine in such a way to reflect what *regulators* refer to as their *regulatory mandate*.

(see also: Authorising Environment; Regulatory Mandate)

Jurisprudence

Jurisprudence is the study of *law* and the principles on which *laws* are based, as opposed to *law* making.

Jurisprudence can also be seen as the legal philosophy underpinning a legal system.

When deciding on matters, decision-makers (usually judges and magistrates) not only consider the *law*, they also consider how other decision-makers have interpreted the *law*.

Jurisprudence assists with greater consistency and stability of decisions and *decision-making*.

(see also: Case Law; Precedent)

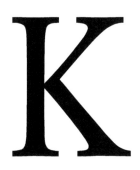

Key Performance Indicators (KPIs)

Generally, *regulators* see *KPIs* as measures used to evaluate their effectiveness in performing their *regulatory functions* and achieving *regulatory outcomes.*

An example of *KPIs* for *regulators* were contained in the Australian Government's *Regulator Performance Framework (RPF).*[68] The *KPIs* included:

'KPI 1 Regulators do not unnecessarily impede the efficient operation of regulated entities

KPI 2 Communication with regulated entities is clear, targeted and effective

KPI 3 Actions undertaken by regulators are proportionate to the regulatory risk being managed

KPI 4 Compliance and monitoring approaches are streamlined and co-ordinated

KPI 5 Regulators are open and transparent in their dealing with regulated entities

KPI 6 Regulators actively contribute to the continuous improvement of regulatory frameworks'.[69]

The items below are also indicators of *regulator* performance:
- 'Achieving objectives;
- Costs;
- Use of different strategies;
- Cost-effectiveness of different strategies;
- Timeliness;

- Communication and education;
- Consultation and stakeholder feedback;
- Staff capacities and performance;
- Continuous improvement; and
- Dispute resolution'.[70]

(see also: Regulator Performance and Evaluation; Regulator Performance Framework)

Knowledge

Knowledge is a mental or *fault element* that must be proven in many criminal matters.

Equally, *knowledge* can impact the decisions made and *sanctions* applied in *administrative matters* and *civil matters*.

The three most common states of awareness, in ascending order, are often discussed in terms of suspicion, belief and knowledge. Other states of awareness include, but are not limited to probable, recklessness, and negligence.

(see also: Burden of Proof; Intent; Mens Rea [Latin])

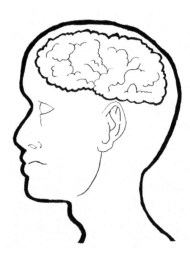

Law/s

Are the enforceable rules that govern a society to regulate behaviour.

Laws within a *jurisdiction* regulate the actions of its members and may be enforced by the imposition of penalties.

Laws are made by the *legislature* and are sometimes referred to as *primary legislation*.

Laws can operate at the local, sub-national, national, and/or international level of government.

Laws are part of a system where *rules* are created and enforced through social or governmental institutions.

(see also: Act of Parliament; Common Law; Legislation; Primary Legislation; Regulation; Rules; Statute)

Law Enforcement Agency (LEA)

Law Enforcement Agency has both a broad and narrow meaning:
- broadly – it can be a reference to any agency which enforces the *law* (or *regulations*); or
- narrowly – it can be a reference to those agencies that are considered the mainstream or premier *law enforcement agencies* within a *jurisdiction*, and typically include:
  - police (local, state, federal);
  - customs and border protection;
  - specialist *enforcement* agencies;[71] and
  - international organisations such as Europol and Interpol.

It is important that *regulators* are clear, and can clearly articulate and justify, which agencies are *law enforcement agencies*, as this often has restrictions and implications when it comes to exchanging data, *evidence*, and *intelligence* between agencies.

(see also: Regulatory Agency)

Lawful

Is something that is allowed or permitted by *law*.

The term is two directional in that *lawful* can be a reference to a requirement or *obligation* that is placed on either or both the *regulated* and the *regulator*. For example, the:

- *regulated* – frequently need to demonstrate that they have acted and operated lawfully, most often this will be achieved by complying with relevant *authorisations* etc., and/or in some other instances positively demonstrating that their actions were not *unlawful*.
- *regulator* – equally, and regularly, need to demonstrate that anything they 'ask' of and especially 'require' of a *regulated entity* is something that is within their *lawful* authority, and which is permitted by their authority. If a *regulator* goes beyond their power or authority, they are said to be acting *ultra vires*.

(see also: Ultra Vires; Unlawful)

Lead Agency

Is a reference to the *regulatory agency* (or body) with a clear mandate to take the lead in terms of a *regulatory response* and intervention. It should be noted that the *lead agency* might have a total and complete 'cradle to grave' responsibility, i.e., from receiving the initial *allegation/* notification right through to finalisation by prosecuting the matter themselves in court.

Equally, the *lead agency* can be different across different phases. For example:

- *Agency A* – may have the lead responsibility in terms of **policy** development or administratively – e.g., under Administrative Arrangements Order (AAOs);[72]

- *Agency B* – may have the lead responsibility at point of **detection** – e.g., a customs or border agency at an international border;
- *Agency C* – may have the lead responsibility at point of **seizure** of an item – e.g., an animal protection, biosecurity, or quarantine agency (especially when specialist skills, knowledge, experience, and equipment is needed to effectively complete the seizure, like that necessary for securing and seizing live and dangerous animals);
- *Agency D* – might have the lead responsibility for the formal **investigation** process – e.g., staff within the *regulatory agency* who are *authorised officers* or *investigators*, or it may fall to staff from another *law enforcement agency* depending on the nature of the *breach*;
- *Agency E* – might have the lead responsibility for the formal **interrogation** – e.g., a different and more intense form of questioning and interview (noting: Agency D and Agency E are often different agencies in some countries);
- *Agency F* – might have the lead responsibility for preparing the formal **brief of evidence** (or prosecution file). Given the descriptions above this could be Agency A, D, or E;
- *Agency G* – might have the lead responsibility for **conducting** the *prosecution*; and
- *Agency H* – might have the lead responsibility for **follow up** actions – which could relate to the payment of *fines, remediation,* and reparation.

There are numerous permutations of the above, which involve the 'lead' responsibility toggling back and forth between agencies and organisations.

(see also: Competent Authority; Regulatory Agency)

Legal Model, of regulation

The *legal model, of regulation* focusses on *compliance,* as the overarching *framework* for *regulatory activities* and operations.[73]

(see also: Expert Model, of regulation)

Legislation

Legislation relates to the process of making and enacting *laws*.

It is typically reference to an *act of parliament*. It can also be a term to describe *laws* collectively (i.e., the *regulated entity* has *obligations* under several pieces of *legislation*).

For those *regulators* involved in *regulatory delivery*, the term *legislation* is most often seen and considered to be the *law* which has been enacted and which can now be implemented (i.e., administered, monitored, and enforced).

(see also: Act/s; Act of Parliament; Primary Legislation; Regulation/s; Statute; Secondary Legislation)

Legislative Instrument/s

Legislative instruments are made by a person or body authorised to do so by relevant enabling *legislation*. The most common form of enabling *legislation* is an *act of parliament*.

Examples of *legislative instruments* include *regulations, rules,* and determinations.

A *legislative instrument* is defined as an instrument in writing, which is:

- of a legislative character, and
- that is or was made in the exercise of a *power* that has been *delegated* by the parliament.

(see also: Act/s; Code/s; Legislation; Regulation/s; Rules; Schedule/s; Standard/s; Statute)

(The) Legislature

The *legislature* is one of the three branches of government in a Westminster System of government.

Legislative powers are one of three powers subject to separation under the Westminster System of government. The other two are *executive* and judicial powers.

The role of the *legislature* is to make *laws* of the country (or *jurisdiction*) that *regulators* administer. The making of *laws* usually occurs through deliberative parliamentary process.

(see also: (The) Executive; (The) Judiciary)

Letter of Expectations
(see Regulatory Statement of Expectations)

Liability

Is a legal duty or *obligation* for something.

For example, a *regulated entity* has legal *liability* for the safety of staff and visitors on a worksite, under the work health and safety *laws*.

(see also: Obligation; Vicarious Liability)

Licence

Is a formal *authority* to do something which would otherwise be *unlawful*.

Licences are a form of *authorisation* that *regulators* provide to a *person* or *regulated entity* to enable them to engage in certain activities, or to operate within a regulated industry, sector, market, or scheme.

For example, a:

- *person* – may be issued a *licence* from a health *regulator* to practice as a chiropractor; or
- *regulated entity* – may be issued a *licence* from an education *regulator* to operate a chain of child day-care facilities.

Licences are often subject to or based upon a set of (standard and non-standard) conditions or requirements.

(see also: Approval; Authorisation; Licence Condition/s; Permit)

Licence Condition/s

Licence conditions form part of a *licence*.

Licence conditions can be standard, non-standard (often referred to as bespoke or customised) or a combination of the two. For example:

- standard *licence conditions* – tend to be used for issues or processes that do not change between similar places, and similar *regulated entities*,
  - a standard *licence condition* for a work health and safety *regulator* might be that all staff working on an oil refinery platform need to wear protective and anti-static overalls; or

- non-standard *licence conditions* – tend to be used for issues or processes that do or may change between similar or different places, and similar or different *regulated entities,*
  - a non-standard *licence condition* for a work health and safety *regulator* might be that all staff working on an oil refinery platform **at sea** need to wear protective overalls which are fitted with a water activated EPIRB.[74]

(see also: Approval; Authorisation; Licence; Permit)

Licensee/s (see Regulated/Regulated Entity/ies)

A *licensee* is a *regulated entity* (whether an individual or a company) that has been issued with a *licence* by a relevant authority to engage in an activity/ies that without a *licence* would be *unlawful.*

(see also: Duty Holder/s; Regulated Commodity/ies; Regulated; Regulatees)

Licensing and Approvals

Licensing and approvals are a *regulatory activity* which covers various entry controls through which *regulatory agencies* can authorise individuals or *regulated entities* to undertake certain activities. These *authorisations* can be general or specific in nature, and at times can involve a combination.

Licensing and approval mechanisms reinforce and clarify, in a tangible way, the *advice and guidance* information previously provided to *regulated entities* by the *regulator.* It includes more specific information relating to:

- the background, history, and general intent of the *regulations* (i.e., *regulatory regime, regulatory scheme*);
- the general nature and type of any *approvals* (or similar) that are required to operate or function within the regime or scheme;
- any general and/or mandatory conditions associated with any *approval*;
- any specific conditions, that may be put in place depending on a range of factors (see *licence conditions*); or
- any general or specific *advice and guidance* to:
  - assist a *regulated entity* to avoid instances of *non-compliance*, and
  - assist a *regulated entity* to return to *compliance.*

In a linear sense, it is the third of six phases contained in the *Extended Regulatory Spectrum.*

Licensing and approval mechanisms cover all types of *authorisations.* They effectively enable and authorise a *regulated entity* or participant to enter, and participate within a *regulated* industry, sector, market, or scheme. Examples include, but are not limited to:

- *approvals;*
- *licences;*
- *permits;* and
- *registrations.*

(see also: **Extended Regulatory Spectrum**; Licence Conditions; Non-standard Permit/s)

Light-touch regulation

A light touch reflects a delicate, careful, or sensitive approach to dealing with something.

In a *regulatory* context *light-touch regulation* is a *regulatory approach* that:

- provides greater discretion to *regulated entities* in how they can act, while still complying with their regulatory duties and *obligations;* and
- enables *regulators* to take a less prescriptive- and more principles-based approach.

For *regulators, light-touch regulation* is considered the least intrusive intervention by government, that is needed to achieve the underlying policy objective. *Light-touch regulation* is often associated with efforts to minimise *regulatory burden* or *red tape* costs.

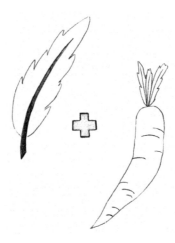

Light-touch regulation is most often seen in self-regulatory or co-regulatory *regimes/schemes*, but it may also be used where the *regulatory regimes/schemes* are operating well with minimal need for involvement by *regulators*.

It is important that *regulators* do not consider *light-touch regulation* to be a one size fits all – even when it is appropriate, *monitoring* and *verification* remain central pillars to *compliance*. The term *light-touch regulation* can be problematic. Not only because it can send the wrong message that the *regulator* is hands-off or reluctant, but it could also be an early indicator of *regulatory capture*. For this reason, the author prefers the term *right-touch regulation*. *Right-touch regulation* recognises that the *right-touch* could be heavy, moderate, light, or non-existent – but it is always context dependant.

(see also: Right-touch Regulation; Types of Regulation)

Limitation of Time (see Statute of Limitations)

Litigation

Litigation is the process of taking legal action in a court or tribunal. It typically involves each party having to appear, and to present evidence and arguments.

(see also: Model Litigant; Prosecution; Trial)

Macrory Review

The *Macrory Review* was a review that occurred in the United Kingdom in 2006, under the auspice of the UK Cabinet Office.

The focus of the *Macrory Review* was on effective *regulatory sanctions*. With *sanctions* seen as being both a deterrent and catalyst for improved rates of *compliance* amongst *regulated entities*.

The *Macrory Review* outlines six principles of an effective *sanction*, and seven characteristics of a successful sanctioning regime.

The six principles suggest that to be effective, a *sanction* should:

1. '... aim to change the behaviour of the offender;
2. ... aim to eliminate any financial gain or benefit from non-compliance;
3. ... be responsive and consider what is appropriate for the particular offender and the regulatory issue, which can include punishment and the public stigma that should be associated with a criminal conviction;
4. ... be proportionate to the nature of the offence and the harm caused;
5. ...aim to restore the harm caused by regulatory non-compliance, where appropriate; and
6. ... aim to deter future non-compliance'.[75]

The seven characteristics of a successful sanctioning regime suggest that *regulators* should:

1. '... publish an enforcement policy;
2. ... measure outcomes not just outputs;

3. ... justify their choice of enforcement actions year on year to stakeholders, Ministers and Parliament;
4. ... follow-up their enforcement actions where appropriate;
5. ... enforce in a transparent manner;
6. ... be transparent in the way in which they apply and determine administrative penalties; and
7. ... avoid perverse incentives that might influence the choice of sanctioning response'.[76]

The way that *sanctions* are designed, developed, used, and ultimately explained and justified is important for *regulators* – as *sanctions* are often the most visible projection of *regulator independence* and the *regulatory posture* of a *regulator,* as seen from the perspective of *co-regulators, regulated entities, stakeholders,* and the *wider community.*

The way that *inspection* and *enforcement* activities are conducted, prior to the use of *sanctions* is also important, see *Hampton Review.*

(see also: PACTT; Principles of Good Regulation; Regulator Independence; Regulatory Posture)

Mens Rea [Latin]

A Latin phrase translating to 'guilty mind'. A more modern term used would be the *mental element* or *fault element* of an *offence.*

Fault elements include *intent, knowledge, recklessness,* and *negligence.*

(see also: Actus Reus [Latin]; Fault Element)

Mental Element (see Fault Element)

Merits Review

A *merits review* is a mechanism that is specified in some *jurisdictions* for the review of decisions made by government, by someone else in government, who was not the original decision-maker. *Merits review* is distinct from *judicial review.*

Merits review can be internal or external. Internal reviews are conducted by another senior official within the same agency. External reviews are conducted by an external body such as a tribunal or other agency/ministry.

(see also: Judicial Review)

Meta-regulation

A particular style of *regulation/regulatory approach* which involves oversight of, or greater governance of *regulation*, as opposed to *direct regulation*.

For example, *meta-regulation* might occur through use of an environmental management system (EMS). Under an EMS the *regulator's* main role is to oversee and *audit* the plans which are developed and managed by the *regulated entity*.

Meta-regulation can also involve third parties, and use the market, as key drivers of *self-regulation* which is in the public interest.

(see also: Types of Regulation)

Ministerial Statement of Expectations
(see Regulatory Statement of Expectations)

Model Litigant

The *model litigant* rules and *obligations* are guidelines for how government, through its *regulators* and *prosecuting authorities*, should behave at all stages (before, during, and after) of *litigation*.

The rules apply irrespective of whether the *litigation* involves an individual *person*, *regulated entity*, business entity of any type, or even another government agency or body.

In Australia, at the Federal (or national) and State and Territory (sub-national) levels of government, most *jurisdictions* have a *model litigant* policy or similar. Noting that in some *jurisdictions* it is referred to as a legal practice direction.

The *model litigant* rules are essentially additional rules and *obligations* that are aimed at ensuring that there is good governance and effective administration associated with the *litigation* that governments engage in.

Listed below is an edited extract from the Australian Government's Legal Services Direction 2017.[77] It outlines the nature of the *model litigant's obligations*, relating to:

a) 'dealing with claims promptly and not causing unnecessary delay in the handling of claims and litigation …

b) paying legitimate claims without litigation, including making partial settlements of claims or interim payments, where it is clear that liability is at least as much as the amount to be paid

c) acting consistently in the handling of claims and litigation

d) endeavouring to avoid, prevent and limit the scope of legal proceedings wherever possible, including by giving consideration in all cases to alternative dispute resolution before initiating legal proceedings and by participating in alternative dispute resolution processes where appropriate

e) where it is not possible to avoid litigation, keeping the costs of litigation to a minimum …

f) not taking advantage of a claimant who lacks the resources to litigate a legitimate claim

g) not relying on technical defences …

h) not undertaking and pursuing appeals unless the Commonwealth or the agency believes that it has reasonable prospects for success or the appeal is otherwise justified in the public interest, and

i) apologising where the Commonwealth or the agency is aware that it or its lawyers have acted wrongfully or improperly.'

It is important for *regulators* when initiating or continuing *litigation* (or *prosecutions*), that they can justify or demonstrate that they are pursuing – the right cases, for the right reasons, at the right time, in the right way, in pursuit of the right outcomes – as this can reflect and impact upon their *regulatory posture*, and influences their overall regulatory credibility amongst *co-regulators, regulated entities, stakeholders,* and the *wider community.*

(see also: Litigation; Prosecuting Authority; Prosecution; Zealous Witness)

Modern Regulation

What constitutes *modern regulation* is context dependant. However, the focus of *modern regulation* generally includes:

- achieving (regulatory) outcomes, in the most effective way;
- having fewer, or minimal burdens on *regulated entities*;
- prioritising effort and resources, on areas of higher risk; and
- using a broad suite of regulatory and non-regulatory tools, with high levels of nuance and expertise.

(see also: Regulatory Posture; Types of Regulation)

Modern Regulator

The concept of what constitutes a *modern regulator* is context dependant.

Being modern (or contemporary) can vary across *jurisdictions*. What constitutes 'modern' can also vary greatly within a *regulatory agency*, especially if it administers multiple *regulatory regimes/schemes* (with different: commencement dates, that span decades; and *types of regulation*, i.e., from *command and control* though to *self-regulation*).

Fundamentally, the concept of the *modern regulator* allows *regulators* to decouple themselves from the historical (and often fixed) viewpoint of what their regulatory role entails.

While there is no formula, to be considered a *modern regulator* a *regulator* should be able to demonstrate that it:

- is using modern thinking;
- has access to, is using, and is proficient in the use of modern tools; and
- is solving (or at least improving) modern problems.

(see also: Regulatory Posture; Types of Regulation)

Monitoring Compliance

Monitoring compliance is a *regulatory activity* which involves the monitoring of a *regulated entity,* to determine its conformance or adherence with regulatory requirements, to determine the entity's *compliance* status. And if *non-compliance* is detected then working with or managing an entity's return to *compliance.*

Monitoring compliance activities reinforce, check, and verify in a tangible way the *licensing and approvals* conditions previously agreed to by the *regulated entities,* or required by the *regulator.* It includes a specific focus on:

- monitoring – whether by the *regulated entity* themselves; the *regulator;* or by a *third party;* and
- compliance – whether they are *compliant* or *non-compliant.*

In a linear sense, it is the fourth of six phases contained in the *Extended Regulatory Spectrum.*

Monitoring activities include, but are not limited to:

- *audits,*
- certification,
- data collection and analysis,
- evaluations,
- *inspections,*
- observations,
- recertification,
- reporting, and
- verification.

Compliance relates to either a current or end-state for a *person* or *regulated entity:*

- if *compliant* – whether this was a result of: voluntary; assisted; directed; or enforced means; and
- if *non-compliant* – whether this is despite: assisted; directed; or enforced means.

(see also: ***Extended Regulatory Spectrum; VADE Model***)

Monitoring Warrant

A *monitoring warrant* is a tool which enables the monitoring powers of a *regulator* to be accessed in certain circumstances.

A *monitoring warrant* is used to check *compliance* with the provisions of an *act* or *authorisation*. This means there **is no need** to suspect that a specific *offence* or *breach* has been, is being, or is about to be committed – as is the case for obtaining an *investigation warrant* or *search warrant*.

The process for obtaining a *monitoring warrant* usually involves an *authorised person* or *authorised officer* providing information (on oath or affirmation), to a *judicial officer*, that it is reasonably necessary that the *regulator* should be given access to certain *premises* for the purpose of determining whether:

- a provision that is subject to monitoring under an *act* or relevant *authorisation* has been, or is being, complied with; or
- information subject to monitoring under an *act* is correct.

If issued, the *monitoring warrant* then provides the *regulator* with access to their usual *regulatory powers*.

(see also: Investigation Warrant; Offence-related Warrant; Search Warrant)

Name and Shame (colloquial term)

Occurs when the activities of wrongdoers are publicised.

Name and shame type publications occur when:

- the *regulator* – publishes an outcome or information about the event, or
- the *regulated entity* – publishes either proactively (as part of damage control, and/or in an attempt to reduce penalties), or reactively (based upon a legal requirement) some form of admission or apology for a *breach* of *compliance*.

For example, from time to time you will see a full page add taken out in a broadsheet paper where Company X (the *regulated entity*):

- admits to some wrongdoing;
- apologises for any discomfort and impact on customers; and
- outlines how they will (either in addition to a penalty, or in lieu of) rectify the occurrence and seek to prevent it from re-occurring.

(see also: Adverse Publicity Order; Sanction)

Natural Justice

An *administrative law* concept which relates to fairness, with *natural justice* often referred to as 'the right to a fair hearing'.

There are three main components or requirements to *natural justice*, including:

- adequate notice – means that people affected by the decision need to be told about the central issues and be provided with sufficient *information* in order that they can meaningfully participate in the *decision-making* process;
- fair hearing – means that people affected by the decision are provided with the opportunity to present their viewpoint and respond to alternate views or counterpoints; and
- no bias – means that the decision-maker must not have any relationships or conflicts of interest which could impact upon their ability to act impartially.

Natural justice is used interchangeably with the term *procedural fairness*. However:

- *natural justice* tends to be associated more with procedures used by *courts* or tribunals; and
- *procedural fairness* is more often used when talking about administrative *decision-making* processes.

(see also: Administrative Law; Procedural Fairness)

Negligence

Negligence is considered a failure to take proper care over something.

Generally, *negligence* refers to a state of mind which sits behind an action which influences how a person acts or does not act in a certain way.

Negligence sits lower than *recklessness* which in turn sits lower than *intent*.

Negligence of a *person* or *regulated entity* (whether an *accused* or an *offender*) is a factor that influences a *regulator's decision-making* at critical times:

- initially – as part of the initial *triaging* process, to determine the priority of response to a *breach* or *allegation* of *non-compliance*;

- ongoing – throughout various *compliance* activities, but especially *audits*, *inspections*, and *investigations*; and
- finally – as part of determining the nature and quantum of penalty submissions.

For a *regulator* the term *negligence* is usually considered in terms of the level of *knowledge* (or associated *mental element* or *fault element*) that must be proven in proceedings or *contested matters*.

Further, *negligence* and other levels of awareness (including belief; carelessness; *knowledge*; probable; recklessness; and suspicion) are based upon the 'reasonable person test'. The 'reasonable person test' measures the anticipated decisions and actions, against what a reasonable citizen would do in the same or similar circumstances.

(see also: Burden of Proof; Guilty Knowledge; Intent; Mens Rea [Latin]; Recklessness)

Network/s

In this book *network/s* is used interchangeably with *enforcement networks* and/or *regulatory networks*.

For the purposes of this book, a *network* is a reference to:
- a set of relationships that involve 'formal and informal ties between members of a profession or people working in similar jobs';[78] and
- ongoing multi-member forums linked by subject matter, professional knowledge, and areas of concern and practice.[79]

Networks tend to operate at multi-agency, cross-jurisdictional, and cross-disciplinary levels.[80] For this reason, *networks* tend to focus on generic aspects, such as:
- training of *regulatory officers*;
- development of high-level *regulatory policies*; and
- development of high-level *regulatory processes*.

Whereas *communities of practice* tend to focus on more practical and applied aspects, such as:
- training of *regulatory officers* – that is contextualised, for a specific *regulatory domain*, industry, sector, commodity, and/or *jurisdiction*;
- operationalisation of high-level *regulatory policies*; and
- modification and adaption of *regulatory processes*.

Regulators engage with *networks* to:

- share resources, knowledge, and experiences;
- advance their practices, professionalise their roles, and improve their *regulatory tools*; and
- maximise the effectiveness of their *enforcement* responses.[81]

It is important for *regulators* to be clear about the similarities and differences between *networks* and *communities of practice*. Their similarities are that they both provide forums for *regulators* and regulatory staff to share experiences and develop strategies to deal with common challenges. It is particularly important that *regulators*, and *regulatory executives*, pay particular attention to their differences and note that by their nature:

- *networks* tend to be more formal and fixed – in terms of their focus and work, their *regulatory activities* generally span those which are *strategic* and *operational* in nature; and
- *communities of practice* tend to be more informal, organic, and transitory – in terms of their focus and work, their *regulatory activities* generally span those which are *tactical* and *operational* in nature.

(see also: Communities of Practice/s; **Working Together**)

Noble Cause Corruption

Noble cause corruption is a form of corrupt behaviour that occurs when a person tries to produce or contrive a just outcome, through use of illegal or unjust methods or means.

A noble cause, such as wanting to make the world a safer place, is a central reason why many people join regulatory, *enforcement*, and *policing agencies*. But in extreme cases this can lead to what is referred to as the 'warrior culture', which is based around an 'us and them' mentality.

Noble cause corruption is based upon an 'ends justifies the means' and/ or 'it is for the greater good' approach.

Examples of *noble cause corruption*, from a *law enforcement* and regulatory perspective, include:

- manipulating or fabricating *evidence*;
- exaggerating *statements* in written reports and;
- making false *statements* or lying whilst giving testimony in *court*.

It is important for *regulators* to keep a look out for early signs or indicators of *noble cause corruption*. Terms (or rationalisations) like those listed below, if heard in the workplace, can be red flags and warning signs:
- 'well, they got what they deserved';
- 'they were overdue' or 'their time is coming'; and
- 'well, there is no real victim' or 'no one was hurt'.

It is also suggested that arrogance, a lack of administrative accountability, and/or weak supervision can contribute to a degree of *noble cause corruption* existing in regulatory and *law enforcement* work.[82]

(see also: Corruption; Regulatory Capture)

Non-Binding Precedent
(also known as Persuasive Precedent)

A *non-binding precedent* is one that should be seriously considered but is not required to be followed in later cases.

A *non-binding precedent* may be of sufficient importance to assist or shape the thinking of a *judicial officer* (in the *court* setting) or a *regulatory* decision-maker (in the administrative setting).

(see also: Binding Precedent; Precedent)

Non-Compliance

Is a failure or refusal to comply.

Non-compliance occurs when a *regulated entity* fails to adhere with a regulatory requirement or their regulatory *obligations*.

(see also: Breach; Offences; Non-Compliant)

Non-Compliant

To be *non-compliant* can include:
- failing to act in accordance with a request or command for some reason;
- failing to comply with any required regulatory duties and *obligations*, or agreed/pre-determined standards; or
- being wilfully defiant and resistant to some form of authority.

For a *regulator* it tends to refer to a binary state of being of how they see *regulated entities* – i.e., are they *compliant* or *non-compliant*?

(see also: Compliant)

Non-Expert Opinion

Non-expert opinion is *evidence* that is given by a person, who is considered a layperson. Such a person does not possess any specific expertise, but can provide opinions which can be relied upon, on limited matters.

Examples of *non-expert opinions* being given and admitted into *evidence*, could include:
- a liquor and gaming *inspector* – in relation to a patron's level of intoxication; and
- a road traffic *inspector* – in relation to the speed of a motor vehicle.

(see also: Evidence; Expert Evidence; Opinion Evidence)

Non-Standard Permit/s

Non-standard permits (sometimes referred to as bespoke) are issued to a *person* or *regulated entity* where standard or generic conditions are not suitable or appropriate.

Often the conditions attached to a *non-standard permit* are negotiated between the *regulator* and the *regulated entity*.

(see also: Bespoke Permit; Permits; Standardised Permit)

Nudge/s

Nudge techniques are intended to achieve higher levels of voluntary compliance.

Nudge techniques are shaped around the acronym EAST. Meaning that the techniques are based upon the precursor, that the *decision-making* process for the *person* or *regulated entity,* to choose to comply, is:

- Easy;
- Attractive;
- Social; and
- Timely.

An example of a *nudge* might include a *regulator* sending a letter to a *regulated entity* whose behaviour is making them an outlier, relative to their peers.

(see also: Behaviour Change; Behavioural Insights; Targeting Interventions)

Obligation

An *obligation* is something that a person is bound or required to do, out of a sense of duty, custom or *law*.

From a *regulator's* perspective, an *obligation* is a legal duty or requirement for a *person* or *regulated entity* to do something, for which there is the possibility of the *regulator* initiating a *regulatory response* for *non-compliance*.

Broad examples of *obligations* might include a *person* or *regulated entity*:

- being accredited, to participate in a regulated market, regime, or scheme;
- reporting to government (*regulators*) periodically; and
- having certain systems and processes in place.

A specific example might include a *regulated entity* having legal *obligations* to take precautions (which could include combinations of systems, equipment, training, processes, and procedures) that protect the safety of staff and visitors on a worksite, under the work health and safety laws.

(see also: Liability; Vicarious Liability)

Offence/s

An *offence* might be considered to be or involve a *breach* of a *law, rule,* or some form of illegal act.

Regulators tend to refer to *crimes* and regulatory *breaches* as *offences*.

(see also: Breach/es; Crime/s; Indictable Offence; Summary Offence/s; Violation/s)

Offence-Related Warrant (see Investigation Warrant)

Offender

The term used to describe the *person* or *regulated entity* who has committed a *crime*, regulatory *breach*, or some form of illegal act.

(see also: Accused; Defendant; Suspect)

Official Warning

Is a *regulatory response* that is available to *regulators* under most *regulatory regimes/schemes*.

Official warnings, if available, typically form part of a *regulator's* choices/options as an *administrative response*. However, an *official warning* can also be part of a penalty or *sanction* (either civilly or criminally) following the admission or finding of *guilt*.

Regulators typically issue *official warnings* for instances of *non-compliance* that are considered minor or technical in nature. That said, the criteria for issuing an *official warning*, for accountability and transparency reasons, should be documented and contained in a *compliance and enforcement policy* (or equivalent).

(see also: Administrative Remedy/Response/Sanction; Verbal Caution; Warning Letter; Warnings and Cautions)

On-the-spot fine (colloquial term)
(see Fixed Penalty Notice)

Operational

Amongst *regulators*, *operational* can be a term to describe one of three levels (or types) of *regulatory activity* that forms part of *regulatory practice*.

For example, *operational* can reflect:
- a group of *breaches* or cases, involving either multiple sites for the same *regulated entity*, and/or multiple (inter-related) *regulated entities*.

The other two levels (or types) of *regulatory activity* are *tactical* and *strategic*.

For more detailed explanation of the similarities, overlaps, and differences between the three levels of *regulatory activity* see the *Three Levels of Operational Activity*.

(see also: Strategic; Tactical; ***Three Levels of Operational Activity***)

Operational Regulatory Functions

For the purposes of this book, *operational regulatory functions* are those that are contained within the four central phases of the *Extended Regulatory Spectrum*.

(see also: ***Extended Regulatory Spectrum***; Regulated Activity/ies; Regulatory Delivery; Regulatory Functions; Regulatory Practice)

Operational Risk Appraisals (OPRA)

Developed by the Environment Agency UK, OPRA scores and categorises the overall *risks* associated with a *regulated premise* that is subject to licensing approvals. The *assessment* of *risk* is based upon various factors including:

- complexity – of the *regulated entity's* operations;
- emissions and inputs – from and into the *regulated entity's* installation or factory;
- location/s – of the installation or factory, relative to environmentally sensitive areas; and
- operator performance – in terms of their *compliance* record/history.

Participation in *OPRA* provides:

- *regulated entities* – with an opportunity to assess and improve their performance, to reduce their overall *regulatory* and/or *administrative* *burdens* including reduced annual *licence/permit* fees; and
- *regulators* – the opportunity to better direct their limited resources to areas of higher risk.

(see also: Risk Criteria; Earned Autonomy/Recognition)

Opinion Evidence

Opinion evidence is evidence that is given by a person, based upon what they think, believe, or can reasonably infer from observable facts.

Witnesses are generally prevented from providing *opinion evidence* unless it is in the form of *expert evidence* or *non-expert opinion*.

(see also: Evidence; Expert Evidence; Non-Expert Opinion)

OPRA (see Operational Risk Appraisals)

Oral Evidence

Is *evidence* that is spoken, as opposed to written (i.e., *documentary evidence*).

(see also: Documentary Evidence; Evidence)

Ordinance/s

An authoritative order.

(see also: Code/s; Determinations; Directive; Standard/s)

Organised Crime

The definition for *organised crime* varies across *jurisdictions*.

Despite differences, definitions of *organised crime* routinely require that the:

- *crime* involves two or more people;
- criminal activities are undertaken for financial or other gain;
- criminal *offences* meet the definition of serious *crime*; and
- offending is planned and often ongoing.

Examples of *organised crime* that intersect with the work of *regulatory agencies* include:

- drug importation;
- money laundering;
- people trafficking; and
- transnational wildlife smuggling.

(see also: Crime)

Outcome

An *outcome* is generally a reference to the (end) result of a matter which is subject to regulatory consideration. Common permutations include that the matter is:

- not pursued – because the matter does not satisfy the *criteria* or elements contained in the relevant *compliance and enforcement policy* (or equivalent);
- not yet known – because the matter is either still being assessed as to whether it should be pursued, or if it is being pursued it is still under active *investigation*; and
- finalised – resulting in either no action being taken, or some form of *sanction* being applied.

(see also: Regulatory Outcome/s)

Outcomes-based Approach

Is an overarching philosophy or approach that some *regulators* use. This approach has the following aspects:

- *aim* – to clearly define the *regulatory outcomes* that the *regulator* seeks to achieve;
- *purpose* – to assess the efficiency and effectiveness of *regulatory activities* and *regulatory outcomes*; and
- *benefits* – documenting and reporting on *regulatory outcomes* enables greater transparency, accountability, and increases understanding of what the *regulator* is seeking to achieve, which in turn provides opportunities for *continual improvement*.

(see also: Regulatory Approaches; Regulatory Outcome/s)

Outcomes-focused Approach

(see Outcomes-based Approach)

Out-of-System (Regulation)

Means a *regulated entity* is operating within a regulated industry, sector, market, regime, or scheme **without** the *authorisation* that is required as part of scheme entry.

173

Out-of-system includes those entities who are operating illegally, or who are actively seeking to avoid participating in a scheme, to evade its requirements.

For example, an unlicensed panel beater (a 'backyard' operator) will most-likely be operating *out of-system*, whereas a licensed panel beater operating in a commercial workshop as part of a national chain will most-likely be operating *in-system*.

(see also: Gaming the system; In-System Regulation)

Outsourced Regulation

In some circumstances an *outsourced regulation* arrangement may be appropriate for some *regulatory functions* that would normally be performed by a government.

An *outsourced regulation* arrangement can be appropriate where detailed sector, industry, technical, or commodity specific knowledge is required as part of managing or monitoring a *regulatory regime*.

An example from Australia, includes the role performed by the Australian Refrigeration Council (a *peak industry body*), which administers refrigerant handling *licences* and refrigerant trading *authorisations* on behalf of the Australian Government under the *Ozone Protection and Synthetic Greenhouse Gas Management Act 1989.*[83]

(see also: Co-regulation; Licensing and Approvals; Monitoring Compliance)

PACTT

In this book, *PACTT* is an acronym which refers collectively to the *Principles of Good Regulation*, which are:

- **P**roportionate;
- **A**ccountable;
- **C**onsistent;
- **T**ransparent; and
- **T**argeted.

(see also: Principles of Good Regulation)

PBR (Performance-based Regulation)

PEACE Model
(a framework for investigative interviewing)

The *PEACE Model* is a framework or method for approaching, conducting, and evaluating investigative interviews.

The *PEACE Model* involves five steps, which act as prompters throughout the different phases of an investigative interview.

As an acronym PEACE stands for:

- **P**reparation and Planning;
- **E**ngage and Explain;
- **A**ccount clarification and challenge;
- **C**losure; and
- **E**valuation.

The *PEACE Model* of investigative interviewing uses conversation management, instead of adversarial questioning (or interrogation).

With the *PEACE Model,* interviewers seek to build rapport with the interviewee and provide them with an opportunity to provide a full and uninterrupted account.

The focus of a *PEACE Model* interview is more aligned with comprehensive *information* gathering, as opposed to purely (and aggressively) seeking a confession or admission of guilt.

It is important for *regulators* to understand that an investigative interview is a critical part of the *investigation* process. An investigative interview should only be conducted (i.e., led, supported, and overseen) by staff with the appropriate *authorisation*, skills, knowledge, training, and equipment.

Given the necessity to use *regulatory powers,* especially any *coercive powers,* and the issues associated with the *admissibility of evidence* – investigative interviews[84] tend to be conducted by *authorised officers.*

(see also: Authorised Officer; Coercive Powers; Evidence; Investigation)

Peak Body/Peak Industry Body
(see Industry Representative Organisation)

Peer-regulation

Is reference to a *regulatory regime/scheme* which involves co-management and/or co-delivery with *peer-regulators.*

For example, *peer-regulation* would see the respective local, state/territory (provincial), and national *regulators,* or national and international *regulators,* for a given sector, industry, or commodity, work together to deliver *regulatory outcomes.*

(see also: Peer-regulator)

Peer-regulator

A *peer-regulator* is a *regulator* that regulates the same matters and issues in another *jurisdiction.*

For example, all *regulators* that regulate food safety and hygiene in commercial restaurants, irrespective of whether at the local, state/provincial, or federal/central level of government, would be *peer-regulators* of one another.

Whereas a *co-regulator* is a *regulator* whose regulatory activities and interests span or overlap with another *regulator*, either in terms of the *regulatory domain*, sector, or commodity.

For example, for *regulators* that regulate food safety and hygiene in commercial restaurants their *co-regulators* would typically include:
- labour/wage inspectorate – relating to wages and worker entitlements;
- liquor inspectorate – relating to responsible service of alcohol; and
- workplace health and safety inspectorate – relating to the safety of staff and patrons.

Peer-regulators are included as *regulators* as one of the four main groups that provide key regulatory perspectives, the others are: *regulated*; *stakeholders* and *wider-community*.

(see also: Co-Regulator; Jurisdiction; *Four Key Regulatory Perspectives*)

Penalty Infringement Notice (see Fixed Penalty Notice)

Penalty Notice (see Fixed Penalty Notice)

Penalty Provisions

For most *acts* this means any provision for which there is a corresponding penalty (or *sanction*) listed for contravention of that provision.

(see also: Fine/s; Infringement Notice; On-the-spot-fine).

Performance-based Regulation (PBR)

Reflects a *regulatory approach* that describes, signals, and focuses on desired measurable *regulatory outcomes*, as opposed to a prescriptive approach involving excessive processes, techniques, and/or procedures.

Performance-based regulation leads to defined results without specific direction regarding how those results are to be obtained.[85]

(see also: Types of Regulation)

Permission/s

A broad (often all-encompassing) term/phrase referencing some type of *permission* for a *regulated entity* to undertake a particular activity, which without a specific *permission* would otherwise be *unlawful*.

(see also: Approval; Authorisation; Licence; Permit)

Permit/s

A *permit* is an official *licence* or legal document that allows a *person* or *regulated entity* to do something that would otherwise be *unlawful*. A *permit* is a form of *authorisation*.

Permits can be:

- completely standard (that is generic);
- completely non-standard (that is extensively customised, sometimes referred to as bespoke); or
- a combination (that is largely standard, with only a few non-standard modifications).

For example, a *regulator* involved in wildlife protection may issue a *permit* to a *person* or *regulated entity* so that an animal or specimen (that is subject to the *legislation*) can be moved across:

- local and internal borders;
- state/territory and provincial borders; or
- national and international borders.

(See: Approval; Authorisation; Licence)

Permit Cycle (and process)

Permits form a key part of the *regulatory cycle,* and has its own cycle.

There can be differences in the *permit cycle* across *jurisdictions* and regulated industries and sectors. However, the *permit cycle* will generally include the following stages:[86]

- *regulator* – defining, articulating, and communicating the requirement for a *permit*;

- *regulator* and *regulated entity* – pre-application discussions;
- *regulated entity* – preparing and submitting the application for *permit*;
- *regulator* – checking the *permit* application;
- *regulator* and *regulated entity* – dealing with any confidentiality issues;
- *regulator* – consulting interested parties and *stakeholders*;
- *regulator* – determining and developing *permit* conditions;
- *regulator* – issuing or refusing the *permit*;
- *regulator* – subsequently varying, suspending, or revoking the *permit*; and
- *regulator* – ongoing review of the *permit*.

(See also: Authorisation; Regulatory Cycle)

Person

A *person* can be, and is usually, a reference to an individual – acting as an individual. For example, a road traffic *statute* might state that 'a *person* must not drive a motor vehicle on a road without a driver's licence'.

A *person* can also be a reference to a *person* who is operating as a *regulated entity*, in their own right (i.e., as a natural *person*/sole trader), or as part of a *regulated entity* (perhaps a company).

Some *offences* or *breaches* of *legislation* may extend the definition of *person* to include corporate entities.

(See also: Regulated Entity/ies)

Person Assisting

From time-to-time *regulatory officers* will require assistance as they perform their regulatory duties and functions.

In certain circumstances, *legislation* allows that a *regulatory officer* may be assisted by other persons, if certain criteria are met. For example, the:

- *regulatory officer* must be exercising powers and functions under the specific piece of *legislation*; and
- assistance sought is both necessary and reasonable; and
- specific piece of *legislation* that the *regulatory officer* is acting under allows for assistance.

The nature of the assistance might typically be confined to assistance with *monitoring* or *investigation*.

Regulators will often utilise the *person assisting* function where their *regulatory officer* does not have, or the *regulatory activity* (usually, *audit*, *inspection*, or *investigation*) requires some form of expertise (whether technical or scientific) or the use of specialist equipment.

(see also: Authorised Officer; Inspector; Investigator; Regulatory Officer; Warden)

Person of Interest (POI) (see Suspect)

Physical Act (see Actus Reus)

Plaintiff

The *person* (or entity) that brings a *case* or legal proceedings against another, in a *court* or tribunal.

A term used especially in *civil matters*.

Before proceedings have officially commenced the *plaintiff* will be referred to as the *claimant*.

(see also: Claimant; Defendant)

POI (see Person of Interest)

Police/ing Agencies (role in regulation)

Given their mandate, *police agencies* are appropriately focussed on *crime*, especially serious *crime*, and *organised crime*. However, *police agencies* are becoming increasingly involved in regulatory matters. For example, they:

- have **direct** roles – as they are often appointed as *authorised officers* (either *ex-officio* or directly);
- have **overlapping** roles – as often regulatory matters (i.e., alleged *regulatory breaches*) can overlap with *criminal matters* (i.e., *fraud* and dishonesty); and

- have **support** roles – as they are often called to support and/or provide assistance to other *regulatory officers*. This is commonly referred to as standing by to prevent a 'breach of the peace' where police attend to protect and/or act as a deterrent for unco-operative or aggressive *persons* or *regulated entities*.

(see also: Regulatory Agency/ies)

Post-Market Surveillance

Is a term that is commonly used in the medical and pharmaceutical *regulated* sectors, and matters intersecting with product safety and consumer *law*.

Post-market surveillance relates to the practice of *monitoring* the safe use of medical devices or pharmaceutical drugs after they have been released to the market for sale or use.

The *regulatory activities* that typically occur as part of *post-market surveillance* are most closely aligned with those functions that occur in the *monitoring compliance* phase of the *Extended Regulatory Spectrum*.

(see also: **Extended Regulatory Spectrum**; Monitoring Compliance; Surveillance).

Precedent/s

In literal terms, a *precedent* is something that precedes, or comes before.

For *regulators* a *precedent* might be reference to a:

- *precedent* set by a *regulator* itself – where they demonstrate consistency over time, which is reflected in their *operational decision-making*, consistency, and objectivity; and
- legal *precedent* in the *court* and judicial sense – which depends on the level of the *court*, the *jurisdiction*, and the legal issues involved.

Precedents can be:

- informative – in that it is more of an example, from a previous matter or *case*, that can be considered to inform a subsequent decision or action involving a matter with similar circumstances; or
- instructive – in that it is more directive, and the guidance comes from a decision from a superior body, like a delegated decision-maker or a *court*.

There are two types of legal *precedent*:

- *binding* – which is sometimes referred to as *authoritative precedent*; and
- *non-binding* – which is sometimes referred to as persuasive *precedent*.

(see also: Binding Precedent; Non-Binding Precedent)

Preliminary Investigation (see Initial investigation)

Premise/s

What is classed as a *premise* is shaped by many factors including:

- the nature and role of the *regulator*;
- the *regulator's* operating environment (e.g., industries, sectors, and commodities); and
- how and where *regulated entities* are conducting their business.

The *legislation* that the *regulator* is operating under usually provides a definition for *premise/s*.

Premise/s can include aircraft, buildings, caravans, cars, homes, offices, ships, and trains etc.

Prima Facie [Latin] (Case, or Evidence)

A Latin phrase translating to 'on the face of it' or 'at first look' and is usually something which is accepted as correct until proved otherwise.

(see also: Burden of Proof; Contested Hearing; Prosecution)

Primary Legislation

Acts of parliament are sometimes referred to as *primary legislation* which are made by the *legislature*, the legislative branch of government.

Primary legislation can also authorise a *person* or body (e.g., the responsible minister) to make other *laws* in the form of *secondary legislation* that relate to matters of detail.

(see also: Act/s; Act of Parliament; Delegated Legislation; Legislative Instruments; Regulation; Secondary Legislation; Statute; Subordinate Legislation)

Principles-based Regulation

Is based upon 'principles' or higher-level broadly stated *rules*, which operate at a high level of generality. [87]

Principles-based regulation, like *performance-based regulation* avoids detailed and prescriptive rules and associated processes, techniques, and/or procedures.

(see also: Types of Regulation)

Principles of Good Regulation

The *Principles of Good Regulation*, based on the work of the UK's Better Regulation Taskforce,[88] listed alphabetically are:

- Accountable;
- Consistent;
- Proportionate;
- Targeted; and
- Transparent.

In this book, when referred to collectively, the principles appear as the acronym *PACTT*.

(see also: Accountable/Accountability; Consistent/Consistency; PACTT; Proportionate/ Proportionality; Targeted/Targeting; Transparent/Transparency)

Private Prosecution (see Third Party Action)

Probation Order/s

Is a *regulatory response* that is available to some *regulators* under certain *regulatory regimes/schemes*.

Probation orders, if available, typically form part of a *regulator's* choices/options as a *criminal response*. *Probation orders* are a form of supervised order and can be part of a penalty or *sanction* following the admission or finding of guilt.[89]

Examples of a *probation order* for a juvenile *offender* would include mandatory conditions such as:

- 'reporting to the Secretary [or delegate] within two working days after the Court makes the order;
- reporting to a youth justice officer as required;

183

- not re-offending during the period of probation;
- not leaving the State without the Secretary's [or delegate's] written permission;
- notifying the youth justice officer of any change in where the offender lives, studies or works within 48 hours after the change;
- obeying all reasonable and lawful instructions of the youth justice officer'.[90]

(see also: Administrative Remedy/Response/Sanction; Exclusion Order)

Problem-Solving approach to regulation

The *problem-solving approach to regulation* is based upon the philosophy which suggests that *regulators* should be 'picking important problems and fixing them'.[91]

The *problem-solving approach to regulation* is based upon a six-stage problem-solving protocol:

'Stage 1: Nominate & Select Potential Problem for Attention
Stage 2: Define the Problem Precisely
Stage 3: Determine How to Measure Impact
Stage 4: Develop Solutions/Interventions
Stage 5(a): Implement the Plan
Stage 5(b): Periodic Monitoring/Review/Adjustment
Stage 6: Project Closure, and Long Term Monitoring/ Maintenance'.[92]

(see also: Regulatory Craft; Types of Regulation)

Procedural Fairness

An administrative *law* concept which relates to fairness of the procedures used by a decision-maker during the process of arriving at a decision, rather than the actual outcome of the decision itself (i.e., the outcome).

Procedural fairness is often used interchangeably with the term *natural justice*. However:

- *procedural fairness* is used more often when talking about administrative *decision-making* processes, and

- *natural justice* tends to be associated more with procedures used by *courts* or tribunals.

(see also: Administrative Law; Natural Justice)

Proof Beyond Reasonable Doubt
(see Beyond Reasonable Doubt)

Proportionate/Proportionality

From a *regulator's* perspective, to be *proportionate* or act with *proportionality*, is a reference to demonstrating *compliance* with the:

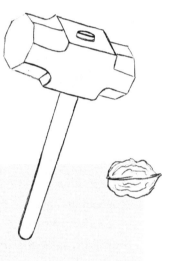

- *Principles of Good Regulation*; and
- forms the **P** in the associated *PACTT* acronym.

It is important for *regulators* that *proportionality* is considered holistically, with the *regulator* being *proportionate* across all its *regulatory functions* and activities, but paying particular attention to:

- the *regulatory risks* and harms they are seeking to control or mitigate;
- the antecedents and culpability of individuals or *regulated entities*; and
- the fact that the overall *regulatory response* or intervention is considered *proportionate* from the perspective of *co-* and *peer- regulators*, *regulated entities*, *stakeholders*, and the *wider community*.

(see also: ***Four Key Regulatory Perspectives***; PACTT; Principles of Good Regulation; Problem-Solving approach to regulation)

Prosecuting Authority

For *regulators, prosecuting authority* is a reference to a body or organisation that is authorised by *law* to initiate proceedings (whether administrative, civil, or criminal) on behalf of the *regulator*.

Examples of public *prosecuting authorities* include:
- Australia – Crown Solicitors Office, Director of Public Prosecutions;
- Canada – Crown Attorney, Crown Counsel;
- England and Wales – Crown Prosecution Services;
- New Zealand – Crown Prosecution Services;
- Scotland – Procurator Fiscal; and
- United States – District Attorney, State Attorney.

The main functions of a *prosecuting authority* include providing advice on whether to:
- commence or not commence proceedings;
- amend or substitute charges;
- discontinue proceedings; and
- accept and/or negotiate plea bargains.

(see also: Litigation; Prosecutorial Discretion; Trial)

Prosecution

A *prosecution* refers to the commencement and conduct of legal proceedings against a *person* or *regulated entity*.

The term *prosecution* is predominantly used for a *breach* of criminal provisions as opposed to administrative or civil *breaches*. However, in practice the term tends to be used interchangeably.

The steps in a *prosecution* can vary between *jurisdictions*, however most will include and involve the aspects listed below: [93]
- completing an *investigation* and producing a *brief of evidence*;
- brief assessment and/or decision to charge;
- charging or commencing proceedings;
- committal proceeding;
- hearing;
- *trial*;
- sentencing; and
- appeals.

(see also: Litigation; Trial)

Prosecution File (see Brief of Evidence)

Prosecution Policy

Irrespective of its final form, a *prosecution policy* is based upon a two-step test which must be conducted prior to commencement of a *prosecution*.

Step 1 – the *regulator* (if they are conducting the *prosecution*) or *prosecuting authority* must be satisfied that:
- there is sufficient *evidence* to prosecute the case; and

Step 2 – it must be evident from the facts of the case, and all the surrounding circumstances, that:
- the *prosecution* would be in the *public interest*.

If a *regulator* does not have their own dedicated *prosecution policy*, they:
- will most likely defer to any overarching *prosecuting policy* published by the relevant *prosecuting authority* in their *jurisdiction*; or
- may incorporate the relevant principles of such a *prosecution policy* into a *compliance and enforcement policy* or similar.

(see also: Compliance and Enforcement Policy; Enforcement Policy; Prosecutorial Discretion; Regulatory Policy)

Prosecutor

A *prosecutor* is responsible for presenting the case for the *prosecution*.

A *prosecutor* is usually a lawyer or someone who is legally trained. However, in some *jurisdictions*, especially for lower *court* matters, the *prosecutor* may be a (non-lawyer) civil/public servant.

(see also: Litigation; Prosecution; Prosecutorial Discretion; Trial)

Prosecutorial Discretion

Prosecutorial discretion is a broad discretion that is available to a *prosecutor* (or *prosecuting authority*) to:
- commence or not commence proceedings;
- amend or substitute charges;
- discontinue proceedings; and
- accept and/or negotiate plea bargains.

There are a range of factors that influence a *prosecutor's* use of *prosecutorial discretion*. Factors include, but are not limited to, considerations around:
- admissibility, reliability, and sufficiency of *evidence*;

- availability of *witnesses;*
- efficacy and efficiency in concluding matters;
- proper use of prosecutorial resources; and
- *public interest.*

(see also: Discretion; Public Interest)

Protracted investigation

Is reference to an *investigation* that takes place over a prolonged or extended period.

(see also: Investigation; Initial Investigation; Statute of Limitations)

Public Benefit

The terms *public benefit; public good;* and *public value* are often used individually and in combination to explain or justify why *regulation* is:

- necessary;
- appropriate; and
- generally beneficial in advancing the interests of society.

(see also: Investigation; Initial Investigation)

Public Good (see Public Benefit)

Public Interest

For *regulators* the term *public interest* can have both a broad and narrow meaning:

- broadly – it can be a reference to a thing or matter being of value, benefit and in the interests of the *wider-community;* and
- narrowly – it can be a reference to one of the primary *criteria* on which regulatory matters are assessed, prioritised, and pursued, especially in terms of *enforcement* and *litigation.*

(see also: Public Benefit; Prosecutorial Discretion)

Public Value (see Public Benefit)

Quality Assurance

Quality assurance broadly involves systematic *monitoring* and evaluation of something (e.g., a process, activity, or facility) to ensure relevant requirements or *standards* are being met.

Quality assurance activities tend to be based on time frames ranging from daily, weekly, monthly, quarterly, or annually.

Quality assurance can be focussed and directed inward or outward. For example:

- *Regulated entities* – tend to have inward focussed *quality assurance* that assists them to adhere to and demonstrate their *compliance* with regulatory *obligations*, and
- *Regulators* – tend to have outward focussed *quality assurance* that assist them to both:
  - enable and support *regulated entities* to meet their regulatory *obligations*, and
  - detail how they will undertake (including identifying, prioritising, resourcing, implementing, and evaluating) their *regulatory activities* as part of delivering the *regulatory outcomes* they have been charged with.

(see also: Regulatory Cycle; Regulatory Excellence; Regulatory Professionalism)

Quasi-Legislation/Quasi-Regulation

Quasi-legislation includes and describes a wide variety of arrangements where government influences a *person* and *regulated entities* to comply, but which do not form part of explicit (or direct) government *regulation*.

Quasi-regulation is sometimes referred to as *soft law*.[94] This is because in some instances it may simply involve the mere threat of government *regulation* if the industry or sector does not take action to effectively *self-regulate*.

Arrangements that can be considered *quasi-legislation* include:

- *codes*;
- instruments;
- guidelines;
- *rules*;
- rulings; and
- *standards*.

An example of *quasi-regulation* in Australia saw an agreement by internet service providers to voluntarily filter a list of sexually explicit websites, based upon a list of website URLs, that were compiled and maintained by the telecommunications *regulator*. This arrangement occurred and was agreed to by *regulated entities*, based upon signalling by the *regulator* that they were considering proposing a system which involved mandatory filtering by the internet service provider.

(see also: Legislation; Regulation)

Ranger (see Authorised Officer)

In a *regulatory* context, a *ranger* is a *person* who has supervisory responsibilities in a specific geographic location.

The title of *ranger* is most often associated with *authorised officers* whose work involves the protection of a forest, nature reserve or national park.

The term is increasingly being used by local government to describe *regulatory officers*, especially those who are engaged in parking and traffic management and animal control.

(see also: Authorised Officer; Inspector; Investigator; Regulatory Officer; Warden)

RBP (see Risk-based Prioritisation)

RBR (see Risk-based Regulation)

Really Responsive Regulation

Really responsive regulation requires *regulators* to go beyond being responsive to the *compliance* rates and performance of *regulated entities*,[95] and consider:

- the *regulated entity's* operating environment;
- the broader authorising and operating environment of the *regulatory regime/scheme*;
- the performance of the *regulatory regime/scheme* itself;

- the reasons sitting behind the use of different *regulatory tools* and strategies; and
- any changes to the points above.

(see also: Responsive Regulation; Types of Regulation)

Reasonable Belief

A *reasonable belief* is the legal standard that must be met before *authorised officers/regulatory officers* can exercise certain *regulatory powers* or authority.

A *reasonable belief* is sometimes referred to as *reasonable grounds to believe*.

A *reasonable belief* is more than a *reasonable suspicion*.

It is important for regulatory agencies, supervisors, and managers to ensure that the requisite belief **must** be formed in the mind of the *authorised officer*, or *person* exercising the relevant *regulatory powers* or authority – without any undue influence or pressure being placed upon them.

(see also: Coercive Powers; Reasonable Suspicion; Regulatory Powers)

Reasonable Cause to Suspect
(see Reasonable Suspicion)

Reasonable Grounds to Believe
(see Reasonable Belief)

Reasonable Suspicion

A *reasonable suspicion* is the legal standard that must be met before *authorised officers/regulatory officers* can exercise certain *regulatory powers* or authority.

A *reasonable suspicion* is sometimes referred to as *reasonable cause to suspect*.

A *reasonable suspicion* is less than a *reasonable belief*.

It is important for regulatory agencies, supervisors, and managers to ensure that the requisite suspicion **must** be formed in the mind of the *authorised officer*, or *person* exercising the relevant *regulatory powers* or authority – without any undue influence or pressure being placed upon them.

(see also: Coercive Powers; Reasonable Belief; Regulatory Powers)

Re-certification

The process of being re-certified can relate to both the *regulated* and *regulators*.

For those *regulated* it usually forms part of a broader *authorisation* process, but it also intersects with *licensing and approvals*, and *monitoring compliance*.

For example, *re-certification* might involve a:

- *regulated entity* who holds the *authorisation* to undertake the *regulated activity* – to establish that the plant equipment they are using has been appropriately maintained (i.e., serviced, repaired, or calibrated) and the factory or plant where the activity occurs continues to meet the requirements; or
- *person* who holds the *licence* or qualification to undertake the *regulated activity* – has maintained the appropriate skills, qualifications, and certifications (i.e., re-qualification to use equipment, medical health examination, and membership to a relevant professional body).

For the *regulator*, it usually relates to the need for *authorised officers* to maintain the skills, qualifications, and certifications to perform their regulatory work. For example, *re-certification* might involve the *authorised officer* who operates in the:

- aviation environment – maintaining currency of their aeronautical engineering qualifications;
- maritime environment – maintaining currency of their safety-at-sea qualifications; or
- child protection environment – maintaining their working with vulnerable persons accreditation.

Noting also, that *authorised officers* are generally employed by the civil/ public service, so many have a general requirement to be of good character and not have any criminal convictions. Periodic *re-certification*, especially for those *authorised officers* that have access to sensitive or protected information, will often include a criminal history check.

(see also: Certification).

Recklessness

Generally, *recklessness* refers to state of mind which sits behind an action which influences how a person acts or does not act in a certain way.

Recklessness sits lower than *intent* but higher than *negligence*.

Recklessness of a *person* or *regulated entity* (whether an *accused* or an *offender*) is a factor that influences a *regulator's decision-making* at critical times:

- initially – as part of the initial *triaging* process, to determine the priority of response to a *breach* or *allegation* of *non-compliance*;
- ongoing – throughout various *compliance* activities, but especially *audits*, *inspections*, and *investigation*; and
- finally – as part of determining the nature and quantum of penalty submissions.

(see also: Burden of Proof; Guilty Knowledge; Intent; Mens Rea [Latin])

Record of Decision (ROD)

A *record of decision* has broad and narrow applications for *regulators* and regulatory staff. For example:

- broadly – regulating is a function of government, therefore anything that shows the thinking, working and factors behind a decision or outcome is a public record. And public records must be managed in accordance with the legal requirements and policies of the *jurisdiction*; and
- narrowly – a *record of decision* is critically important for:
  - *regulatory officers* (usually *investigators* or case officers) to record the circumstances surrounding, and the rationale for decisions they have made, especially at critical stages of an *investigation* or matter; and

■ a range of regulatory staff including managers, supervisors, or *decision-making* bodies (usually *case management committees* or similar), irrespective of whether endorsing, modifying, or over-riding a decision made by a *regulatory officer.*

It is important for *regulators* that *records of decisions* are maintained and form a central part of the *regulator's* culture as they:

- demonstrate a commitment to proper record keeping;
- reflect best practice in (*inspection* and *investigation*) case management; and
- advance *accountability, transparency* and other aspects of the *Principles of Good Regulation.*

(see also: Accountable/Accountability; Case Decision Record; Decision/s; Decision-Making; Decision-Review; PACTT; Principles of Good Regulation; Transparent/Transparency)

Red Tape

Red tape is typically taken to mean *regulation* (including regulatory processes, regulatory procedures, regulatory reporting, and/or other administrative requirements of government) that impose or create burdens for *regulated entities* – which are considered:

- unjustified;
- unnecessary; or
- excessive.

During the initial stages of the *red tape* reduction movement governments generally directed their efforts towards removing *regulatory burdens*. This often centred around repealing *legislation,* as part of reducing the stock and flow of *regulation.* This led to the practice (and sometimes an explicit requirement) to remove one rule before introducing another, which was sometimes referred to as the 'one rule out – one rule in' model, and in extreme cases involved 'two rules out – one rule in'.

In more recent times, governments around the world have generally moved away from using the term *red tape* and binary or formulaic approaches to reducing *regulatory burdens.* Now instead they tend to talk in terms of a more sophisticated de-regulation agenda.[96]

It is important for *regulators* that they do not become myopic on the issue of *red tape*, causing them to confuse or conflate those *regulations*, processes, or administrative requirements that are justified, necessary, and not excessive.

It is important to keep and maintain *regulations* that are appropriate to deliver *regulatory outcomes* which are in the *public interest* and advance the *public good*.

(see also: Beige Tape; Green Tape; Grey Tape; Regulatory Burden; Stock, Flow and Effectiveness (of regulation))

Registration

Registration can take the form of an *authorisation* – either in its own right – or as part of another form of *authorisation*.

For example, a transportation company may:

- have a *licence* to carry demolition and building waste, and
- also be registered to handle dangerous substances such as asbestos.

(see also: Approval; Authorisation; Licence; Licence Condition/s; Permit)

Regulated

The term used to describe an entity (*person*, body, or organisation) who is subject to *regulation* by a *regulator/regulatory body*.

The *regulated* are one of the four main groups that provide key regulatory perspectives, the others are: *regulators*; *stakeholders*; and *wider community*.

(see also: **Four Key Regulatory Perspectives;** Person; Regulated Commodity/ies; Regulated Sector/s)

Regulated Activity/ies

Is an activity or activities that are subject to some form of *regulation* or regulatory oversight, and for which it is necessary or required for a *person* or *regulated entity* to obtain and maintain a relevant *authorisation*. A *regulated activity* can be specific or general in nature. For example:

- a business that possesses and sells restricted or prescribed chemicals would be involved in a specific *regulated activity*; and

- all businesses that sell products, irrespective of their nature, are involved in a general *regulated activity* as they are subject to consumer protection/fair trading requirements.

(see also: Authorisation; Regulated)

Regulated Commodity/ies

Regulated commodities can be confined to one, or span several, *regulatory domains*. The examples below are confined to single domains:
- economic – i.e., cash transactions, as part of money laundering;
- environmental – i.e., possessing endangered animals, as part of wildlife trafficking; or
- social – i.e., possessing certain types of medicines, as part the broader health care system.

(see also: Regulated; Regulated Sector)

Regulated Entity/es (see Regulated)

Regulated Party/ies (see Regulated)

Regulated Sector/s

Is a reference to the grouping of *regulated entities* into similar or related groups.

Regulated sectors can be divided across the following broad *regulatory domains*:
- economic – the financial sector;
- environmental – the environment sector; or
- social – the health and welfare sector.

Regulated sectors can be further divided into sub-sectors, for example the:
- financial sector – might be considered in terms of personal and commercial lines;
- environment sector – might be considered in terms of air, water, land; and waste; and

- health sector – might be considered in terms of medical equipment, medical services, and pharmaceutical products.

(see also: Regulated; Regulated Commodities)

Regulated Self-Assurance
(see Earned Autonomy/Recognition)

Regulatees (see Regulated)

Regulation (definitions)

The definition for what constitutes *regulation* varies across *jurisdictions* and often within *jurisdictions*. For example, *regulation* is defined by the:
- Australian Government –

  '[as] any rule endorsed by government where there is an expectation of compliance';[97]
- New Zealand Government –

  '[as] the promulgation of rules by government accompanied by mechanisms for monitoring and enforcement, usually assumed to be performed through a specialist public agency';[98] and
- Organisation for Economic Co-operation and Development (OECD) –

  '[as] the diverse set of instruments by which governments set requirements on enterprises and citizens. Regulations include laws, formal and informal orders and subordinate rules issued by all levels of government, and rules issued by non-governmental or self-regulatory bodies to whom governments have delegated regulatory powers';[99] or more succinctly

  '[the] imposition of rules by government, backed by the use of penalties that are intended specifically to modify the economic behaviour of individuals and firms in the private sector'.[100]

(see also: Act/s; Act of Parliament; Code/s; Legislation; Primary Legislation; Regulation (in practice); Rules; Statute)

Regulation (in practice)

Regulation involves the administration of any *law* or *rule* which is put in place by government, with government authority (or support), where there is a reasonable expectation of *compliance*.

Regulation seeks to influence or compel specific behaviour by a *person* or *regulated entity*, whether operating as an individual or as part of a commercial enterprise.

Regulation is expansive and includes a range of activities, see *Regulation (Big 'R')* and *regulation (Little 'r')* below.

(see also: Act/s; Code/s; Determination; Directive; Legislation; Rules; Schedule; Standard; Statute)

Regulation (Big 'R')

The term *Regulation (Big 'R')* refers to a specific type of *legislative instrument* which is a form of delegated *legislation*.

Regulation (Big 'R') is typically made by an executive authority (e.g., Government Minister) under powers given to them by *primary legislation* (an *act*) to implement and administer the requirements of that *act*.

Several examples include:
- Australia – Therapeutic Goods Regulations, 1990;
- Canada – Migratory Birds Regulations, 2020;
- New Zealand – Health and Safety at Work (General Risk and Workplace Management) Regulations, 2016; and
- Scotland – The Milk and Healthy Snack Scheme (Scotland) Amendment Regulations, 2021.

(see also: Delegated Legislation; Primary Legislation; Secondary Legislation)

regulation (Little 'r')

The term *regulation (Little 'r')* is a broad term to describe the totality of government requirements, including legally binding *codes, licence* conditions, ministerial orders and directions, and planning schemes, as well as *acts* and *regulations*.

(see also: Code/s; Determination; Directive; Ordinance/s; Standard/s)

Regulation Impact Statement (RIS)

A *regulation impact statement* (or *RIS*) is a document prepared by the entity responsible for a *regulatory policy* proposal, whether a department, agency, *statutory authority*, or board. The *RIS* formalises the analysis of the likely impacts of *regulatory policy* proposals and includes information and assessment of the costs and benefits of each option considered.

In some *jurisdictions*, a *RIS* is the product that results from the *regulatory impact assessment/analysis* process.

A *RIS* is a statement that agencies (whether a regulatory or non-regulatory agency) are required to produce as part of the policy making process, when certain types of decisions or regulatory changes will or are likely to have a regulatory impact on a *person*, business, or element of the *wider community*.

A *RIS* informs and relates to the flow of new *regulation*, as such it would fall under flow in the *stock, flow, and effectiveness (of regulation)* process.

(see also: De-regulation; Regulatory Impact Analysis; Regulatory Impact Assessment; Stock, Flow and Effectiveness (of regulation))

Regulator

Is a broad term which is used individually and collectively to describe an entity (whether a *person*, body, or organisation) who has the *statutory authority* and mandate to administer and enforce *regulation*.

The main examples of a *regulator* include:

- individual person – i.e., a specific and named person, usually in the form of a statutory office holder. For example, Ms Jane Doe is the National Water Office Holder – in this role she is the ultimate decision-maker in respect to allocation and management of environmental water flows;
- individual agency or Ministry – i.e., a single and specific *regulatory agency* in a specific context. For example, the Environmental Protection Agency – is the *regulator* for the protection of the environment from dust emissions from factories; or

- multiple agencies – i.e., two or more *regulatory agencies* (even though they are standalone *regulators*) might be considered collectively to be the *regulator* in a specific context. For example:
  - geographically, at an international airport – some *regulated entities*, *stakeholders*, and elements of the *wider community* would see biosecurity agencies, border and customs agencies, and police agencies as 'the *regulator*' at international borders; and
  - on an overlapping issue, like ensuring that migrant/immigrant workers are not exploited – some *regulated entities, stakeholders,* and elements of the *wider community* would see the Department of Labour, together with the Inland Revenue Service, and Department of Immigration as 'the *regulator*'.

Regulator is one of the four main groups that constitute the *Four Key Regulatory Perspectives* the others are: *regulated*; *stakeholders*; and *wider community*.

(see also: ***Four Key Regulatory Perspectives***; Statutory Authority)

Regulator Independence

In many ways, *regulators* perform a role for society which is like that of a referee in a sporting event – and just like the referee who can annoy or frustrate someone every time they blow their whistle, so too can the *regulator* when they make a decision or take action.

Therefore, just like the referee, it is important that *regulators* can demonstrate independence.

It is an oversimplification to think that being an independent regulator or having *regulator independence* is achieved purely (or largely) by institutional design.

For *regulators* the issue of independence is a challenging one and there are many variables. For example, the nature of the issues impacting upon *regulator independence* might vary between *jurisdictions* and could be further shaped by the type of industry, sector, or commodity being *regulated*.

There are several areas where *regulators* are susceptible to undue pressure and influence, which can impact upon their independence. Areas of concern and those that require special attention include:

- a lack of clarity from the *executive* arm of government, in relation to the *regulator's* role and functions;
- the nature of the relationships the *regulator* has with *regulated entities* and *stakeholders*;
- the way *regulators* attract, recruit, and maintain staff; and
- how *regulators* are funded, including whether by government, industry, or a combination[101, 102]

(see also: Independence; Statutory Authority; Type of Regulatory Agency)

Regulator Performance and Evaluation

Regulator performance and evaluation is a *regulatory activity* which involves the *regulator* being accountable for its own performance. It involves a process whereby the *regulator's* performance is evaluated and is reported, often against *key performance indicators* or some predetermined measures.

The *regulator's* performance can be self-assessed, assessed by a *peer-regulator*, or by an independent third party.

The evaluation and subsequent report can be:

- internal – restricted to the *regulator* itself;
- partially-public – de-identified, in terms of *regulated entities*; and with sensitive *operational* information removed; and
- fully-public – often being tabled in parliament or equivalent or available on an open access website.

Regulator performance and evaluation is important in terms of *regulator* accountability and transparency and plays a critical part in the *continuous improvement* process of the *regulator*. It typically involves *regulators* demonstrating how their *regulatory priorities, capability, processes,* systems, and relationships are fit for purpose. It also enables the achievement of targets and the successful delivery on government objectives or solving specific problems.

In a linear sense, it is the last of six phases contained in the *Extended Regulatory Spectrum*.

An example from Australia comes in the form of the *Regulator Performance Framework* which provided a practical example for *regulator performance and evaluation*, across six *key performance indicators (KPIs)*.[103]

(see also: ***Extended Regulatory Spectrum;*** Key Performance Indicators)

Regulator Performance Framework (RPF)

The *Regulator Performance Framework*[104] *(RPF)* is a document that provided guidance to both policy-makers and *operational regulatory* staff, on how to minimise their impact on *regulated entities,* while undertaking their mandated *regulatory functions.*

Although superseded, by the *Regulator Performance Guide (RPG),* a central and useful component of the *RPF* was its six *key performance indicators (KPIs).* These six *KPIs* continue to have utility for *regulators* as they provide a basis for (internal) reflection and/or (external) demonstration of the *regulator's* performance.

(see also: Key Performance Indicators; Regulator Performance Guide; Regulator Performance Management)

Regulator Performance Guide (RPG)

The *Regulator Performance Guide*[105] *(RPG)* is a document that provides guidance to both policy-makers and *operational regulatory* staff, on how to minimise their impact on *regulated entities,* while undertaking their mandated *regulatory functions.*

The *RPG* transitions *regulators* from the 2014 *Regulator Performance Framework (RPF)* based upon six *key performance indicators (KPIs)* to a Guide that encourages a more outcomes-focused, principles-based service. Specifically relating to:

- a proportional approach to risk;

- genuine engagement with *regulated entities* and the broader community; and
- the importance of maintiaing trust and confidence.

The *RPG* contains three principles of regulator *best practice*:

- 'Continuous improvement and building trust – regulators adopt a whole-of-system perspective, continuously improving their performance, capability and culture to build trust and confidence in Australia's regulatory settings.
- Risk-based and data driven – regulators manage risks proportionately and maintain essential safeguards while minimising regulatory burden, and leveraging data and digital technology to support those they regulate to comply and grow.
- Collaboration and engagement – regulators are transparent and responsive communicators, implementing regulations in a modern and collaborative way'.[106]

(see also: Regulator Performance Framework; Regulator Performance Management)

Regulator Performance Management

Regulator performance management is linked to the measurement of *regulatory outcomes*.

Firstly, it is acknowledged that measuring *regulatory outcomes* can pose real challenges, for it is often difficult to determine causation and then attribute improvements to *regulatory activities* or intervention.

Secondly, attempts to measure the performance of *regulators* are often measured against several indicator categories, including:

- inputs (resources);
- outputs (activities);
- intermediate outcomes (measures of knowledge and behaviour of the regulated community); and
- final outcomes.[107]

Several examples, where central governments have developed guidance to assist *regulators* with performance include:

- in Australia – the Government developed the *Regulator Performance Framework (RPF)*[108] which used six *key performance indicators* to measure the performance of *regulators*;

- in New Zealand – *regulatory stewardship* is at the centre of *regulator performance management*, with the three key components being:
    - performance assessment;
    - evaluation; and
    - review.
- in the United Kingdom – where a good practice guide[109] suggests that performance measurement *frameworks* used or developed by *regulators* should include the following characteristics:[110]
    - focused;
    - appropriate;
    - balanced;
    - robust;
    - integrated; and
    - cost-effective.

(see also: Key Performance Indicators; Regulator Performance Framework; Regulatory Stewardship)

Regulators' Code

The *Regulators' Code* sets out the expectations of government for *regulators* in the United Kingdom, especially in terms of *regulatory delivery*.

The *Regulators' Code,* is based heavily upon the *principles of good regulation*, and is comprised of six broad principles:

1. 'Regulators should carry out their activities in a way that supports those they regulate to comply and grow;
2. Regulators should provide simple and straightforward ways to engage with those they regulate and hear their views;
3. Regulators should base their regulatory activities on risk;
4. Regulators should share information about compliance and risk;
5. Regulators should ensure that clear information, guidance and advice is available to help those they regulate meet their responsibilities to comply; and
6. Regulators should ensure that their approach to their regulatory activities is transparent'. [111, 112]

It is important for *regulators* to be held accountable. The *Regulators' Code* concludes by stating that 'the Government is committed to making sure the Regulators' Code is effective. To make sure that the Code is being used effectively, we want businesses, regulated bodies and citizens to challenge regulators who they believe are not acting in accordance with their published policies and standards. It is in the wider public interest that regulators are transparent and proportionate in their approaches to regulation.'[113]

(see also: Principles of Good Regulation; Regulator Performance; Regulatory Culture; Regulatory Delivery)

Regulatory Activity/ies

Is a term which can be used by *regulators* in very broad, broad, and narrow contexts. For example, when used:

- very broadly – it might be reference to **any and/or all** *regulatory activities* that a *regulatory agency* engages in as part of administering, regulating, and enforcing *legislation*;
- broadly – might be reference to **the main areas or types of** *regulatory activity* that a *regulator* engages in, for example it may group them as:
  - *registration* and *approvals*;
  - *licensing* and *permits*;
  - *monitoring compliance*; and
  - *investigation* and *enforcement*; and
- narrowly – might be reference to the *regulator* modifying (i.e., increasing overall, decreasing overall, or maintaining the current level, but moving the focus) **a single type of** *regulatory activity*, for example in relation to *inspections*.

Regulatory activities can be *operational*, *strategic*, and/or *tactical* in nature.

(see also: Operational; Regulatory Delivery; Regulatory Functions; *Three Levels of Operational Activity*)

Regulatory Acumen

The term acumen refers to an ability to make good (and correct) judgements and take quick decisions. It includes the ability to demonstrate a nuanced application around a particular subject and especially on practical matters. For example, acumen is often preceded by the word business or political, to suggest that a person has business acumen or political acumen.

Regulatory acumen therefore is considered to involve a combination of awareness and practice.[114]

If *regulation* is to become a recognised profession, *regulators* will need to demonstrate increased *regulatory acumen* as part of being a *regulatory professional.*

(see also: Regulatory Literacy; Regulatory Profession; Regulatory Professional)

Regulatory Advisory Panel
(see Internal Regulatory Body/ies)

Regulatory Agency/ies

Depending on the *jurisdiction* they are operating in, and the approach government takes to establishing regulatory and oversight bodies, a *regulatory agency* can take various forms.[115]

The three main types of *regulatory agency* or body, include those that are a:

- **standalone regulatory function** which is embedded within another agency or department – for example:
  - Australia (national level) – the Commonwealth Water Holder in Australia is located within a Division of the Department of Agriculture and Water;
  - Canada (sub-national level) – the Alberta Energy Regulator; and
  - New Zealand (central level) – the Real Estate Authority in New Zealand, as a Crown Entity.
- **standalone regulatory agency** or body within a portfolio or ministry – for example:
  - Australia (sub-national level) – the Environmental Protection Authority in Victoria;

- Canada (sub-national level) – the Ontario Securities Commission; and
- New Zealand (regional level) – Environment Waikato.
- **standalone statutory authority** within a portfolio or ministry – for example:
  - Australia (national level) – the Great Barrier Reef Marine Park Authority;
  - Netherlands (national level) – the Netherlands Authority for the Financial Markets; and
  - Scotland (national level) – the Scottish Housing Regulator.

(see also: Regulator; Regulator Independence; Statutory Authority)

Regulatory Approach/es

Is reference to the overarching philosophy or main approach/es that a *regulator* uses.

The main *types of regulation* and *regulatory approaches* are:
- Command and control;
- Harms-based;
- Intelligence-based/led;
- Outcomes-focused;
- Performance-based;
- Principles-based; and
- Risk-based.

Some *regulators* identify with one main approach, while others will use two or more. Listed below are examples of the different types of approaches that *regulators* identify with:
- a *risk-based regulator;*[116]
- an *intelligence-led* and *risk-based regulator;*[117]
- an *intelligence-led, risk-based regulator,* and *outcomes-focused regulator.*[118]

As is evident, *regulatory approach/es* and *types of regulation* can overlap and be used somewhat interchangeably.

(see also: Regulatory Method/s; Regulatory Tool/s; Types of Regulation)

Regulatory Board/s

Regulatory boards are a governance and oversight mechanism for *regulators*.

Regulatory boards provide:
- advice and guidance on strategic direction to the *regulator*;
- advice and guidance on policies being developed by the *regulator*; and
- a means of monitoring and reporting on the performance of the *regulator*.

In descending order, the work of a *regulatory board* is generally focussed on matters that are *strategic*, *operational*, and *tactical* in nature.

The precise nature of the role of a *regulatory board* will vary, depending on the size, structure, and culture of the *regulatory agency*. However, a *regulatory board* will usually:
- work extremely closely with and have very frequent interactions with the head of the *regulatory agency* – and in some instances the head of the *regulatory agency* is a member of the board;
- have frequent interactions with *regulatory executives* – through papers or issues that the *regulatory executive* tables and speaks to at board meetings;
- have infrequent interactions with *regulatory managers* – through papers or issues that the *regulatory manager* tables and speaks to at board meetings directly, or as part of attending and speaking as a subject matter expert on a topic or issue being considered by the board;
- have little or no direct contact with *regulatory practitioners* unless they are supporting a *regulatory executive* or *regulatory manager*.

The membership of a *regulatory board* varies between *regulatory agencies*. A *regulatory board* may include representatives from:
- *co-* or *peer- regulators*;
- *peak industry bodies*;
- *stakeholders*;
- the *wider community*;
- academic or research institutions; and

- other professions, disciplines, businesses, and sectors that are relevant to the *authorising environment* of the *regulator*.

(see also: Regulator Independence; Regulatory Executive; Regulatory Manager; Regulatory Practitioner)

Regulatory Body/ies (see Regulatory Agency/ies)

Regulatory Burden/s

As an overarching concept, *regulatory burdens* are those direct burdens placed on *regulated entities* by government *regulation*.

Definitions of *regulatory burdens* may vary, but generally they include both direct *administrative* and *compliance* burdens such as applying for *permits* and reporting requirements, and in some cases include delay and opportunity costs.

Regulatory burdens are typically considered to comprise both the burden of the *regulatory requirements* themselves, and how they are given *operational* effect by the *regulator*.

Regulators will be criticised or accused of subjecting *regulated entities* to a *regulatory burden* if:

- the *regulator's* – processes, procedures and requirements are perceived as being unnecessary complex, duplicative, or redundant; and/or
- the *regulated entity* – will incur additional (financial or resource) costs.

(see also: Beige Tape; Grey Tape; Red Tape; Stock, Flow and Effectiveness (of regulation))

Regulatory Capability

Capability is a term which is defined as the power or the ability to complete or do something.

Therefore, *regulatory capability* can be a reference to the ability of a:

- *regulator* – to perform the *regulatory functions* they are responsible for across the *Extended Regulatory Spectrum,* in such a way that they deliver the *regulatory outcomes* they are charged with delivering, and
  - will often be considered at an individual, team, agency, portfolio/ministry, or whole-of-government level; or

- *person* or *regulated entity* – to meet/achieve their regulatory duties and *obligations*, and
  - will often be considered in terms of a specific *regulatory regime/ scheme* level, or an ability across all *regulatory regimes/schemes*.

The terms capability and capacity are often used interchangeably, especially when the issue of *regulatory culture* is discussed.

(see also: ***Extended Regulatory Spectrum***; Regulatory Capacity; Regulatory Competence; Regulatory Culture)

Regulatory Capacity

Capacity is a term which is defined as the amount that something can contain and/or produce.

Therefore, *regulatory capacity* can be a reference to the ability of a:

- *regulator* – to undertake and perform those *regulatory functions* that they are responsible for across the *Extended Regulatory Spectrum,* in such a way that they deliver the *regulatory outcomes* they are charged with, and
  - will often be considered at an individual, team, agency, portfolio/ministry, or whole-of-government level; or
- *person* or *regulated entity* – to undertake and complete their regulatory duties and *obligations*, and
  - will often be considered in terms of a specific *regulatory regime/ scheme* level, or an ability across all *regulatory regimes/schemes*.

The terms capacity and capability are often used interchangeably, especially when the issue of *regulatory culture* is discussed.

(see also: ***Extended Regulatory Spectrum***; Regulatory Capability; Regulatory Competence; Regulatory Culture)

Regulatory Capture

Is a form of misconduct, unique to the regulatory sphere, by a *regulator* or its regulatory staff.

Regulatory capture comes in three main forms including when:

- *regulators* over-identify with the industry, sector, or commodity of *regulated entities* they regulate;

- *regulators* over-sympathise with the problems and issues the industry or *regulated entities* being regulated are dealing with; and
- there is an absence of toughness being demonstrated by *regulators*.[119]

Regulatory capture is insidious and often arises when *regulators* have an inappropriate focus on regulatory assistance. For example, this can occur when *regulators*:

- conflate and/or overly focus on their *engage* and *educate* roles, which is exacerbated if combined with a reluctance to *enforce* – see *engage, educate, and enforce*; or
- prioritise *advice and guidance,* and *licensing and approvals* work over *monitoring compliance,* and *enforcement* work – see the *Extended Regulatory Spectrum.*

(see also: Agency Capture; Corruption; Engage, Educate and Enforce (as a mantra and approach); **Extended Regulatory Spectrum**; Noble Cause Corruption; Regulator Independence)

Regulatory Competence/y

Regulatory competence is multifaceted and occurs across several dimensions.

For example, *regulatory competence* can be, and is perhaps most often, considered at:

- an individual, team, agency, portfolio/ministry, or whole-of-government level – especially in terms of specific *regulatory regimes/ schemes.*

However *regulatory competence* can usefully, and perhaps should be, considered in terms of a:

- level – i.e., beginner/novice, basic/introduction, intermediate, advanced/specialist, or expert;
- role – i.e., practitioner, manager, executive, senior executive, or board member;
- function – i.e., *regulatory regime design, advice and guidance, licensing and approvals, monitoring compliance, enforcement,* or *regulator performance and evaluation;*
- topic – i.e., industry, sector, sub-sector, or commodity.

It is important that *regulators* consider and approach *regulatory competence* holistically, this is because *Regulatory Capacity + Regulatory Capability = Regulatory Competence.*

(see also: **Extended Regulatory Spectrum**; Regulatory Capability; Regulatory Capacity)

Regulatory Compliance Officer

Inside some *regulated entities* there is an internal position of *regulatory compliance officer* (sometimes called a *compliance officer*).

This is an **inward** facing role, which focusses on the regulatory requirements of the *regulated entity.*

This position and positions like it, should not be confused with the **outward** facing roles performed by *regulatory officers.*

(see also: Compliance; Compliance Officer (in Regulatory Agencies); Compliance Officer (in Regulated Entity/ies)

Regulatory Craft

Regulatory craft is an overarching concept which suggests that being a *regulator*, and/or a *regulatory professional*, requires a certain type and amount of 'craftmanship'.

The ability to effectively engage in the *problem-solving approach to regulation* is considered central to committing to and advancing the *regulatory craft.*[120]

(see also: Regulatory Profession; Regulatory Professionalism; Problem-Solving approach to regulation)

Regulatory Creep

Regulatory creep occurs when *regulation* (and its associated regulatory requirements) extends to areas and/or activities beyond what is justified, intended, and deemed necessary within the original policy objective. As such *regulatory creep* intersects with *regulatory mandate.*

(see also: Red Tape; Regulatory Burden; Regulatory Mandate; Ultra Vires)

Regulatory Culture

Regulatory culture is a ubiquitous concept which can be difficult to describe and articulate, with many describing *regulatory culture* as something they can 'feel' or 'sense', but not easily put into words.

Regulatory culture can describe the shared norms, values and beliefs that exist within, and influence the behaviour of staff working within, a *regulatory agency*.

Regulatory culture is shaped and informed by several key issues including the:

- *authorising environment* in which the *regulator* operates;
- type of *regulatory agency* that the *regulatory agency* is; and
- level and nature of regulatory leadership.[121]

The extent to which *regulatory culture* has permeated within an agency can be reflected by:

- artefacts – which are the visible indicators and easily observable aspects of a regulator's culture. Examples of which include published policies, procedures, and practices;
- espoused beliefs and values – which may be more aspirational than actual. An example of which might be *regulatory statements of intent* and *regulatory strategies*; and
- basic underlying assumptions – which largely occur at an unconscious or sub-conscious level. An example would include the beliefs and values that are strongly held by a group.[122]

It is important that *regulators* understand that *regulatory culture* is a pervasive issue and one that influences and impacts upon nearly every aspect of a *regulator's* work.

The agency executive and *regulatory executives* play a large part in determining the *regulatory culture* of a *regulatory agency*, so it is critically important for them to set clear expectations and model the desired regulatory attitudes and behaviours.

Regulatory culture can be visible and/or recognisable in the areas including *regulatory delivery*, *regulatory practice*, *regulator performance and evaluation*, and *regulatory posture*.

(see also: Regulatory Posture; Type of Regulatory Agency)

Regulatory Cycle

There is no single or universally accepted or agreed *regulatory cycle*.

A *regulatory cycle* generally commences with problem identification, a decision by *government* to *regulate*, then the subsequent design, development, and delivery of *regulation*, and concludes with evaluation as part of *continuous improvement*.

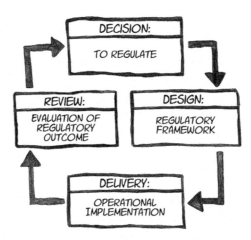

Two examples of *regulatory cycles*, with their corresponding chronological elements are listed below.

At a more command-and-control level
- legislative development
- strategic planning
- permitting
- monitoring
- inspection
- enforcement
- reporting[123]

At a more systematic level
- problem identified
- decision to regulate
- legislative development
- interpreted
- administered
- enforced
- assessment[124]

(see also: **Extended Regulatory Spectrum**; Regulatory Regime Design; Regulator Performance and Evaluation)

Regulatory Delivery

Regulatory delivery refers to the activities a *regulator* directs towards the delivery of its *regulatory functions*, and associated *obligations* and duties, under a *statute*, as opposed to activities associated with development, implementation, and review of *regulatory policy*.[125]

Regulatory delivery is reflected by those more *operational regulatory functions* that are contained in the four central phases of the *Extended Regulatory Spectrum*.[126]

(see also: **Extended Regulatory Spectrum**; Regulatory Functions; Regulatory Implementation; Regulatory Practice)

Regulatory Domain

Regulatory domain is a reference to the three main domains that *regulators* tend to operate within and across.

The three main domains are economic, environmental, and social. With:

- economic *regulators* – being those that focus on regulating financial markets and systems;
- environmental *regulators* – being those that focus on regulating environmental and natural resource management issues; and
- social *regulators* – being those that focus on regulating matters that impact upon individuals and groups within society.

The reality, however, is that *regulatory domains* are rarely if ever truly one dimensional. Instead, much like a formal qualification or area of study, *regulators* will have a major and a minor. For example:

- economic *regulators* – while primarily focussing on regulating financial markets and systems, will intersect with and impact upon matters associated with social *regulation*;
- environmental *regulators* – while primarily focussing on regulating environmental and natural resource management issues, will intersect with economic *regulation*; and
- social *regulators* – while primarily focussing on regulating matters that impact upon individuals and groups within society, will intersect with economic *regulation*.

Equally, from time to time, a *regulator* will regulate and/or operate at the intersections of all three *regulatory domains*.

(see also: Authorising Environment)

Regulatory Excellence (RegEx)

Regulatory excellence (or *RegEx*) is a concept that is based around the acronym TAO which stands for:

- Traits;
- Actions; and
- Outcomes.

When these three elements align, *regulatory excellence* is more likely to be achieved.

Outlined below is what each element of TAO might look like from the perspective of *regulators* and *regulated entities*. For example:

- Traits
  - that a *regulator* generally possesses, promotes, and projects – e.g., beliefs, values, and resources, and
  - of a *regulator*, as perceived by *regulated entities* – e.g., honest and trustworthy, credible and competent, and adequately funded;
- Actions
  - that a *regulator* performs – e.g., developing and issuing *rules*, performing *audits* and *inspections*, and conducting *litigation* and *enforcement*, and
  - of a *regulator*, as perceived by *regulated entities*– e.g., evidence-based and reasonable, firm but fair, vigilant and thorough;
- Outcomes
  - that a *regulator* achieves or advances – e.g., improved financial markets, environmental quality, and social protections, and
  - of a *regulator* as perceived by *regulated entities* and the *wider community* – e.g., in terms of publicly valued and improved economic, environmental or social outcomes.[127, 128]

It is important that *regulators* understand and maintain alignment across the three elements of TAO. The three elements are inexorably linked to the success and failure of a *regulator*, for example:

1. 'Traits without aligned actions are hypocrisies (the agency is not what it says it is) ...
2. Traits without aligned outcomes are platitudes (the agency is what is says it is, but that does not do society any good)

3. Actions without aligned traits are signs of capture (the agency "goes along to get along") …
4. Actions without aligned outcomes are drudgery (the agency is very busy, but probably just moving sand from one proverbial pile to another) …
5. Outcomes without aligned traits are capricious, easily undone or reversed (the agency is effecting change for change's sake) …
6. Outcomes without aligned actions are signs of inertia and easily become raw material for a self-satisfied agency …' [129]

(see also: Regulatory Capability; Regulatory Capacity; Regulatory Competence; Regulatory Posture)

Regulatory Executive

A *regulatory executive* is responsible for effective *regulatory delivery* and the achievement of *regulatory outcomes* – most simply, they 'lead the do'.

The work of a *regulatory executive* is reflected by those more *operational regulatory functions* that are contained in the four central phases of the *Extended Regulatory Spectrum*, and from time to time they will be asked to input or comment on the bookend phases of the *Extended Regulatory Spectrum*.

The precise nature of the role of a *regulatory executive* will vary, depending on the size, structure, and culture of the *regulatory agency*. However, a *regulatory executive* will usually:

- not be an *authorised officer,* and if they are will rarely step into that space and will vary rarely carry a caseload themselves, however they may be a statutory decision-maker;
- lead and support the activities and duties of a *regulatory manager*; and
- report to the head of the agency or a *regulatory board*.

It is important for *regulators* to fully understand the extent of overlap and nature of any interrelationships between *regulatory practitioners, managers, executives,* and *boards*. As the nature of these roles can vary greatly, depending on many factors, which have flow on effects to *tactical, operational,* and *strategic* activities, which in turn impact upon effective *regulatory delivery* and achieving *regulatory outcomes*.

(see also: Regulatory Board; Regulatory Manager; Regulatory Practitioner)

Regulatory Failure

Regulatory failure is a relative term, and one which will vary based upon many factors, central to which include:
- which viewpoint of the *Four Key Regulatory Perspectives* (i.e., *regulator, regulated, stakeholders,* or *wider community*) is considered;
- the *regulatory domain* (i.e., economic, environmental, or social) in which the *regulation* is primarily directed or focused on; and
- what the nature of the *regulatory objectives* and *regulatory outcomes* sought are or were.

Examples of *regulatory failure* from a *regulator's* perspective at a:
- *tactical* level – might relate to the ineffective use or misapplication of a *regulatory power* in a single case or matter,
  - resulting in an inability to obtain sufficient information or evidence to progress a *regulatory response* or intervention;
- *operational* level – might include the *regulator* not being able to increase *voluntary compliance* levels or influence *regulated entities* in a defined area,
  - such as a *regulator* being unable to sufficiently achieve its *regulatory objectives* within a regulated industry, sector, sub-sector, or in relation to a *regulated commodity*; and
- *strategic* level – might include the total or near total failure of a *regulatory regime/scheme* to deliver its intended *regulatory outcomes*, or where *regulation* fails to evolve and keep up with the operating and/ or *authorising environment* it is meant to regulate,
  - such a systemic failure is usually associated with significant economic, environmental, and social impacts for *regulated entities, stakeholders,* and the *wider community*.

Regulatory failure is often attributed to *regulation* which is poorly designed, developed, or delivered.

However, there are numerous factors that can contribute to *regulatory failure*. These factors include, but are not limited to:

- bad design of the *regulation/s*;
- inadequate consultation across those affected by *regulation/s*;
- poor or ineffective regulatory implementation;
- conflict and confusion;
- failure to clearly identify appropriate targets for *regulation*;
- poor tool choice;
- poor or ambiguous *rules* or *laws*;
- ambiguity in forms of *regulation*;
- procedural injustice; and
- *regulatory capture.*[130]

(see also: Authorising Environment; **Four Key Regulatory Perspectives**; Regulatory Outcomes; Statutory Authority)

Regulatory Frameworks

The purpose of a *regulatory framework* is to explain and clarify how a *regulator* will generally approach and perform its regulatory role.

A *regulatory framework* is usually comprised of several documents that a *regulator* has produced.

These documents combine to form an overarching framework that detail:

- What – *regulation* the *regulator* is responsible for administering;
- Who – the *regulation* is directed towards and impacts upon;
- How – the *regulator* will interact with those *regulated* (*persons* or *regulated entities*) or impacted (*stakeholders* and *wider community*);
- Where – the *regulator's* overarching principles and approaches are anchored;
- When – the *regulations* and the *regulators* themselves will be evaluated; and
- Why – the *regulation* and *regulatory intervention* is deemed necessary.

(see also: Regulatory Outcomes; Regulatory Policy (document); Regulatory Policy Framework)

Regulatory Functions

What constitutes *regulatory functions* can vary between *jurisdictions*, however at a high-level most will include and involve the type of functions listed below:

- making *rules* and/or *standards*;
- informing and educating;
- approving and banning activities;
- promoting and *monitoring compliance*;
- receiving and handling complaints; and
- enforcing *compliance* where *breaches* have occurred or are suspected.[131]

Regulatory functions can often be confused, conflated, and used interchangeably with the descriptors or functions that are used to describe *regulatory activity*; *regulatory delivery*; and *regulatory practice*.

(see also: Operational; Regulatory Activity; Regulatory Delivery; Regulatory Practice)

Regulatory Impact Analysis (RIA[a])

Regulatory impact analysis (RIA[a]) is a systematic approach to critically assessing the likely (positive and negative) impacts of regulatory proposals, and the relative net benefit of the policy options under consideration.

Regulatory proposals here are considered broadly and include both developing new *regulations* and modifying existing *regulations*. They also extend to non-regulatory alternatives, and/or light-touch *regulatory interventions*.

Importantly, the *RIA*[a] process incorporates a range of methods that when combined bring an evidence-based approach to policy making.

(see also: Regulation Impact Statement; Regulatory Impact Assessment; Stock, Flow and Effectiveness (of regulation))

Regulatory Impact Assessment (RIA[b])

Regulatory impact assessment (RIA[b]) is considered by the OECD as a core regulatory management tool.

A *RIA*[b] provides information to *regulated entities, regulators, stakeholders,* and the *wider community* on the cost and benefits of the potential impacts associated with the regulatory solution/s.

A *RIA*[b] considers costs and benefits across the triple bottom line which include economic, environmental, and social impacts.[132]

(see also: Regulation Impact Statement; Regulatory Impact Analysis)

Regulatory Implementation

Once a *regulation* or *regulatory regime/scheme* has been designed, developed and is in place, it needs to be implemented or operationalised.

The four central phases of the *Extended Regulatory Spectrum* (*advice and guidance, licensing and approvals, monitoring compliance*, and *enforcement*) would be considered *regulatory implementation* activities. *Regulatory implementation* activities have a strong link with *regulatory practice*.

(see also: **Extended Regulatory Spectrum**; Regulatory Delivery)

Regulatory Intelligence

Intelligence is a process which involves the collection, collation, analysis, and dissemination of *information* to assist with *decision-making*.

Regulators primarily use *intelligence* to support decision-makers as they determine *regulatory intervention* priorities whether *strategic, operational,* or *tactical* in nature.

Regulatory intelligence has been described as an 'umbrella term' for 'intelligence that supports and services regulatory decisions responding to at-risk behaviours within the regulator's sphere of interest'.[133, 134]

Some *regulators* describe their *regulatory approach* as being *intelligence-based* or *intelligence-led*.

(see also: Intelligence; Intelligence-Based/Intelligence-Led; Intelligence Cycle; Regulatory Approach/es)

Regulatory Intervention/s (see Regulatory Response)

Regulatory Landscape

Regulatory landscape refers to the landscape, or operating environment, that a *regulator* operates within and across.

The factors that contribute to *regulatory landscape* are diverse and can be classified in different ways. For example, a government study of selected *regulators* in England, considered *regulatory landscape* in terms of:

- the differing size of the regulators by expenditure;
- who is regulated;
- who is protected; and
- the standards used for regulation.[135]

Regulatory landscape can also be shaped by issues including the:

- nature and type of *legislation* administered;
- *risks*, harms, and impacts the *regulations* seek to address;
- relationships with *co-* and *peer-* *regulators*; *regulated entities, stakeholders,* and *the wider community*;
- commodities, sectors, industries, and issues regulated; and
- overall state and stability of the *authorising environment*.

(see also: Authorising Environment; Regulatory Mandate; Regulatory Posture)

Regulatory Language

Regulatory language is a reference to the professional language used by staff working within and across the *regulatory profession*.

In simple terms *regulatory language* is a common and shared language which enables *regulators* to communicate with each other, around the core or foundational issues of *regulation* and *regulatory delivery*. It also allows *regulators* to communicate with each other, irrespective of the *regulatory domain* in which they operate and/or the specific industries, sectors, or commodities they regulate.

However, at present, *regulators* operate **without** a fully common and shared language. Their current language:

- produces limited and sub-optimal outcomes across *jurisdictions*, industries, sectors, and commodities; and
- can lead to or result in regulatory confusion, duplication, and failure.

Establishing a distinguishable *regulatory language* forms a critical pathway to establishing an identifiable *regulatory profession,* which in turn is required to advance the concept of *regulatory professionalism.*

It is important for *regulators* to ensure that their regulatory recruiting, onboarding, training, and continuing professional development of staff (wherever possible) establishes and/or reinforces a common *regulatory language.*

An example is the Core Knowledge (Level 3) qualification developed by New Zealand's Government Regulatory (G-Reg) Initiative, as it provides learners with a common language drawn from regulatory theory, legal knowledge, and regulatory compliance activities.[136]

(see also: Regulatory Failure; *Regulatory Language*)

Regulatory Literacy

Literacy, most simply, relates to being able to read and write.

One definition of literacy is that it is:

- 'having the ability, confidence and willingness to engage with language to acquire, construct and communicate meaning in all aspects of daily living'.[137]

Another defines literacy as:

- 'the ability to identify, understand, interpret, create, communicate and compute, using printed and written materials associated with varying contexts. Literacy involves a continuum of learning in enabling individuals to achieve his or her goals, develop his or her knowledge and potential and participate fully in community and wider society'.[138]

Drawing on the definition immediately above, *regulatory literacy* seeks to assist those operating within and across the regulatory field to:

- increase their ability to more fully understand, interpret, and communicate with one another – across a more common and shared *regulatory language;* and
- develop their individual and collective knowledge and potential to participate more efficiently and effectively – in terms of *regulatory*

practice, regulatory delivery, and (advancing or achieving) *regulatory outcomes.*

New Zealand's Government Regulatory (G-Reg) Initiative, considers increasing *regulatory literacy* as providing practitioners with insights into a variety of regulatory theories and then enabling them to develop and implement practical *regulatory interventions.*[139]

Regulatory literacy is important for all staff including those staff who develop *regulations* or *regulatory policies*, and who may not identify as *regulators*. High levels of *regulatory literacy* increase alignment between policy design and the ability to successfully implement and operationalise *regulation*, which assists in achieving successful *regulatory outcomes.*

(see also: Regulatory Acumen; **Regulatory Language**)

Regulatory Manager

Distinct from a *regulatory executive*, a *regulatory manager* is actively engaged in management and oversight of *regulatory delivery* – most simply, they 'manage the do'.

The work of a *regulatory manager* is reflected by the more *operational regulatory functions* contained in the four central phases of the *Extended Regulatory Spectrum*, and very rarely are they asked to input or comment on the bookend phases of the *Extended Regulatory Spectrum*.

The precise nature of the role of a *regulatory manager* will vary depending on the size, structure, and culture of the *regulatory agency*. However, a *regulatory manager* will usually:

- be an *authorised officer* (of some description) but carry a caseload less than that of a *regulatory practitioner;*
- manage directly and/or oversee the activities and duties of a *regulatory practitioner;* and
- report to a *regulatory executive.*

It is important for *regulators* to fully understand the extent of overlap and nature of any interrelationships between *regulatory practitioners, managers, executives,* and *boards.* The nature of these roles can vary greatly, depending on many factors, which have flow on effects to *tactical, operational,* and *strategic* activities, which in turn impact upon effective *regulatory delivery* and achieving *regulatory outcomes.*

(see also: Regulatory Board; Regulatory Executive; Regulatory Practitioner)

Regulatory Mandate

Regulatory mandate primarily relates to the:
- *regulator's* purpose for existing or being; and
- *regulatory outcomes* or *regulatory objectives* that a *regulator* seeks to advance or achieve.

It is important that *regulators*:
- receive a clear *regulatory mandate* from government;
- operate within their *regulatory mandate*; and
- clearly define, maintain, and communicate their *regulatory mandate* to *regulated entities*; *co-* and *peer- regulators*; *stakeholders* and the *wider community.*

It is important for *regulators* to ensure they have the minimum components of a *regulatory mandate* which include:
- clear *legislation*;
- implementable *regulation*;
- a *statement of expectations* from government; and
- appropriate regulatory powers and remedies.

(see also: Authorising Environment; Regulatory Objectives; Regulatory Outcomes; Regulatory Posture)

Regulatory Maturity

Regulatory maturity is a term used to describe how a *regulatory agency* evolves, matures, and sometimes regresses over time.

Given the diversity of *regulatory agencies* and the nature of their work, the ability to accurately assess *regulatory maturity* can be difficult.

However, it is possible, through use of different *frameworks*, for an agency to map and assess the stages of its *regulatory maturity*. While the levels or stages referred to in the different *frameworks* vary, they tend to range from nil/absent through to well-established/optimal.

The mapping and assessment process, however conducted, enables the identification of areas within the agency requiring improvement and/or additional capability and capacity. Key areas for consideration include: systems; processes; and people.

It is important for *regulators* to fully understand that:
- the aim of assessing *regulatory maturity* is not to produce a league table for comparison against other *regulators*. Instead, it is a moment in time assessment which provides *regulators* with the opportunity to stop and reflect, and then develop a plan to increase its capability and capacity; and
- *regulatory maturity* is not a linear process, there will be situations and factors that both positively and negatively impact upon a *regulator* establishing, maintaining, and sustaining its *regulatory maturity*.

(see also: Regulatory Posture)

Regulatory Method/s

Regulatory method/s intersect with *regulatory tool/s* and sometimes the terms are used interchangeably.

The concept of what constitutes a *regulatory method* and *regulatory tool* is a broad one, and often come together under the broad umbrella of *regulatory intervention*.

One way to delineate or distinguish between *regulatory methods* and *regulatory tools*, is to consider that methods tend to be broader in nature while tools tend to be narrower, in terms of their application.

For additional context, consider also *regulatory approaches*. [140]

(see also: Regulatory Approaches; Regulatory Tools)

Regulatory Networks (see Networks)

Regulatory Objectives (see Regulatory Outcome/s)

Regulatory Officer/s

Regulatory officers are usually authorised under one or more pieces of *legislation*, with reference to a corresponding 'Authorised Officers Powers and Provisions' section clearly identifiable within the *legislation* or *regulations*.

The powers and provisions, typically provide *regulatory officers* and those assisting them ('officer/*person assisting*') the ability to enter *premises*, inspect *premises*, and search *premises* (buildings, persons, vehicles, vessels etc.).

(see also: Authorised Officer; Inspector; Investigator; Warden)

Regulatory Outcome/s

Simply put, *regulatory outcomes* are those outcomes that the *regulator* or *regulatory agency* has been charged with, in achieving for the community.

It is important for *regulators* to ensure that their *regulatory outcomes* are:
- clearly defined and achievable;
- within the *regulator's* legislative mandate;
- able to be articulated and justified to *regulated entities, co-* and *peer-regulators; stakeholders,* and the *wider community*; and
- aligned with the broader strategic context and the options that are available to implement regulatory initiatives.[141]

(see also: Annual Operational Plan; Operational; Regulatory Activity/ies; Regulatory Mandate; Regulatory Objectives, Regulatory Strategy; Strategic; Tactical)

Regulatory Pendulum

For *regulators* the *regulatory pendulum* is reference to the feeling that they experience when oscillating between the extremes. For example, when they are asked to:
- reduce *regulation/regulatory activity* (de-regulating); or
- increase *regulation/regulatory activity* (without over-regulating).

The parameters, scope, or mandate that shape what a *regulator* is 'allowed' to do, or is 'supported' to do, is set, and influenced by its *authorising environment*.

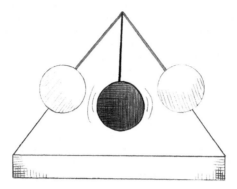

Equally, there are often significant swings (or adjustments) to the *regulatory pendulum* caused by factors including:

- change of government;
- change of Minister;
- a *regulatory failure*;
- the *regulator* being subject to significant public criticism; or
- a change in public expectations and the 'social licence' for the activities regulated, or in fact the broader *regulatory regime/scheme*.

(see also: Authorising Environment; Regulatory Mandate; Regulatory Posture)

Regulatory Policy (definition)

The OECD describes *regulatory policy* as being 'about achieving government's objectives through the use of *regulations, laws,* and other instruments to deliver better economic and social outcomes and thus enhance the life of citizens and business'.[142]

To avoid doubt, and to ensure that *regulation* and *regulatory frameworks* are in the best interests of the public,[143] the OECD suggest that governments should have an explicit policy. A policy that ensures that the government:

- adopts a continuous policy cycle for regulatory *decision-making*;
- only uses *regulation* when it is appropriate to achieve policy objectives;
- maintains a regulatory management system to assess pre and post regulatory impacts;

- clearly articulates the policy aims and objectives, and strategies used to achieve them;
- actively monitors the *stock, flow, and effectiveness (of regulation)*; and
- maintains ongoing support for the goals and benefits of regulatory quality.[144]

(see also: Regulatory Policy Frameworks)

Regulatory Policy (document)

A *regulatory policy* can be a public (outward facing) document that a *regulator* produces to convey to *co-* and *peer- regulators, regulated entities, stakeholders,* and the *wider community,* what policy objectives it seeks to achieve, and the *regulatory methods* and *approaches* it will use to advance them.

A *regulatory policy* can be a standalone document, or elements of it may be incorporated across several documents including, but not limited to a:
- *compliance policy;*
- *compliance and enforcement policy;*
- *enforcement policy;*
- *regulatory strategy;* and
- *regulatory statement of intent.*

(see also: Compliance Policy; Compliance and Enforcement Policy; Enforcement Policy; Regulatory Policy (definition); Regulatory Strategy)

Regulatory Policy Cycle (see Regulatory Cycle)

Regulatory Policy Framework

A government's (or *regulator's*) *regulatory policy framework* is aimed at assisting the country's (or jurisdiction's) economy to be as efficient, effective, flexible, and responsive as possible. *Regulatory policy frameworks* often include *de-regulation* or *red tape* reduction initiatives and guidance on how *regulatory agencies* should behave.

For example, in Australia, key *regulatory policy frameworks* include:

- *Regulatory impact analysis (RIA[a])* – requires that policy makers proposing to introduce or abolish *regulation* first develop a *regulation impact statement (RIS)*.
- The Australian Government Guide to Regulatory Impact Analysis [145] – provides guidance to policy makers around the process and requirements for developing a *RIS*.
- The Commonwealth Regulatory Burden Measure (RBM)[146] – assists policy makers in calculating the compliance costs of regulatory proposals, and where and who those costs impact upon.
- The *Regulator Performance Guide (RPG)*[147] – provides guidance to both policy makers and *operational* regulatory staff on how to minimise their impact on *regulated entities* while undertaking their mandated *regulatory functions*.

(see also: Regulatory Policy)

Regulatory Posture

Regulatory posture is the approach or stance that a *regulator* adopts towards those it regulates.

Regulatory posture involves the *regulator* balancing primary tensions between being:

- proactive vs reactive;
- co-operative vs combative; or
- discretionary vs prescriptive.

Regulatory posture involves the *regulator* balancing secondary tensions relating to the:

- nature and type of *legislation* administered;
- *risks*, harms, and impacts the *regulations* seek to address;
- relationships with *co-* and *peer- regulators; regulated entities, stakeholders*, and *the wider community*; and
- overall state and stability of the *authorising environment*.

Regulatory posture can also involve the *regulator* balancing tertiary tensions relating to the:

- *regulatory regime or scheme* – including whether it is a new scheme, a settled scheme, or a scheme in transition; and
- *person* or *regulated entity* – including whether they are a new, recent, or a longstanding participant to the scheme; and/or
- nature of any alleged or proven *breach* – including whether this is the *regulated entity's* first *breach*, subsequent *breach*, or is a particularly egregious *breach*.

Regulators may state and project either a general and/or specific posture. For example, a:

- general *regulatory posture*, is one that could be described as:
  - 'firm but fair'
  - 'trust and verify'.
- specific *regulatory posture*, (in specific circumstances such as domestic violence, one-punch assaults, or *offences* against children) is one that could be described as:
  - 'zero tolerance'
  - 'worthy of the full weight of the *law*'.

(see also: Authorising Environment; Regulatory Statement of Intent; Regulatory Strategy)

Regulatory Powers

The term *regulatory powers* are sometimes used as a sweeping and all-inclusive term.

What amounts to *regulatory powers* varies, dependent upon a range of factors including:

- how they are interpreted or perceived from different perspectives or viewpoints, primarily those of *regulators, regulated entities, stakeholders,* and the *wider community*;
- the circumstances in which they are accessed, used, and applied; and
- their underpinning legislative basis.[148]

Regulatory powers have a broad and narrow meaning:

- broadly – it can be a reference to all the powers (regulatory and non-regulatory) that the State has access to, and can bring to bear on individuals or *regulated entities* through its *regulatory agencies*; or
- narrowly – it can be a reference to those powers and/or authorities that *regulators* have access to under *legislation,* which typically and most simply relate to the powers to *licence, monitor,* and *enforce.* Notably, in the narrow sense, the application of individual *regulatory powers* may be obligatory or discretionary.

It is important that *regulators* are clear about and can clearly articulate:
- what *regulatory powers* they have access to, may use, or are using as part of their *regulatory activities*: and
- that they have formed the requisite grounds (suspicions or beliefs) to access and use them.

(see also: Coercive Powers; PACTT; Principles of Good Regulation; Reasonable Belief; Reasonable Suspicion; Ultra Vires)

Regulatory Practice

Regulatory practice is distinguishable from *regulatory policy* and regulatory design. *Regulatory practice* focusses on the capability of *regulators* in terms of their ability to implement *regulation.*[149]

Regulatory practice relates to and involves the more *operational* activities that 'front-line' *regulatory officers* perform and carry out. Therefore, *regulatory practice* is strongly connected to and should be considered in conjunction with *regulatory delivery.*[150]

The key principles to support effective *regulatory practice,* by *regulators,* include:
- understanding their operating and *authorising environment;*
- deciding on an appropriate *regulatory strategy;*
- educating *regulated entities* about the *regulatory regime;*
- *monitoring compliance* with regulatory requirements and managing *non-compliance;* and
- assessing the effectiveness of the *regulatory regime* in achieving the government's policy goals and any unintended consequences arising.[151]

It is important that *regulators* use and embrace the term *regulatory practice*.[152] To do so recognises that administering *regulation* to a high standard is a skill (in its own right) and further, it is a skill that requires staff to be appropriately trained, resourced, and supported in.

(see also: Regulatory Delivery; Regulatory Implementation; Regulatory Profession; Regulatory Professionalism)

Regulatory Practitioner

A *regulatory practitioner* is actively engaged in *regulatory delivery* – most simply, they 'do the do'.

The work of a *regulatory practitioner* is reflected by the more *operational regulatory functions* that are contained in the four central phases of the *Extended Regulatory Spectrum*.

The precise nature of the role of a *regulatory practitioner* will vary depending on the size, structure, and culture of the *regulatory agency* that they work for. However, a *regulatory practitioner* will usually:

- be an *authorised officer* (of some description); and
- be managed directly or have their duties overseen by a *regulatory manager.*

It is important for *regulators* to fully understand the extent of overlap and nature of any interrelationships between *regulatory practitioners, managers, executives,* and *boards.* As the nature of these roles can vary greatly, depending on many factors, which have flow on effects to *tactical, operational,* and *strategic* activities, which in turn impact upon effective *regulatory delivery* and achieving *regulatory outcomes.*

(see also: Regulatory Board; Regulatory Executive, Regulatory Practitioner)

Regulatory Praxis

Praxis is variously described as:

- transferring theory into practice; or
- the exercise or practice of an art, science, or skill; or
- an accepted practice or custom, which is then translated into action.

Therefore, *regulatory praxis* is the process and conversion of skills, theory, and concepts into application – which translates into enhanced *regulatory practice* and *regulatory delivery*.

Regulatory Priorities

Regulatory priorities are the priorities that *regulators* either have set for them by their governing bodies or boards, set themselves, or set in consultation with *co-* and *peer- regulators*.

At a high-level, *regulatory priorities* can be:

- short term, medium term, or longer term in nature;
- *regulatory domain*, industry, sector, or commodity specific;
- for an entire *jurisdiction*, region, or sub-region;
- limited to one or more phases of the *Extended Regulatory Spectrum*; and
- directed towards static and ongoing and/or new and emerging risks.

Some *regulatory agencies* will publish their *regulatory priorities*:

- as a standalone document;[153]
- as part of a strategic plan,[154] or
- in response to changes brought about by extreme and unexpected circumstances, such as those associated with COVID-19.[155]

Regulatory priorities will often inform and be referred to in *tactical, operational*, and *strategic* documents. For example, *annual operational plans* and *regulatory strategies* – the latter typically covering a three-to-five-year period, and which are updated annually.

It is important for *regulators* to understand and/or acknowledge that in some instances their *regulatory priorities* may:
- be self-evident, and set by the *regulator* itself;
- in some cases, be set by the *executive* arm of government; or
- be modified by the *regulator* and *executive* arm of government, based upon changes to the *authorising environment*.

(see also: Annual Operational Plan; Authorising Environment; Operational; Regulatory Activities; Regulatory Outcomes; Regulatory Strategy; Strategic; Tactical)

Regulatory Process

The *regulatory process* is a broad and inclusive term covering the process of regulating by *government*. It is also referred to as the *regulatory policy cycle* and occasionally the 'cycle of regulatory activities', both of which involve the broad steps of:
- legislating;
- administering *regulation*; and
- reviewing *regulation/s*.

(see Regulatory Cycle)

Regulatory Profession

Before considering the *regulatory profession* directly, it is necessary that we consider and establish what a profession is.

There are four aspects that are generally recognised as constituting a profession:
- firstly, the professional usually holds a recognised qualification – a qualification which is acquired once the requisite knowledge, skills and experience in a defined field or area have been established,
  - for example, a certified practising accountant;
- secondly, the professional activities of the individual are overseen by an industry, peak, or professional body – these bodies pay particular attention to the code of ethics, standards of service, and general level of accountably to users/clients, the general-public, and the profession broadly,
  - for example, Certified Practising Accountant (CPA) Australia;

- thirdly, the professional undertakes ongoing or continuing professional development (CPD) – which is a commitment to maintaining and improving their professional skills and knowledge,
  - for example, many professions have a CPD model which is point based, meaning practitioners/professionals must earn points by attending webinars, conferences or similar and/or completing assessments, assignments or similar; and
- fourthly, the profession needs to be recognised, accepted, and acknowledged by the public as a profession,
  - for example, the public recognise accountants, engineers, lawyers, and medical doctors as all belonging to their respective professions.

The importance of defining and establishing a *regulatory profession* has gained momentum over recent years.[156] *Regulators* need to satisfy the four pre-conditions above and establish that they are engaged in *regulatory practice* and/or *regulatory delivery*, to establish that they are part of a *regulatory profession*.[157]

(see also: Continuing Professional Development; Regulatory Professionalism; Training)

Regulatory Professionalism

Irrespective of whether it is considered that a recognised *regulatory profession* exists (see immediately above), the issue of *regulatory professionalism* is a standalone issue.[158]

Regulatory professionalism is an important and necessary consideration for *regulatory practitioners, managers,* and *executives.*

While there are numerous areas where *regulatory professionalism* comes into sharp focus, the following are worthy of special mention. For example, the need for staff to maintain:

- professional relationships – with *co-* and *peer- regulators, regulated entities, stakeholders,* and the *wider community* – to assist with avoiding or reducing the likelihood of *regulatory capture;*
- complete records – to make appropriate decisions which maintain and enhance the credibility of the *regulator;*

- core skills, knowledge, and experience – to perform their *regulatory roles* and *regulatory functions*;
- an in-depth or at least working knowledge – of relevant *regulatory domains*, industries, sectors, and commodities; and
- continually project professional competence – in words, actions, and deeds.

(see also: Regulatory Capture; Regulatory Profession)

Regulatory Reform

Regulatory reform is a process undertaken by governments to improve regulatory quality, especially so in terms of enhancing its overall effectiveness.

Regulatory reform can be narrow or broad. For example, *regulatory reform* that is:

- narrow – might relate to the revision of a single *regulation*; and
- broad – might relate to removing and/or rebuilding an entire *regulatory regime/scheme*.

De-regulation is a subset of *regulatory reform*.[159]

(see also: De-Regulation; Red Tape; Regulatory Regime Design; Stock, Flow, and Effectiveness (of regulation))

Regulatory Regime/Scheme

In this book *regulatory regime* and *regulatory scheme* are used interchangeably and will usually appear as *regulatory regime/scheme*.

Regulatory regime/scheme is a reference to any regime or scheme that is established, administered, supported, or overseen by government that seeks to regulate or control a specific activity.

(see also: Act/s; Legislation; Regulated Activity/ies; Regulation; Statute)

Regulatory Regime Design

Regulatory regime design is a *regulatory activity* which involves designing and developing a *regulatory regime* or *scheme*. The *regulatory regimes* or *regulatory schemes* are deemed necessary to address problems which are not (or cannot) be controlled by usual market forces.

Regulatory regime design is often a lengthy process. It involves *regulators* developing *regulation* in accordance with the principles of better regulatory design. The principles that *regulators* should follow in this area include:

- conducting or commissioning a *regulatory impact assessment;*
- developing or commissioning *a regulation impact statement;*
- consulting and collaborating with: (other) *regulators;* (existing and potential) *regulated entities;* (existing and potential) *stakeholders;* and the *wider community;*
- drafting and modifying the *regulatory regime* or *regulatory scheme* (as a *bill, act,* or *legislative instrument*) based upon the activities listed above; and
- successfully having the relevant body (parliament or *legislature*) in their *jurisdiction* pass it and enact it as *law.*

In a linear sense, it is the first of six phases contained in the *Extended Regulatory Spectrum.*

Regulatory regime design is most often undertaken when a *regulatory regime* or *scheme* is established and first comes into being. However, it can also be revisited and occur when a *regulatory regime* or *scheme* is reviewed. These reviews can be either pre-planned and scheduled (often at five- or ten-year intervals) or because of a *regulatory failure* or some other external driver.

(see also: **Extended Regulatory Spectrum**)

Regulatory Response

A *regulatory response* is a broad overarching term that can be used interchangeably or in conjunction with terms such as *regulatory intervention/s* or *regulatory sanction/s.* For example, *warning letters,* infringement notices, licence revocations and court proceedings might all constitute *regulatory responses.*

A *regulatory response* is a response used or initiated by a *regulator,* which is intended to modify the behaviours of a *person* or *regulated entity* to bring them back into *compliance.*

The nature of the *regulatory response* will be informed by a range of factors including, but not limited to the:

- relative importance of the *regulatory outcome* being sought;
- nature, level, and type of *regulatory risk* being addressed;
- *compliance posture* of the alleged wrongdoer (whether a *person* or commercial *regulated entity*);
- likely impact and response to the *regulatory intervention;* and
- type of (general and specific) *deterrence* that might be achieved.

(see also: Administrative Remedy/Response/Sanction; Civil Remedy/Response/Sanction; Criminal Remedy/Response/Sanction; Sanction)

Regulatory Risk

Given the nature of *risk, regulatory risk* can apply to both the *regulator* and the *regulated.* For example:

- a *regulator* – tends to consider a *regulatory risk* as something that interferes with or impacts upon their ability to deliver upon a *regulatory policy* objective or achieve a *regulatory outcome;* and

- those *regulated* – tend to consider a *regulatory risk* as something that decreases their ability to comply with regulatory *obligations* or requirements.

(see also: Risk; Risk Matrix; Risk Ratings)

Regulatory Sandbox/es

A *regulatory sandbox* is a *framework* which participants in a *regulatory regime/scheme* can test new or innovative concepts. With the testing occurring:
- on a time-limited basis, and not necessarily aligned with their existing *authorisation*;
- at a smaller scale, than their normal operations; and
- with fewer and/or relaxed regulatory duties and *obligations*, such as having a *permit* instead of requiring a full *licence* or *registration*, and having reduced and less frequent reporting requirements.

Regulators will develop and use *regulatory sandboxes* when they want to:
- encourage or support innovation in and amongst their *regulated entities*;
- remove regulatory barriers, especially those associated with trials; and
- make use of existing and new *regulatory tools*, in a narrower and more controlled environment.

(see also: Compliance History; Earned Autonomy/Recognition)

Regulatory Scheme (see Regulatory Regime/Scheme)

Regulatory Stance (see Regulatory Posture)

Regulatory Statement of Expectations

A statement prepared by the *executive* arm of government outlining certain expectations of *regulatory agencies* regarding their regulator performance.

In recent years these expectations have become increasingly codified. While described by different names across *jurisdictions*, these expectations can also be referred to as a:

- *letter of expectations;*
- *ministerial statement of expectations;* or
- *statement of expectations.*

The aim and objective of these statements is to establish clear expectations around *regulator performance*, regulator improvement, and regulatory best practice, to achieve and deliver *regulatory outcomes* – and where possible reduce costs and burdens for *regulated entities, stakeholders,* and *the wider community.*

As part of good practice, a *regulatory statement of expectations* should be updated periodically. The review and update process should form part of the scheduled performance cycle and ideally should occur at least every two years.

There can be other triggers for reviewing and updating a *regulatory statement of expectations,* including:

- appointment of a new minister or head of a *regulatory agency;*
- in response to or as required following a *regulatory failure;*
- a significant change in the *authorising environment;* or
- a change in government policy (for any number of reasons that impact upon one or more of the points above).

In line with *best practice,* the *regulatory statement of expectations* should be publicly available as part of increased transparency and accountability.

Note: in response to receiving a *regulatory statement of expectations* from a minister, a *regulator* will develop a *regulatory statement of intent.*

(see also: Regulatory Statement of Intent)

Regulatory Statement of Intent

As mentioned above, a *regulator's* response to a *regulatory statement of expectations* will be to develop a *regulatory statement of intent.*

The *regulatory statement of intent* is typically broad in nature and will relate to a *regulatory regime.* Generally:

- detailing how the *regulator* will deliver upon the expectations of government; and

- including an outline of the approaches (usually principles based) that the *regulator* will use or deploy.

In line with *best practice*, the *regulatory statement of intent* should be publicly available as part of increased transparency and accountability.

A *regulatory statement of intent* is more specific than a *statement of regulatory intent* and clarifies a *regulator's* approach to certain legislative matters in certain circumstances.

(see also: Annual Operational Plans; Regulatory Posture; Regulatory Statement of Expectations; Regulatory Strategy; Statement of Regulatory Intent)

Regulatory Stewardship

Regulatory stewardship was designed and developed in New Zealand.[160]

Fundamentally, *regulatory stewardship* treats *regulation*, and each *regulatory regime* or *regulatory scheme*, as an asset.

The benefits of *regulatory stewardship* include that:
- it takes a system-wide approach, to the design, implementation, and maintenance of *regulation*;
- long-term sustainability is at its core;
- it involves regular and ongoing review and *continuous improvement*; and
- it ensures the entire regulatory system remains fit for purpose.

Regulatory agencies in New Zealand have a statutory *obligation* to engage with and advance *regulatory stewardship*.

(see also: Stewardship)

Regulatory Strategy/ies

Regulatory strategies typically cover a three-to-five-year period and tend to be updated annually or following a major incident or event.

The contents and intent of a *regulatory strategy* will often cascade into and inform other regulatory documents such as *annual operational plans*. *Regulatory strategies* can be focussed on:
- the entire *regulated sector*, or sub-sectors;
- all *regulated entities*, or sub-elements;
- all *regulatory functions*, or selected functions; and

- *regulatory* and *enforcement* activities, and/or their intersection with policy and programmatic activities.

(see also: Annual Operational Plan; Regulatory Outcomes; Regulatory Policy; Regulatory Priorities; *Three Levels of Operational Activity*)

Regulatory Tool/s

Regulatory tools intersect with *regulatory methods* and sometimes the terms are used interchangeably.

The concept of what constitutes a *regulatory tool* and *regulatory method* is a broad one, and often come together under the broad umbrella of *regulatory intervention*.

One way to delineate or distinguish between *regulatory tools* and *regulatory methods*, is to consider that tools tend to be narrower, while methods tend to be broader in nature, in terms of their application.[161]

For additional context, consider also regulatory approaches.

(see also: Regulatory Approaches; Regulatory Methods)

Remedy

A *remedy*, in a *regulatory* and *enforcement* context is a broad term that seeks redress or relief for an infringement or *breach* of *law* or *regulations*.

(see also: Administrative Remedy/Response/Sanction; Civil Remedy/Response/Sanction; Criminal Remedy/Response/Sanction; Sanction)

Reparation Order/s

Reparation orders may be issued by a *court*, based upon:
- the *court's* own initiative;
- an application by the victim/s; or
- an application by the *prosecuting authority*.

Reparation orders require a party (typically the *offender* or a third party) to make some form of payment or restitution, either in part or full for damages.

Reparation orders, and the associated payments or compensation, are often made to victims of *crime*.

(see also: Remedy)

Repealing Regulations

From time to time, it is necessary to repeal *regulations* to ensure that the stock of *regulations* on hand are fit for purpose and continue to contribute to the delivery of *regulatory outcomes*.

Regulations may be repealed because they:

- are no longer necessary;
- are obsolete or have become outdated;
- have been superseded by updated *regulations*;
- are subject to *sunsetting* provisions and are automatically repealed at their *sunsetting* date; and
- may be subject to disallowance by the *legislature* after having been made by the *executive*.

Whatever the reason, the process of *repealing regulations* would fall under stock in the *stock, flow, and effectiveness (of regulation)* process.

(see also: De-regulation; Regulatory Impact Analysis; Stock, Flow and Effectiveness (of regulation))

Reporting

When used in a *regulatory* context, *reporting* tends to be used as a broad and inclusive term. It usually relates to a *person, regulated entity, regulator,* or *stakeholder* providing a verbal or written account of their *regulatory duties* and *obligations* or their involvement in a regulatory matter.

For example, *reporting* requirements for a:

- *person* – might require them to advise the *regulator* if they no longer satisfy/meet a condition of their *authorisation* (e.g., health, maintaining a driver's licence, or security clearance);
- *regulated entity* – might be required to periodically (e.g., three, four, six, twelve monthly) report their *regulatory activities* to a *regulator,* and/or self-report notifiable *breaches* and near-misses to the *regulator* within a specified time, particularly to demonstrate *compliance* with regulatory requirements. Noting that the burden of *reporting obligations* often features prominently in discussions on *red tape* and administrative costs;
- *regulator* – is required to periodically report to parliament or other oversight bodies (e.g., ombudsman's office) about their progress

on general and specific *regulatory activities* and matters and/or use of *coercive powers*; and

- *stakeholder* – especially those involved in *self-* or *co-regulation* might need to report on their *regulatory activities* and/or those of their membership (e.g., if they are an industry or *peak body*).

In terms of the *Extended Regulatory Spectrum*, most *reporting* would occur within or across *licensing and approvals* and *monitoring compliance*.

(see also: Earned Autonomy/Recognition; **Extended Regulatory Spectrum**; Licensing and Approvals; Monitoring Compliance)

Respondent

Respondent is a term which can be used to describe the *person* or *regulated entity* against whom legal proceedings have been commenced.

(see also: Accused; Claimant; Defendant; Plaintiff; Suspect).

Responsive Regulation

To be responsive is to be able to react quickly and positively.

Responsiveness is at the heart of *responsive regulation*, with responsiveness depending on the ability of a *regulator* to have:

- an ongoing relationship with *regulated entities*;
- an understanding of the different motivators and factors that impact on a *regulated entity's* ability to comply; and
- a clear and full appreciation of the *authorising environment* in which they are operating.

Responsive regulation is a particular style of *regulation/regulatory approach*, which suggests that the best *regulatory outcomes* will be achieved if *regulators* use a blend of persuasion and coercion, with the actual mix being adjusted to the circumstances, and/or motivations, particular to the *regulated entity*. [162, 163]

Responsive regulation is shown diagrammatically in adaptions of the *compliance pyramid/triangle*.

Responsive regulation was influenced by the *tit-for-tat* approach.

(see also: Compliance Pyramid/Triangle; Tit-for-Tat; Types of Regulation)

Restorative Justice

It is suggested that there are three pillars to *restorative justice*:
- harms and needs;
- *obligations* (to put right); and
- engagement (of *stakeholders*).[164]

Restorative justice therefore:
- focuses on the harm caused by *crime*, regulatory *breaches*, and broader wrongdoing;
- involves *frameworks* and processes to bring victims, *offenders*, and affected communities together to address harms caused and prevent future harms; and
- seeks to move beyond blame and punishment, and instead it reflects a move towards strengthening relationships through mutual respect and understanding, to enable healing.

For *regulators* the benefits of a *restorative justice* approach include:
- preventing or reducing re-offending rates;
- providing a voice to and empowering victims;
- benefiting criminal justice (and regulatory) agencies by providing them with *alternate dispute resolution* mechanisms; and
- increasing *stakeholder* and community involvement in dispute resolution processes.

(see also: Alternate Dispute Resolution)

Revocation/Revoke (of Authorisation)
(see Cancellation (of Authorisation))

RIAª (see Regulatory Impact Analysis)

RIAᵇ (see Regulatory Impact Assessment)

Right-touch Regulation

Right-touch regulation requires having sufficient understanding of a regulatory problem or issue before proceeding to implement a solution or response.

Right-touch regulation reflects adherence to the *Principles of Good Regulation* in both a theoretical and applied sense.

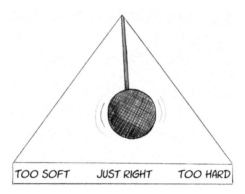

The eight elements listed below are considered to sit at the heart of *right-touch regulation*:

- identify the problem before the solution;
- quantify and qualify the risks;
- get as close to the problem as possible;
- focus on the outcome;
- use *regulation* only when necessary;
- keep it simple;
- check for unintended consequences; and
- review and respond to change.[165]

(see also: Light-touch Regulation; Principles of Good Regulation; Types of Regulation)

RIS (see Regulation Impact Statement)

Risk/s

Risk is variously defined and described as:
- 'the effect of uncertainty on objectives';[166]
- 'the chance of something happening that will have an impact on objectives';[167] and
- 'the effect of uncertainty on objectives. An effect is a deviation from the expected – positive and/or negative. Risk is often expressed in terms of a combination of the consequences of an event (including changes in circumstances or knowledge) and the associated likelihood of occurrence.'[168]

Regulators predominantly consider *risk* in terms of likelihood and consequence (or impact). They therefore develop and incorporate a *risk matrix* into their *decision-making* and regulatory documents.

(See also: Risk Analysis; Risk-based Prioritisation; Risk Control; Risk Criteria; Risk Management; Risk Matrix; Risk Rating)

Risk Analysis

Risk analysis involves identifying and assessing the likelihood and consequence of a *risk* or adverse event occurring.

Risk analysis is often presented in a *risk matrix*.

Risk analysis together with *risk management* and *risk communications* are said to combine under the broad term of *risk control*.

(see also: Risk Assessment; Risk Control; Risk Management; Risk Matrix)

Risk Appetite

Risk appetite is sometimes referred to as *risk tolerance* and relates to the amount or level of *risk* that an entity is prepared to:
- accept in the first instance, and not treat; or
- retain after the *risk/s* have been treated, this is referred to as residual *risk*.

Combined, the level of *risk* accepted and retained can be seen as an indicator of the entity's overall approach and attitude towards *risk*.

(see also: Risk Criteria; Risk Profile)

Risk Assessment

Risk assessment is a three-step process involving:

- *risk* identification;
- *risk analysis*; and
- *risk* evaluation.

(see also: Risk Analysis; Risk-based Prioritisation; Risk Control; Risk Criteria; Risk Management; Risk Ratings)

Risk-based Prioritisation (RBP)[169]

Risk-based prioritisation fundamentally relates to identifying, understanding, measuring, and treating the *risks* that have the potential to impact upon the:

- *regulatory activities* of a *regulator*; and
- *regulatory outcomes* a *regulator* seeks to achieve or advance.

The major aspects and elements of *risk-based prioritisation* that inform and influence *regulatory delivery* and *regulatory practice* include:

- identification of *risk*;
- assessing *risk*;
- managing *risk*;
- *risk* and *enforcement*.[170]

(see also: Regulatory Risk; Risk Assessment; Risk-based Regulation)

Risk-based Regulation (RBR)[171]

Risk-based regulation involves a *regulator* targeting or directing regulatory resources and activities towards the most serious *regulatory risks* facing them.

The elements of *risk-based regulation* include:

- defining outcomes and identifying *risks*;
- determining the *risk appetite*;
- *risk assessment*;
- prioritising *risks*;
- implementation and the allocation of resources; and
- reviewing outcomes.[172]

Risk-based regulation uses *risk management* methodology to:
- identify *risks*;
- target *risks*; and
- direct resources and effort to *risk*.

Risk-based regulation therefore:
- directs efforts towards the management of 'unacceptable *risks*'; and
- focuses on the actual and most serious *risks* with associated negative effects, rather than those *risks* (real or perceived) that might be more visible or contentious.

Risk-based regulation tends to have multiple meanings which can then be interpreted differently, especially in an applied sense when it comes to implementation.[173]

Most *regulators* will identify with the definition below which describes *risk-based regulation* as:

> 'Systematised decision-making frameworks and procedures to prioritise regulatory activities and deploy resources, principally relating to inspection and enforcement, based on an assessment of the risks that regulated firms [entities] pose to the regulator's objectives.'[174]

(see also: Risk-based Prioritisation)

Risk Communication/s

Having identified, analysed, and evaluated *regulatory risks* it is important that *regulators* then engage in *risk communication*.[175] *Risk communication* is the process of communicating *risks* internally and externally to:
- *co-* and *peer- regulators*;
- *regulated entities*;
- *stakeholders*; and
- the *wider community*.

Risk communication together with *risk analysis* and *risk management* are said to combine under the broad term of *risk control*.

It is important that *regulators*:
- communicate their *regulatory risks* – to the nature and extent that is possible and appropriate, appreciating that there may be limitations

(given *operational* and/or commercial-in-confidence issues) to what can be communicated; and

- having communicated their *regulatory risks* – that *regulators* then monitor, manage and report on the most significant *risks*, as doing so forms part of a *regulator's* accountability and transparency mechanisms and processes.

(see also: Risk Analysis; Risk-based Prioritisation; Risk-based Regulation; Risk Control; Risk Management)

Risk Control[176]

A broad term (or subject) that incorporates:

- *risk analysis*;
- *risk management*; and
- *risk communication.*

(see also: Regulatory Risk; Risk Assessment; Risk-based Regulation)

Risk Criteria

Risk criteria:

- typically include definitions that describe the outcomes of different combinations of impact and likelihood; and
- are shaped and are dependent on the nature of *risks* the *regulator* seeks to mitigate.

Combined, the criteria provide a term of reference by which a *risk* is evaluated. For example, a *regulator* of:

- pharmaceutical products – might frame criteria in terms of the 'probability of failure' – e.g., as a percentage 1%, 5%, 10%, 20%, 50%;
- road safety – might frame criteria in terms of the 'level of injury' – e.g., death, life threatening, serious, moderate, slight; and
- financial services – might frame criteria in terms of the 'level of financial loss or fraud' – e.g., $10k, $50k, $100k, $500k, $1M.

(see also: Risk Assessment; Risk Ratings)

Risk Management

Risk management is variously described as a process which involves at least a four or five step process. For example, representative examples of a:
- four-step process include – identify, assess, control, and review;
- five-step process include – identify, analyse, prioritise, treat, and monitor; and
- five-step process include – identification, assessment, mitigation, monitoring, and reporting.

Risk management together with *risk analysis* and *risk communications* are said to combine under the broad term of *risk control*.

(see also: Risk Assessment; Risk Control)

Risk Matrix

A *risk matrix* is a table (or matrix) that is used as part of the *risk assessment* process, which defines and categorises risk.

Typically, a *risk matrix* is colour coded (often using green, yellow, orange, and red) to demonstrate an increase in *risk*. One axis is labelled 'likelihood' and the other is labelled 'consequence'.

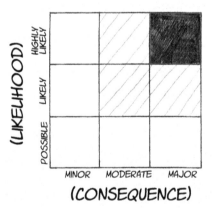

(see also: Risk Ratings)

Risk Profile

A *risk profile* is an analysis, which uses quantitative methods, of the types of *risks* or threats that:

- any entity (e.g., *person* or *regulated entity*) is currently facing or may face in the future; or
- are associated with an activity (e.g., whether unauthorised and *in-system*, or unauthorised, or illegal and *out-of-system*).

The benefit of completing a *risk profile* is that it provides an objective understanding of *risk*. *Regulators* typically develop and describe their *risk profiles* by allocating numbers or points to the variables which represent the different types of *risk* or threat, in terms of the specific *risk* or threat that they pose.

(see also: Risk Criteria; Risk Matrix)

Risk Ratings

For *regulators* the quantification of *regulatory risk* is a core function.[177]

There are two sets of *risk ratings*, one for each axis of the *risk matrix*.

One axis relates to 'likelihood' – with typical ratings including between three to five variables. For example:

- three levels – low, medium, high
- four levels – low, medium, high, extreme
- five levels – rare, low, medium, high, extreme

The other axis relates to 'consequence' – with typical ratings including between three to five variables. For example:

- three levels – low, medium, high
- four levels – low, medium, high, extreme
- five levels – rare, low, medium, high, extreme

The outcome, depending on the variables chosen, typically result in a:

- three by three (3×3) matrix,
- three by four (3×4) matrix,
- four by four (4×4) matrix,
- four by five (4×5) matrix, or
- five by five (5×5) matrix

(see also: Risk Assessment; Risk Criteria; Risk Matrix)

Risk Tolerance (see Risk Appetite)

ROD (see Record of Decision)

RPF (see Regulator Performance Framework)

RPG (see Regulator Performance Guide)

Rules

Rules document and reflect the set of explicit and accepted requirements that control a certain procedure or activity.

Regulators will often develop *rules* as part of the *framework* and processes that need to be met, to satisfy regulatory requirements and *obligations*.[178]

Rules may range from those that are relatively minor technical or procedural requirements set by the *regulator,* to those that are formal *legislative instruments* made under an *act.*

Rules are developed by various bodies, including:

- government;
- *regulated entities* themselves (as part of *self-regulation*); and
- private bodies or industry/sector peak bodies (as part of *co-regulation*).

(see also: Act/s; Code/s; Legislation; Regulation/s; Schedule; Standard)

Sanction

The term *sanction* has two very different, and in fact almost opposite meanings. The examples below highlight how the term *sanction* can be used:

- to approve something – i.e., the *regulator* sanctioned the use of the new equipment as part of the *licence* held by the *regulated entity*; or
- to punish – i.e., the *regulator* seeks to impose a *sanction* against the *regulated entity* for a *breach* of their *licence* for using non-approved equipment.

Regulators tend to use the second example more often, in that they see a *sanction* in the context of punishment, penalty, or as a means of *enforcement*. Equally, *regulators* can use the threat or possibility of a *sanction* as an incentive to achieve higher rates of *voluntary compliance*.

Sanctions can be administrative, civil, or criminal in nature. Examples highlighting the differences between these three types of *sanctions* appear earlier in this book under:

- *administrative remedy/response/sanctions;*
- *civil remedy/response/sanctions;* and
- *criminal remedy/response/sanctions.*

(see also: Regulatory Response)

Schedule/s

A *schedule* often appears as an appendix to an *act*.

Schedules tend to contain greater and finer levels of detail on a range of matters than those that appear in the main body of the *act*.

(see also: Act/s; Code/s; Legislation; Regulation/s; Rules)

Search Warrant (see Investigation Warrant)

Secondary Legislation

Secondary legislation is also referred to as *delegated legislation* or *subordinate legislation* and is made by the *executive* arm of government.

Secondary legislation is *legislation* enabled or authorised by *primary legislation* (generally an Act of Parliament). For example, the *Therapeutic Goods Regulations 1990* are made under the *Therapeutic Goods Act 1989*.

(see also: Legislative Instruments; Primary Legislation; Regulation (Big 'R'); Regulation (Little 'r'))

Self-disclosure

Self-disclosure involves revealing information about oneself to another.

An example of *self-disclosure*, in a regulatory context, is when a *person* or *regulated entity* proactively notifies the *regulator* that they have committed a *breach* or are *non-compliant*.

The reasons and rationale for a *regulated entity* to self-disclose, instead of waiting to be detected by the *regulator*, is that generally the *regulator* will be less likely to pursue a *sanction*, and if they do then they tend to be more lenient.

The reasons and rationale for why many *regulators* encourage *self-disclosure* is that they do not want to create a regulatory system where there is no benefit for a *regulated entity* to bring a *breach* to the *regulator's* attention. The benefit for *regulators* is that they can focus their finite resources on reducing the overall risks and harms to society.

(see also: Earned Autonomy/Recognition; Regulatory Posture)

Self-regulation

A particular style or type of *regulation*.

Self-regulation typically occurs when a *regulated entity*, industry, or sector (either alone or together with a *peak industry body*/professional body or *stakeholders*) is trusted enough to conduct their own *audits* and *inspections* and generally monitor and administer their own regulatory arrangements, including *enforcement*.

However, if *self-regulation* is not effective, the government may elect to implement a *regulatory intervention*.

(see also: Types of Regulation)

Sentencing

Is the process of a *judicial officer* (usually a magistrate or judge) determining what penalty or *sanction* to impose on a *person* or *regulated entity*, who has either pleaded guilty or been found guilty of an *offence* or *breach* of regulatory duties or *obligations*.

When considering *sentencing* matters, *judicial officers* operate within a framework of *sentencing* guidelines that typically require them to weigh up what can be comprehensive and wide-ranging factors. [179]

Given the statutory maximum penalties that apply to *offences*, primary *sentencing* considerations tend to revolve around:

- the nature, level, and type of offending, in terms of its relative degree of seriousness;
- any aggravating or mitigating factors associated with the offending or *offender*;
- the characteristics and prior history (good and bad) of the *offender*;
- the degree of remorse or contrition shown by the *offender*;
- the need for *deterrence* (either specific or general); and
- the level of *public interest* and/or concern for the offending under consideration.

Regulators need to be aware that for a first *offence* the penalty is typically some fraction of the maximum penalty.

It is important for *regulators* that their *compliance and enforcement policy* or *prosecutions policy* (or equivalent) is consistent with the prosecutorial or sentencing guidelines that their *offences* will be considered against.

(see also: Sanction)

Show Cause/Show Cause Letter

From a legal perspective, and in a *court* context, *show cause* involves the:
- applicant (usually the prosecution) – producing satisfactory grounds to justify their application for commencement of proceedings, procedure, or penalty; and/or
- *respondent* (usually the defence) – producing satisfactory grounds to justify why they should be exempted from the application for commencement of proceedings, procedure, or penalty.

From an *operational* and *regulatory practice* viewpoint, and prior to commencing formal *show cause* proceedings in court, a *regulator* may issue a *show cause letter*.

A *show cause letter* might be issued to a *person* or *regulated entity* explaining that with the information presently before them, the *regulator* intends to initiate some form of regulatory or *enforcement* action (possibly *litigation, prosecution,* or remediation focussed). The purpose of the letter is to provide an opportunity for the *person* or *regulated entity* to provide additional *information* that might persuade the *regulator* to not initiate (or continue) an action.

An example of a *show cause letter* might involve a *regulator* detailing several *licence breaches* to a *person* or *regulated entity* suggesting that the *regulator* is contemplating varying, suspending, or revoking the *licence* or *authorisation,* unless the *regulator* can be convinced that there is good reason not to do so.

(see also: Model Litigant; Natural Justice; Procedural Fairness)

Smart Regulation

Smart regulation reflects a wholistic and integrated approach to *regulation* which is based upon the theory that multiple *regulatory interventions* and/ or strategies used in combination, are more effective than standalone strategies.

Smart regulation seeks to use:

- *regulatory policy*, regulatory instruments, and *regulatory activities* in combination; and
- markets, civil society, and other institutions as surrogate *regulators*, and if this is not possible at least leverage off these groups.

The aim of *smart regulation* is to achieve public policy objectives and deliver *regulatory outcomes* in the most effective way, and with the highest possible levels of buy-in and societal support.[180]

(see also: Types of Regulation)

Soft law (see Quasi-Legislation/Quasi-Regulation)

Stakeholder/s

The term used to describe an entity (*person*, body, or organisation) who has an interest in *regulation* and its impacts. *Stakeholders* can include a wide range of individuals and groups, which often take the form of interest groups (i.e., 'friends of') or *peak industry bodies*.

Stakeholders are one of the four main groups that constitute the *Four Key Regulatory Perspectives*, the others are: the *regulated*; *regulators*; and *wider community*.

(see also: ***Four Key Regulatory Perspectives***)

Standard/s

Standards document and reflect the criteria or processes that need to be met to satisfy regulatory requirements and *obligations*.[181]

Standards are developed by various bodies, including:

- government;
- *regulated entities* themselves (as part of *self-regulation*); and
- private bodies or sector/*peak industry bodies* (as part of *co-regulation*).

(see also: Act/s, Code/s; Legislation; Regulation; Rules)

Standard of Proof (see Burden of Proof)

Standard Operating Procedure/s (SOP/s)

A *standard operating procedure* is a set of instructions that are prepared to quite a fine level of detail (often step-by-step) to guide the performance of tasks and functions in a consistent manner.

Both *regulated entities* and *regulators* use *SOPs*. For example:

- *regulated entities* will use *SOPs* to – help them achieve and remain in *compliance*, and if a *breach* occurs will then offer the *SOP* as an example of their efforts to comply, as part of mitigating any prosecutorial or remedial action considered by the *regulator;* and
- *regulators* will use *SOPs* to – bring greater efficiency, effectiveness, and efficacy to their *regulatory activities*, and as part of demonstrating their commitment to *consistency* of approach (which is one of the *Principles of Good Regulation*).

(see also: Consistency; Policies; Principles of Good Regulation)

Standardised Permits

Standardised permits are issued to a *person* or *regulated entity* where the conditions attached to the *permit* are generic and apply to all activities and premises within the *jurisdiction*.

(see also: Conditions; Non-Standard Permit/s; Permits)

Statement (see Witness Statement)

Statement of Expectations
(see Regulatory Statement of Expectations)

Statement of Facts

A *statement of facts* is a document that contains a summary of:

- the core legally significant facts, surrounding the alleged offending; and
- other relevant facts, with relevance determined by the nature of the alleged offending.

The *statement of facts* is prepared by the *prosecutor* and provided to the *accused's* legal representative, or the *accused* if they are unrepresented.

(see also: Agreed Facts; Brief of Evidence; Contested Matter; Trial)

Statements of Regulatory Intent

Statements of regulatory intent are typically used when new or interim regulatory requirements (*obligations* and duties) are introduced.

A *statement of regulatory intent* is issued by a *regulator* to clarify its *regulatory approach* and signal its regulatory intentions to certain legislative matters or in certain circumstances.

Typical circumstances leading to a *statement of regulatory intent* being issued include when:

- new regulatory requirements have been introduced, and *regulated entities* need time to adjust;
- further clarification around the changes to a *regulatory approach* are necessary, which will assist *regulated entities* to comply more fully or easily;
- interim arrangements need to be explained, ahead of upcoming changes to the *regulatory framework*; and/or
- *regulators* require more time to provide *advice and guidance* and other materials to *regulated entities* to support *compliance*.

Statements of regulatory intent display the following characteristics including a clear:[182]

- reference to the *act*, section number, or clause, that is the subject of the statement;
- explanation of the *regulatory approach* (usually *compliance* and *enforcement*) that the *regulator* will take;
- time frames, relating to when the statement starts and ends and any transitionary periods;
- expectations and requirements of *regulated entities*; and
- additional advice, guidance, and support that the *regulator* will provide or facilitate.

Conversely, a *regulatory statement of intent* is typically broad in nature and will relate to a *regulatory regime*.

It is important for *regulators* that their *statement/s of regulatory intent* reinforce their current *regulatory posture*, or accurately signal a conscious and considered change in *regulatory posture*.

(see also: Regulatory Statement of Expectations; Regulatory Approach; Regulatory Posture; Regulatory Response; Regulatory Statement of Intent)

Statute (see Primary Legislation)

Statute of Limitations

Is a reference to the maximum amount of time that parties have to initiate legal proceedings, in a *civil* or *criminal matter*.

In *criminal matters, statute of limitations* is often used interchangeably with the term *limitation of time*, and in *civil matters* it may be referred to as statute-barred or time-barred.

For *regulators*, the *statute of limitations* most often starts from the date of an alleged offence.

The actual length of time that a *statute* allows for proceedings to be commenced, varies between *jurisdictions*, and is based upon the nature and type of offence. However, for most regulatory matters the *statute of limitations* will be six, twelve, or twenty-four months.

Statutes of limitations assist with matters being heard, determined, and finalised in a reasonable time. This is important because the longer the period that passes between an incident and a court hearing, the more likely that:
- *evidence* may be lost, or compromised, and
- *witnesses* availability and reliability (i.e., faded memories), may also be compromised.

It is important for regulators to be mindful of the issues associated with the statute of limitations, because being unable to commence proceedings:
- can subject the regulator to criticism, and affect its *authorising environment;*

- impact on its regulatory credibility; and
- is a waste of regulatory resources which could have been better utilised.

(see also: Protracted Investigation; Triage/Triaging)

Statutory Authority/ies

Is a term which can be used by *regulators* in broad and narrow contexts. For example, when used:

- broadly – it can be reference to the *statutory authority* or *regulatory powers* that a *regulator* has; and
- narrowly – it can be reference to a *type of regulatory agency*[183] (e.g., the Australian Pesticides and Veterinary Medicines Authority (APVMA) is an Australian Government *statutory authority*).

(see also: Independent Regulator; Regulator Independence; Type of Regulatory Agency)

Statutory Decisions

Are decisions made where there is an identifiable statutory provision or instrument that allows/permits/enables the decision-maker to make the decision.

Statutory decisions may be made based upon a general *regulatory power* or formal *delegation*. *Statutory decisions* are usually appealable to an *administrative appeals tribunal (AAT)* or equivalent body.

Examples of *statutory decisions* might include:

- a *regulatory officer* – as an *authorised officer*, issuing an emergency stop work notice;
- a *regulatory manager* – as an *authorised officer*, extending an emergency stop work notice; or
- a *regulatory executive* – as an *authorised officer* or not, issuing an *improvement notice* on the entity that the original emergency stop work notice had been issued.

(see also: Decision-Making; Decision-Review; Internal Regulatory Body/ies)

Statutory Declaration

A *statutory declaration* is a *written statement* that is signed with an associated declaration that the contents are true and correct.

The signing of a *statutory declaration* occurs in the presence of an authorised witness, usually a justice of the peace or commissioner for oaths.

(see also: Affidavit; Statement; Witness Statement; Written Statement)

Statutory Law/Legislation (see Primary Legislation)

Stewardship (see Regulatory Stewardship)

Stock, Flow, and Effectiveness (of regulation)

Is a reference to the dimensions through which *regulation* is assessed or reviewed, particularly as it relates to:
- assessing the *regulatory policy* setting in a *jurisdiction*; and
- influencing *regulatory delivery*.[184]

In simple terms:
- *stock* – relates to an assessment of the current *regulation* that is available for use by the *regulator*, much like the stock which is on the shelf in a store. It is also often used to represent the totality of *regulatory burden* imposed on *regulated entities*,
  - with stock reduced by *repealing regulation*, i.e., de-stocking or removing it from the shelf;
- *flow* – relates to introducing new *regulation*, much like re-stocking the shelf in a store,
  - noting that new stock is subject to *regulatory impact assessment* and *regulation impact statement* processes; and
- *effectiveness* – relates to how effectively and efficiently *regulation* is implemented or delivered,
  - noting effectiveness here usually involves some form of assessment and reporting against regulatory *key performance indicators*, regulatory principles of *best practice* or similar.

(see also: De-regulation; Regulation Impact Statement; Regulator Performance and Evaluation; Regulatory Impact Analysis; Regulatory Impact Assessment)

Strategic

Amongst *regulators*, *strategic* can be a term to describe one of three levels (or types) of *regulatory activity* that forms part of *regulatory practice*.

For example, *strategic* can reflect:

- system-wide/systemic *breaches*, cases or matters that involve multiple: sites, *regulated entities*; and *regulated* industries, sectors, or sub-sectors.

The other two levels (or types) of *regulatory activity* are *tactical* and *operational*.

For more detailed explanation of the similarities, overlaps, and differences between the three levels of *regulatory activity* see the *Three Levels of Operational Activity*.

(see also: Operational; Tactical; *Three Levels of Operational Activity*)

Strict Liability Offence

From a *regulator's* perspective, a *strict liability offence* is an *offence* that:

- the *regulator* is **not** required to prove that the *accused* had any intention (or *mens rea*) to commit the *offence*, but
- the *accused* usually has the defence of mistaken belief (of facts). Notably, no such defence exists under *absolute liability*.

Speeding in a car along a public road and/or driving while their drivers' licence is suspended are examples of *strict liability offences*.

It is important for *regulators*, when considering pursuing a prosecution for an *offence*, that they are not seen as selecting a strict liability offence over other offences – out of convenience because it is perceived as being easier to prove.

(see also: Absolute Liability Offence)

Subordinate Legislation (see Secondary Legislation)

Summary Offence/s

Is a type or classification of *offence*, which in most *jurisdictions* is usually dealt with by a magistrate or justice summarily (i.e., without a jury).

Summary offences are often determined by the penalty (usually reflected by potential imprisonment time) being under two years, or thereabouts.

The classification of *offences* is an important issue for *regulators* to be aware of – as it can affect a range of *regulatory activities*, including:
- how they might be required to collect *evidence* (usually the format of interviews);
- how they might be able to share *information* and *intelligence* with other *law enforcement* and *regulatory agencies*; and
- how these *offences* might meet or satisfy definitions such as 'serious crimes' which form part of a number of international *treaties* and *conventions*.[185]

(see also: Absolute Liability Offence; Indictable Offence; Strict Liability Offence)

Sunsetting (see Repealing Regulations)

Supervision

Supervision is a term used in Europe, especially in The Netherlands, which translates to *regulation* in countries such as Australia, New Zealand, United Kingdom, and USA.

(see also: Supervision/Supervisory Agencies)

Supervision/Supervisory Agencies

As above, a term used in Europe, especially in The Netherlands, which translates to *regulatory agency* in countries such as Australia, New Zealand, United Kingdom, and USA.

(see also: Regulatory Agency/ies)

Surveillance

The use of *surveillance* is common practice in mainstream *law enforcement*, and it involves the close observation of a criminal, *suspect*, or *person of interest*.

Surveillance can be conducted physically or by using technology. Examples of how *regulators* might use *surveillance*:

- physically, by:
  - following someone, on foot or in a vehicle; or
  - being close enough to overhear someone's conversation; or
  - a static observation post to monitor nearby behaviours, movements, or transactions.
- using technology, by:
  - accessing closed circuit television (CCTV); or
  - use of digital trackers on vehicles, or even potentially attached to items being transported (this is used in the illegal waste *regulation*); or
  - listening devices.

Regulators are increasingly using *surveillance* as part of their *regulatory activities*. For *regulators*, *surveillance* is the process of monitoring the movements, behaviour, activities, and information associated with a *person*, group, or *regulated entity*.

It is important for *regulators* when either considering the use of or deploying *surveillance* practices, that they comply with any legislative requirements in their *jurisdiction* or in the *jurisdiction* they are operating in.[186]

Surveillance is a function that requires:

- specialised training and equipment;
- documented policies and procedures; and
- appropriate governance and oversight.

(see also: Monitoring Compliance; Post-Market Surveillance)

Suspect

Is a *person* or *regulated entity* that is suspected of committing an *offence* or involved in wrongdoing (whether a *crime* or *regulatory breach*).

A *suspect* is often subject to further *investigation* and because of that *investigation*, may become an *accused, defendant*, or be exonerated.

In some agencies, *person of interest* (POI) may be used as an alternate term for *suspect*.

It is important that *regulators* do not prematurely (either consciously or sub-consciously) treat a *suspect* like an *accused* or *defendant* before they meet or satisfy the criteria for such definitions.

(see also: Accused; Defendant)

Suspend/Suspension (of Authorisation)

Is when a *regulator* suspends the *authorisation* that allows a *regulatory entity* to operate within certain *regulatory regimes/schemes* and/or conduct certain activities.

Suspension, if available, typically forms part of a *regulator's* choices/options as an *administrative response*. However, *suspension* can also be part of a penalty or *sanction* (either civilly or criminally) following the admission or finding of guilt.

Often a *regulator*, depending on the circumstance, prior to progressing to *suspension*, may have varied the *authorisation* to provide the *regulated entity* with an opportunity to return to *compliance*.

(see also: Administrative Remedy/Response/Sanction; Cancellation (of Authorisation); Vary/Variation (of Authorisation))

Suspended Sentence

A *suspended sentence* is a penalty in the form of a term of imprisonment, which is then suspended for a period.

The suspension is usually contingent upon the *person* completing a period of probation and/or a *community order/community service order*.

If the *person* complies with and successfully completes their probation the *suspended sentence* will not be served.

If the *person* does not comply, and *breaches* their probation, they will most likely be required to serve the sentence that was suspended (or a portion of it, depending on the circumstances that led to the *breach*).

(see also: Community Order/Community Service Order; Fines; Imprisonment)

Suspension Notices

Is a *regulatory response* that is available to some *regulators* under certain *regulatory regimes/schemes*.

Suspension notices, if available, typically form part of a regulator's choices/options as an *administrative response*.

Suspension notices can be issued by a *regulatory officer* or a *regulator*. The *regulatory officer* tends to issue them on site in time-critical situations, while the *regulator* tends to issue them remotely (usually in writing), after taking time to consider preliminary information and potentially seeking additional advice (e.g., legal, scientific, or technical).

Suspension notices are typically used in circumstances where a *person* or *regulated entity* is conducting an activity that is:

- unsafe (e.g., in a work health and safety context); or
- poses a harm to the environment (e.g., in an environmental or natural resource protection context).

Suspension notices require that a *person* or *regulated entity* who has been served with a notice:

- stop the activity – which is the subject of the notice; and
- does not recommence the activity – until the *regulatory officer* or *regulator* is satisfied that the situation has been rectified or remedied.

In some *jurisdictions,* failing to comply with the requirements of a *suspension notice* constitutes an (additional) *offence*. A failure to comply with the requirements of a *suspension notice* may also result in the *regulator* taking action for the initial *breach* (which led to the issuing of the *suspension notice*).[187]

(see also: Administrative Remedy/Response/Sanction; Cancellation (of Authorisation); Exclusion Order; Suspend/Suspension (of Authorisation))

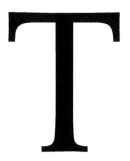

T

Tactical

Amongst *regulators, tactical* can be a term to describe one of three levels (or types) of *regulatory activity* that forms part of *regulatory practice*.

For example, *tactical* can reflect:

• an individual *breach* or case with a single *regulated entity*.

The other two levels (or types) of *regulatory activity* are *operational* and *strategic*.

For more detailed explanation of the similarities, overlaps, and differences between the three levels of *regulatory activity* see the *Three Levels of Operational Activity*.

(see also: Operational; Strategic; *Three Levels of Operational Activity*)

Targeted/Targeting

From a *regulator's* perspective, to be *targeted* or to use *targeting*, is a reference to demonstrating *compliance* with the:

• *Principles of Good Regulation*; and
• forms the second **T** in the associated *PACTT* acronym.

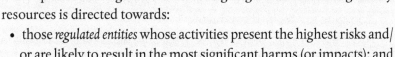

It is important for *regulators* that the *targeting* of their finite regulatory resources is directed towards:

• those *regulated entities* whose activities present the highest risks and/or are likely to result in the most significant harms (or impacts); and
• advancing or achieving the *regulator's* core *regulatory outcomes*.

(see also Intelligence-Based/Intelligence-Led; PACTT; Principles of Good Regulation)

Targeting Interventions

As above, is a reference to directing the *regulator's* resources, effort, and energy to the area of highest need and/or to address specific priorities, risks, or harms.

For *regulators*, the concept of *targeting interventions* was originally and generally associated with *enforcement* effort. However, over time, *targeting interventions* has equally been used to modify behaviour and has broadened to include *nudge/s* and a range of activities captured under the *educate, engage, and enforce* mantra.

(see also: Behavioural Insights; Nudge/s; Regulatory Activity/ies)

Third Party Action/s

Third party actions involve a third party (often an interest group or similar) taking some form of *prosecution* or *litigation,* as part of seeking a *remedy.*

Before a third party can commence or engage in a *third party action,* they are required to demonstrate that they have lawful grounds (or standing). The requirements and process for establishing lawful grounds varies across *jurisdictions.*

Generally, the process of demonstrating standing involves the third party establishing that they have an interest, and more so that their interests may, have, or will be affected.

If grounds exist, the presiding *court* or body will give permission for the third party to make an application or commence proceedings. A key consideration by the presiding *court* or body is whether the action is in the *public interest.*

There are a range of remedies available to third parties, depending on the *legislation.* An example from the environmental regulatory domain, in Australia, contains the following orders:

- restraint – i.e., orders restraining a *person* or *regulated entity* from 'engaging in specified conduct';
- specified acts – i.e., orders that a *person* or *regulated entity* undertake a 'specified act or thing that the court considers reasonably necessary to prevent, minimise or remedy' the *breach* or *non-compliance;*

- financial assurance or sureties – i.e., orders requiring a *person* or *regulated entity* to 'provide a financial assurance as a condition for engaging in specified conduct';
- compensation – i.e., orders 'to pay compensation to the [*regulator*] or the injured person for any injury, loss, or damage as a result of' the *breach* or *non-compliance*;
- specific costs – i.e., orders for 'any costs reasonably incurred by the [*regulator*] or the injured person in the course of taking action to prevent, minimise or remedy any injury, loss or damage suffered by the [regulator] or the injured person as a result of' the *breach* or *non-compliance*; and
- general costs – i.e., orders for 'costs reasonably incurred by the [*regulator*] in the course of taking action to prevent, minimise or remedy any harm to human health or the environment caused by the' *breach* or *non- compliance*.[188]

(see also: Citizen Suit; Complainant: Private Prosecutions)

Three Levels of Operational Activity (3LOA)

Regulatory and *enforcement agencies* tend to describe their *operational regulatory activities* as occurring within and across three levels.

The *three levels of operational activity* are:
- *tactical*;
- *operational*; and
- *strategic*.

The three key elements are considered in greater detail in Part 3.

(See also: Compliance Spectrum)

Tit-for-Tat

Tit-for-tat is an approach or strategy used by *regulatory* and *enforcement* agencies.

A *regulator* using a *tit-for-tat* strategy would be:
- reasonable – towards cooperative *regulated entities*;
- ruthless – towards *regulated entities* who operate outside-of-system, or who engage in criminal behaviour;
- relentless – in pursuit of recidivist offenders; and
- reassuring – toward repentant *regulated entities*. [189]

The *tit-for-tat* approach has the potential to significantly reduce *compliance* and *enforcement* costs, for the *regulator* and *regulated entities*, by encouraging a co-operative instead of confrontational (or even worse combative) relationship.

The *tit-for-tat* approach influenced what would become *responsive regulation*.

(see also: Compliance Pyramid/Triangle; Responsive Regulation)

Training

Staff in *regulatory* (and *enforcement*) *agencies* require and receive various types of *training* and *continuing professional development* relating to their *regulatory* and non-regulatory work.

In relation to their regulatory work, *training* can be grouped in several ways. *Training* can be:
- generalist or specialist in nature;[190]
- provided internally (i.e., in-service training), externally (i.e., by a third party provider), or a combination (i.e., sometimes delivered through a partnership);
- required as part of pre-employment, induction/onboarding, and ongoing employment; and
- mandatory or desirable, noting that there is often minimum and/or mandatory training required to be appointed as an *authorised officer*.

The issue of *training* is critically important for *regulators*. This is because *training* is often linked to the initial appointment of an *authorised officer*.

This particular (initial) *training* is vital in ensuring that an *authorised officer* understands the importance of their *regulatory powers*, especially those powers that are coercive in nature, which if used inappropriately can subject the *regulatory agency* to criticism and external review.

It is often the case that regulatory reviews and inquiries highlight and criticise *regulatory agencies* for not investing enough time and money in staff *training* and *continuing professional development*.

(see also: Authorised Officer; Continuing Professional Development; Regulatory Officer/s; Regulatory Profession; Regulatory Professionalism)

Transparent/Transparency

From a *regulator's* perspective, to be *transparent* or act with *transparency*, is a reference to demonstrating *compliance* with the:

- *Principles of Good Regulation*; and
- forms the first **T** in the associated *PACTT* acronym.

It is important for *regulators* that *transparency* is seen and treated as an essential part of all aspects of the *regulator's* work, including that the *regulator*:

- can demonstrate that it has always acted impartially and with integrity;
- can provide a certain level of comfort to *co-* and *peer- regulators, regulated entities, stakeholders,* and the *wider community* that they have performed their *regulatory activities* (including and especially around *enforcement* decisions) in a *transparent* manner; and
- is comfortable being subjected to scrutiny from third parties.

(see also PACTT; Principles of Good Regulation)

Treaty/ies (see Conventions)

Triage/Triaging

The term *triage* or *triaging* is most often associated with the medical profession. For example, patients are *triaged* in the accident and emergency ward of a hospital, which means they are examined (often quickly, and at a preliminary level) to determine which patients will receive immediate or prioritised treatment.

This *triaging* process is a process that translates to and can be applied to a range of *regulatory* and non-regulatory issues or problems. *Regulators* typically use the *triaging* process to assess:

- *allegations*;
- cases;
- *complaints*;
- *incidents*; and
- a range of other matters.

The *triaging* process involves the consideration of many factors, including but not limited to:

- *criteria*;
- *risk criteria*;
- *risk matrix*;
- *risk profile*; and
- *risk ratings*.

The most usual *outcomes* of a *triaging* process for *regulators* are that the matter (or issue) is:

- not prioritised and the matter is filed/closed – this is often the case when:
  - it simply is not a matter for the *regulator*, i.e., not within their *regulatory mandate* or *jurisdiction*; and/or
  - there is no likelihood that they could effectively resolve the matter, i.e., the *information* or *evidence* required is just not physically possible to obtain; or
- prioritised but the matter is not actioned – in that it may be entered into the system but is awaiting further *information* or resources to become available (i.e., a 'watching brief' if you like); or
- prioritised and the matter is actioned – noting that:

- the action will be allocated a classification within a hierarchy (i.e., low, medium, high; tier 1, tier 2, tier 3; or similar)
- the classification will be subject to ongoing review during the life of the matter, with escalation and de-escalation possible *outcomes.*

(see also: Criteria; Risk Criteria; Risk Matrix; Risk Profile; Risk Ratings; Statute of Limitations)

Trial

A *trial* involves the formal examination of *evidence* by a *judicial officer* (e.g., judge or magistrate).

Trials typically take place in a *court*, and depending on the type, classification, and seriousness of the *offence* (i.e., summary, indictable, or major indictable) may involve a jury.

During a *trial* the *court* (or tribunal) will hear *evidence* from both the *prosecution* and defence to determine whether the prosecution case has been made out (that is proven) to the requisite *burden of proof.*

A *trial* occurs if the *accused* party pleads not guilty, or the matter cannot be resolved by negotiation and/or following an *ADR* process.

(see also: Alternate Dispute Resolution; Contested Hearing/Matter/Case; Litigation; Prosecution)

Type/s of Regulation

The main *types of regulation* are:
- Command and control;
- Harms-based;
- Light-touch;
- Performance-based;
- Principles-based;
- Really responsive;
- Responsive;
- Right-touch;
- Risk-based;
- Self-regulation; and
- Smart.

The different *types of regulation* not only overlap with each other but can be used in combination.

The *types of regulation* can be used somewhat interchangeably with *regulatory approach/es*.

(see also: Regulatory Method/s; Regulatory Tool/s).

Type of Regulatory Agency

The *type of regulatory agency* that an agency is, or might be, is often framed pejoratively. For example, the *regulatory agency* **is not** a:

- *modern regulator;*
- *best practice regulator;* or
- mature regulator.

However, for *regulators* and *regulated entities*, the *type of regulatory agency*, is usually framed around its (relative) level of *independence*. The most common dimensions of *regulator independence* include:

- 'budget independence;
- conditions for dismissal of the head of the regulatory agency;
- appointment of members/head of the regulatory agency by parliament or the legislature;
- accountability and reporting to executive, legislature, or representatives from regulated industry;
- power to set tariffs or price-setting by the executive; and
- power to review or approve contract terms between regulated entities or market actors'.[191]

It is these factors that influence whether a *regulatory agency* is a:

- (Ministerial) Department;
- (Ministerial) Agency;
- Independent Advisory Body; or
- Independent Regulatory Body.[192]

Some *regulators* may identify with one main *type of regulation* while others may identify with two or more *types of regulation*. For example, *regulators* may identify with and therefore describe themselves as being:

- a *risk-based regulator;*[193]
- an *intelligence-led* and *risk-based regulator;*[194]
- an *intelligence-led, risk-based regulator,* and *outcomes-focused regulator.*[195]

What is clear is that the *type of regulatory agency* that an agency is, is a complex issue and intersects with all the factors outlined above. But is particularly influenced by:

- *regulatory mandate;*
- *regulatory culture;*
- *regulatory posture;*
- issues of interoperability when working with *co-* and *peer- regulators;* and
- shared responsibilities or interdependencies when working within and across the *Extended Regulatory Spectrum.*

(see also: Regulator Independence; Regulatory Culture; Regulatory Posture)

Ultra Vires [Latin]

A Latin phrase which translates to 'outside or beyond one's legal power'.

Regulators (and *regulatory officers*) are said to act *ultra vires* when they do something which they have no legal basis or *authority* to do.

Examples of acting *ultra vires* would include:

- a *regulator* – adding a condition to an *authorisation* (usually in a *licence* or *permit*) for which there is no good, proper, or valid reason; or
- a *regulatory officer* – entering and searching a *premise* without permission, whether that permission is based upon *consent, statutory powers,* or written *authority* from a *judicial officer.*

(see also: Accountable/Accountability; Intra Vires; Transparent/Transparency; Regulatory Powers)

Unlawful

Is something that is **not** allowed or permitted by *law.*

The term is two directional, in that *unlawful* can be a reference to a requirement or *obligation* that is placed on either or both the *regulated* and the *regulator.* For example, the:

- *regulated* – frequently need to demonstrate that they have acted and operated lawfully, most often this will be achieved by complying with relevant *authorisations* etc., and/or in some instances positively demonstrating that their actions were not *unlawful.*
- *regulator* – needs to demonstrate that anything they 'ask' of and especially 'require' of a *regulated entity* is something that is within

their *lawful authority*, and which is permitted by their *authority*. If a *regulator* goes beyond their *power* or *authority*, they are said to be acting *ultra vires*.

(see also: Lawful; Ultra Vires)

VADE Model

The *VADE Model* (VADE) is an adaption of the *compliance pyramid/triangle*, it reflects the four states of *compliance* and behaviours of *regulated entities*.

VADE is an acronym for:

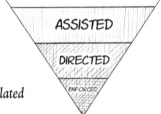

- **V**oluntary compliance, or behaviours
- **A**ssisted compliance, or behaviours
- **D**irected compliance, or behaviours
- **E**nforced compliance, or behaviours

Therefore, the *VADE Model* reflects *regulated entities* who are:

- complying **V**oluntarily, without any additional assistance from the *regulator*;
- complying after they have received some form of additional **A**ssistance from the *regulator*;
- complying after they have been **D**irected to do so by the *regulator*; or
- only complying because they have been **E**nforced to do so by the *regulator* (or other body, i.e., a *court*).

The *VADE Model* is commonly used by *regulatory agencies* in New Zealand government.

(see also: Compliance Spectrum; *VADE Model*)

Vary/Variation (of Authorisation)

Is when a *regulator* chooses to *vary* an *authorisation* that allows a *regulatory* entity to operate within certain *regulatory regimes/schemes* and/or conduct certain activities.

Variation, if available, typically forms part of a *regulator's* choices/ options as an *administrative response*. However, *variation* of an *authorisation* can also form part of a penalty or *sanction* (either civilly or criminally) following the admission or finding of guilt.

Often a *regulator*, depending on the circumstance, will commence with a *variation* of an *authorisation* to provide the *regulated entity* with an opportunity to return to *compliance*.

(see also: Administrative Remedy/Response/Sanction; Cancellation (of Authorisation); Suspend/Suspension (of Authorisation))

Verbal Warning/Caution

A *verbal warning/caution* occurs when a *regulator* raises with a *regulated entity* the need to desist from conduct that has, is, or will *breach* their regulatory *obligations*.

A *verbal warning/caution* is often issued on-site, during an inspection by an *authorised officer*. It typically occurs as part of the lower end activities/responses depicted in the **A**ssisted area of the *VADE Model*.

It is good practice to follow up and record a *verbal warning/caution* with a written record, either by letter or email.

(see also: **VADE Model**; Warnings and Caution)

Verify/Verification

A core part of the operational work of *regulators* is the need to *verify* that a *regulated entity* is complying with their regulatory *obligations*.

Verification can be proactive or reactive and can be undertaken by the *regulated entity* themselves, the *regulator*, or a third party. Irrespective, positive, ongoing, and repeated *verification* assists in establishing and maintaining *earned autonomy*, and/or a current and up to date *compliance history/record*.

Examples of *verification* include:

- self-*verification* – involves the *regulated entity* using internal processes and procedures to *verify* and report to the *regulator*;
- traditional-*verification* – involves the *regulator* itself, conducting *audits, inspections,* or *investigations* to *verify*; and
- third party-*verification* – an independent third party would conduct the *verification* process. Their approach may involve a combination of using the *regulated entity's* documented processes and procedures, and/or conducting an *audit, inspection,* or *investigation* (either own motion/self-initiated, or on behalf of the *regulator*).

(see also: Audit; Compliance History; Earned Autonomy/Recognition; Inspection; Investigation)

Vexatious Complainant

A *vexatious complainant* is a term used to describe a *complainant* who brings baseless allegations or *complaints* to an agency or *complaint* body. Other terms include:
- difficult *complainants*;
- persistent *complainants*; and
- problem *complainants*.

Irrespective of the term, these *complainants* take an inordinate amount of a *regulator's* time and resources to deal with, which is often to the detriment of higher priorities and more pressing matters. For this reason, *regulators* need to be clear of the difference between an *allegation* and a *complaint*.

Regulators can have a person listed/classified as a *vexatious complainant* in order that they can deal with them in a way which would otherwise be inconsistent with their normal (policies, procedures, and practices) *complaint handling* system.

(see also: Allegation; Complainant; Complaint; Complaint Handling)

Vexatious Complaint

A *vexatious complaint* is an isolated *complaint* (but can often form part of a series) that often has no or little basis, and is brought about to cause annoyance, frustration, and emotional and/or financial costs to the other party.

In a *regulatory* context, *vexatious complaints* may be made by entities seeking to distract, disrupt or frustrate the regulatory role and regulatory actions undertaken by *regulators*. In extreme cases, *vexatious complaints*, may even be part of a campaign to have the *regulation* itself overturned.

In a *court/litigation* context, if a *court* is satisfied that a *complaint* is *vexatious* it may stay or dismiss proceedings and make appropriate orders as to costs.

(see also: Allegation; Complainant; Complaint; Complaint Handling)

Vicarious Liability

Refers to the legal liability that one person or entity has for another person or entity.

Examples of where a *regulated entity* might be *vicariously liable* include when:

- liquor is served to an intoxicated person by one of their bar staff, and under the liquor licensing *laws* they have not provided the staff member with appropriate *training*; or
- contaminated food is served in a restaurant by one of the wait staff, and under the food hygiene *laws* management failed to put in place food storage processes.

(see also: Liability)

Victim Impact Statement

A form of *statement*.

Specifically, a *statement* to the *court* by the victim of a *crime* setting out details of injury, loss or damage caused by the *crime*.

(see also: Impact Statement; Statement; Witness)

Violation/s (see Breach/es)

Voluntary Compliance

A *regulator* aims/seeks to maximise the level of *voluntary compliance* amongst its *regulated entities*.

High levels of *voluntary compliance* enables *regulators* to focus their efforts and limited resources to the areas of most need.

Achieving high (or at least increased) levels of *voluntary compliance* can depend on a range of multifaceted issues, that require active management and support by *regulators*. *Regulators* can positively shape and support *voluntary compliance* rates by:

- publishing relevant policies;
- producing and promulgating education and promotional materials;
- establishing and maintaining mutually respectful relationships with the regulated sector; and
- establishing and maintaining multiple communication lines with the *regulated* sector, to enable ongoing dialogue.

Diagrammatically, it is the first and broadest level of four phases contained in the *VADE Model*.

(see also: Assisted Compliance; Directed Compliance; Earned Autonomy/Recognition; Enforced Compliance; *VADE Model*)

Warden (see Authorised Officer)

In a regulatory context, a *warden* is a person who has supervisory responsibilities in a specific geographic location.

The title of *warden* is most often associated with those *authorised officers* whose work involves protection of nature reserves, whether terrestrial or marine.

(see also: Authorised Officer; Inspector; Investigator; Ranger; Regulatory Officer)

Warning (see Warnings and Cautions)

Noting a *warning* can be delivered verbally or in writing.

(see also: Administrative Remedy/Response/Sanction; Official Warning; Verbal Warning/Caution)

Warning Letter

A *warning letter* formalises the fact that the *regulator* has discussed and notified a *person* or *regulated entity* to desist from conduct that has, is, or will *breach* their regulatory *obligations*.

Some *regulators* will follow up a *verbal warning*, which is often issued on-site, during an inspection by an *authorised officer,* with a written *warning letter* or email. This is good practice, for as it has been said 'a verbal warning isn't worth the paper it isn't written on!'

(see also: Official Warning; Verbal Warning/Caution; Warnings and Caution)

Warnings and Cautions

Is a *regulatory response*, widely used by most *regulators*, to warn and notify a *person* or *regulated entity* to desist from conduct that has, is, or will *breach* their regulatory *obligations*.

Warnings and cautions, if available, typically form part of a *regulator's* first or early choices/options, as an *administrative response*. This is because *warnings and cautions* reinforce educative intent and fall within the provision of *advice and guidance*.

Warnings and cautions are often used interchangeably. For example:

- a *warning* or *caution* might be a gentle correction;
- a *formal warning* could also be given in other circumstances, e.g., for cumulative *breaches*; and
- as a last resort a *warning, caution* or *formal warning* may be issued prior to initiating *court* proceedings.

It might also be worth putting these into the context of the *VADE Model. Warnings and cautions* typically occur as part of activities/responses depicted in the **A**ssisted area of the *VADE Model.*

It is good practice for *regulators* to follow up and record a *verbal warning/caution* with a written record, either letter or email.

Breaches for which a *warning* or *caution* may be appropriate, will usually:

- be minor in nature;
- be easily and/or quickly remedied;
- not have caused significant damage or impact;
- not pose any ongoing risk; and
- be covered (explicitly by *breach* or type, certain attributes, or *criteria*) in the *compliance and enforcement policy*, or *prosecution policy*, or equivalent.

Warnings and cautions vary in that they can be:

- formal or informal;
- written or verbal;
- statutory or non-statutory based; and
- publicly recorded.

It is important for *regulators* to record *warnings and cautions* as part of documenting interactions with a *regulated entity* on matters of minor *non-compliance*. This enables the *regulator* to initiate an escalated response (including *prosecution* or *litigation*), for subsequent repeat or similar *breaches*.

Properly recorded *warnings and cautions* also make it more difficult for a *regulated entity* to dispute that they had no prior knowledge, and this also usefully corresponds with higher penalties as the offending or *breach* is seen as aggravated.

(see also: Administrative Remedy/Response/Sanction; Advice and Guidance; Criteria; Official Warning; **VADE Model**; Verbal Warning/Caution; Warning Letter)

Warrant/s

A *warrant* is an official legal document, signed by a *judicial officer*, that allows someone to do something.

Warrants typically give *law enforcement* officers (which includes *authorised officers/regulatory officers*) permission to enter and then search a *premise*.

The most common *warrants* used by *regulatory agencies* are *monitoring warrants* and *search warrants*.

(see also: Investigation Warrant; Monitoring Warrant, Regulatory Powers; Search Warrant, Warrant Card)

Warrant Card

A *warrant card* is proof of identification and authority, carried by officers in mainstream *law enforcement agencies*, the main one being policing agencies, but also includes customs, border protection, and immigration agencies.

Warrant cards are common in Australia, New Zealand, the United Kingdom and a number of other current and former Commonwealth countries.

In other countries, *warrant cards* are known by numerous terms including authority, credentials, or *identification cards*.

Like *identity cards, warrant cards* are a card which contain:

- a photograph of the person named on the card (the card holder);
- reference to the *act/s* or *regulation/s* that the card holder is appointed under;
- the agency or body that the card holder is either employed by or acting on behalf of; and
- any limitations or restrictions to specific powers or authority.

A *warrant card* will usually be supported and corroborated in other formats including gazettal, or some form of written instrument.

(see also: Identification Card; Identity Card)

Wider Community

The term used to describe those individuals who do not identify as being a *regulator, regulated,* or belonging to a specific *stakeholder* group.

Members of the *wider community* are one of the four main groups that constitute the *Four Key Regulatory Perspectives*, the others are *regulated, regulators,* and *stakeholders.*

(see also: Authorising Environment; **Four Key Regulatory Perspectives**)

Witness

A *witness* is a *person* who can give *evidence* at a *trial*, disputed facts hearing, or tribunal/inquiry (or similar).

In court, the *evidence* given by a *witness* is either given under oath or affirmation, and there are *penalties* and consequences if the *evidence* they provide is not true (to the best of their knowledge and ability).

A *witness*, especially civilians or professionals, will often receive a written notification or request, by way of a summons or subpoena, that they are required to attend *court* (or hearing) to provide *evidence*.

However, it is not always the case for *regulatory officers* or other civil/public servants to receive written notification. This is because, as civil/public servants their attendance is mandatory given their role and conditions of employment.

(see also: Affidavit; Evidence; Statement; Statutory Declaration; Witness Statement)

Witness Statement

A *witness statement* is the account/version of events that an individual can (and is able to) provide, relating to the facts in a matter or *case*. It is a written summary of the *evidence* of a *witness*.

A *witness statement* can be confirmed by oath or affirmation, for use as *evidence* in court, or disputed matter.

(see also: Affidavit; Evidence; Statement; Statutory Declaration)

Working Together

Working together is something that *regulators* are increasingly doing, and not only with *co-* and *peer-* *regulators* but with non-regulatory, enforcement, policing, military, and intelligence agencies.[196]

Working together is multi-faceted and can occur in numerous situations. Including:

- involving individuals, teams, and groups within an agency;
- involving agencies within and across portfolios, and at a whole of government level;
- within and across disciplines (e.g., licensing, *audit*, *inspection*, *investigation*, and *prosecution*); and
- within and across professions (e.g., legal, scientific, and technical).

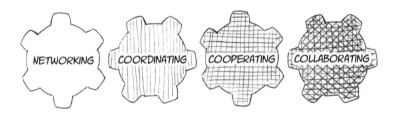

From a *regulator's* perspective, *working together* can take various forms,[197] including:

- networking – exchanging of mutually beneficial *information*;
- co-ordinating – exchanging *information* and altering activities for a common purpose;
- co-operating – exchanging *information*, altering activities, and sharing resources for a common purpose; and

- collaborating – exchanging *information*, altering activities, sharing resources for a common purpose, and enhancing capacity of other partners.

(see also: Network/s; *Working Together*)

Written Statement (see Witness Statement)

Written Warning (see Warnings and Cautions)

XY

Zealous Witness

A *zealous witness* is one that displays excessive or undue favouritism towards one party in a *court* case or proceedings.

A *zealous witness* will often be accused of being biased or lacking objectivity.

Staff in *regulatory agencies* who are overly passionate about a specific industry, sector, and especially commodity are at risk of coming across as a *zealous witness*.

It is important for a *regulator*, that witness impartiality issues are addressed, in the context of staff giving *evidence* in *proceedings*. Especially staff with professional backgrounds and qualifications and/or significant experience and expertise in a particular field or domain.

Sometimes there will be legal practice notes or directives that detail the circumstances when a *witness* can or cannot (or should or should not) be considered as an *expert witness*.

Sometimes this might appear to be overly harsh, or counterintuitive but it is important for *regulators* and *prosecuting authorities* as a *model litigant* to be able to be open and transparent, and be seen to be open and transparent.

(see also: Evidence; Expert Evidence; Model Litigant; Opinion Evidence; Witness)

Zero tolerance

Zero tolerance is a method of enforcing *laws*, even those *offences* or *breaches* that are considered minor.[198]

    Zero tolerance tends to be associated more with *policing agencies* and *enforcement agencies* but has clear application for *regulatory agencies*.

    Examples of *zero tolerance*, across policing, enforcement, and regulation include:

- *policing* – arresting suspects for domestic violence and/or 'one punch' assaults;
- *enforcement* – prosecuting *fraud* offenders where the *fraud* meets a certain criterion (usually including exceeding a defined dollar amount); and
- *regulation* – issuing of parking tickets (*infringement notices*) for vehicles parked in a disabled parking space without a *permit*.

It is important that *regulators* clearly communicate which *breaches* are subject to *zero tolerance*. For example, it would be expected that:

- existing and standard *zero tolerance offences* – would usually be contained in a *regulator's compliance and enforcement policy* or *prosecutions policy* (or equivalent), and
- new and emerging *zero tolerance offences* – would be communicated (broadly or in a targeted and focussed manner) to *co-* and *peer-regulators, regulated entities, stakeholders*, and the *wider community*.

(see also: Criteria; Regulatory Approach; Regulatory Posture)

Part 3

THE SIX KEY REGULATORY CONCEPTS AND FRAMEWORKS

OVERVIEW OF THE SIX KEY REGULATORY CONCEPTS AND FRAMEWORKS

The six key regulatory concepts and frameworks considered in this Part of the book have already been:

- covered alphabetically, and individually, in Part 2 of this book; and
- used as a cross-reference and source of additional information for other words, terms, or concepts covered in Part 2 of this book.

The six key regulatory concepts and frameworks either as a set, or as two groups of three, have been designed in such a way that they can be considered:

- individually;
- in combination; or
- wholistically.

Overview of the two groups

The two groups have been designed to provide users of this book with additional context around the regulatory issues (and associated words, terms, or concepts) they are considering. For example:

Group 1 provides the first level of diagnostics, in terms of:

- which phase or phases of the **Extended Regulatory Spectrum** are fundamental to the regulatory issue at hand;
- which of the **Four Key Regulatory Perspectives** are relevant and/or dominant for the regulatory issue at hand; and

- which of the **Three Levels of Operational Activity** are or may be used on the regulatory issue at hand, and any considerations around using them in parallel, combination, and as to timing and sequencing.

Group 2 provides the second level of diagnostics, in terms of:
- the state of compliance and/or behaviours exhibited by *regulated entities* across the **VADE** *Model*;
- the nature and type of what **Working Together** looks like for *regulators*; and
- the type of **Regulatory Language** and/or professional language being used and needing to be understood by those staff working within and across the regulatory field.

Group 1 and Group 2 combine to become what the author refers to as *the six key regulatory concepts and frameworks*, which when appreciated and more fully understood assists *regulators* to:
- develop a common body of knowledge to better perform a range of *regulatory activities*, which:
  - increases effectiveness and efficiency of those *regulatory activities*; and
  - advances or achieves *regulatory outcomes*; and
- ensure that *regulatory responses* are:
  - appropriate and proportionate;
  - consistent and considerate of *co-* and *peer regulators*; and
  - not diluted or lost in translation due to differences in *regulatory language*.

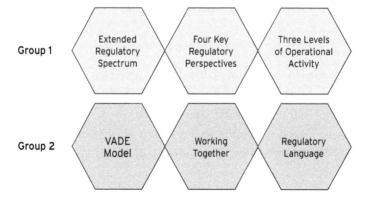

Group 1

| Extended Regulatory Spectrum | Four Key Regulatory Perspectives | Three Levels of Operational Activity |

Group 2

| VADE Model | Working Together | Regulatory Language |

GROUP 1

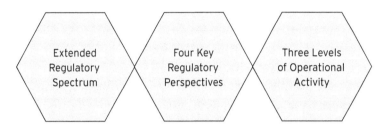

The significance and utility of the Group 1 concepts and frameworks is that they enable the user to quickly triangulate around an issue or matter.

For example, in terms of the:

- **Extended Regulatory Spectrum** – which of the six phases is the *regulatory activity* and/or *regulatory practice* occurring in or related to;
- **Four Key Regulatory Perspectives** – which of the four main regulatory actors, and their respective lenses is the regulatory matter being considered through; and
- **Three Levels of Operational Activity** – which level is the *operational regulatory activities* occurring at, across, or targeted towards.

Extended Regulatory Spectrum

The *Extended Regulatory Spectrum (ERS)* is a framework that describes the six phases of regulatory activity.

Regulatory Regime Design	Advice and Guidance	Licensing and Approvals	Monitoring Compliance	Enforcement	Regulator Performance and Evaluation

(Source: Grant Pink, 2018) [199]

The first and last phases act as bookends, spanning the period from when *regulation* or a *regulatory regime/scheme* is designed through until where the *regulator* evaluates and reports on its own performance.

The four central (shaded) phases reflect activities that are *operational* in nature and are aligned with *regulatory practice* and *regulatory delivery*.

Phase	Key aspects, activities, and personnel
Regulatory Regime Design	• occurs at commencement, and during reviews • led by policy officers, with a focus on *regulatory* effectiveness, efficiency, and possibly *de-regulation*
Advice and Guidance	• communicates requirements to *regulated entities* • provided by non-regulatory and *regulatory officers*
Licensing and Approvals	• an entry control into a *regulatory regime/scheme* • provided by various authorised parties
Monitoring Compliance	• checks and verifies *compliance* of a *regulated entity* • predominantly undertaken by *regulatory officers*
Enforcement	• initiating action to return entities to *compliance* • involves *prosecuting authorities*, and *regulatory executives*
Regulator Performance and Evaluation	• occurs at scheduled review periods • lead by policy officers, with *de-regulation* focus

Four Key Regulatory Perspectives

The *Four Key Regulatory Perspectives* (4KRP) include and reflect the four main regulatory actors, and the respective lenses that they tend to consider regulatory matters through.

The table below provides additional context to the different perspectives across the 4KRP.

Regulator	Regulated
Including co- and *peer- regulators* – whether in the same or different level of government.	**Those directly subjected to regulation** – usually but not always by explicit *authorisation*.
Co-regulators - are *regulators* whose *regulatory activities* and interests span or overlap with another *regulator*, either in terms of the *regulatory domain*, sector, or commodity. ***Peer-regulators***, are *regulators* that regulate the same, or substantially the same matters and issues in another *jurisdiction*.	***Individual persons*** - can be an entity which is subject to regulation. ***Regulated entities*** - can take the form of a body or organisation (e.g., businesses, corporations, or other structure).
Stakeholders	Wider Community
Clear interests and stakes in regulation – include *peak industry bodies*.	**Those in the wider community** – forming part of broader society.
Stakeholders – are an entity (person, body, or organisation) who has an interest in *regulation* and its impacts.	***Wider Community*** – are those individuals who do not identify as being a *regulator*, *regulated* (i.e., for the matter considered), or belonging to a specific *stakeholder* group.

Three Levels of Operational Activity

Regulatory and enforcement agencies tend to describe their *operational regulatory activities* as occurring within and across three levels.

The *Three Levels of Operational Activity* are *tactical, operational,* and *strategic*. In this order or sequence, the activities reflect a move from individual and specific to collective and general. For example:

Level	Type and nature of regulatory activity
Tactical	Individual *breach* or case with a single *regulated entity*.
Operational	Group of *breaches* or cases, involving either multiple sites for the same *regulated entity*, and/or multiple (inter-related) *regulated entities*.
Strategic	System-wide/systemic *breaches*, cases or matters that involve multiple: sites, regulated entities; and regulated industries, sectors, or sub-sectors.

The example below highlights the differences across the three levels:

- a **single supermarket** is non-compliant in respect to its work health and safety (WH&S) obligations. If the *regulator* attends and conducts a site inspection and audits the records of that **individual supermarket**, then that would represent **a tactical response**; and

- during the **tactical response** (above) the *regulator* finds systemic deficiencies in how the **supermarket chain** is approaching its regulatory *obligations* around WH&S. The *regulator* then decides to conduct several unannounced *inspections* and *audits* of **other supermarkets in that chain,** then that would represent **an operational response**; and

- during the **operational response** (above) the *regulator* finds systemic deficiencies in how the **supermarket sector** (as a whole) is approaching its WH&S *obligations*. The *regulator* then decides to conduct numerous unannounced *inspections* and *audits* of other supermarkets, irrespective of (local or national) chain affiliation then that would represent **an example of a strategic response.**

GROUP 2

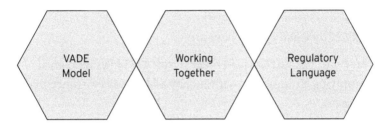

The significance and utility of the Group 2 concepts and frameworks is that they enable the user to quickly triangulate around an issue or matter.

For example, in terms of the:

- **VADE Model** – which provides insights into and reflects the four states of compliance and behaviours of *regulated entities;*
- **Working Together** – for *regulators* is multi-faceted, it can occur in numerous situations and take various forms; and
- **Regulatory Language** – with a common and shared language enabling *regulators* to communicate with each other around the core or foundational issues of *regulation* and *regulatory delivery.*

VADE Model

The *VADE Model* (VADE) is an adaption of the *compliance pyramid/triangle*, it reflects the four states of *compliance* and behaviours of *regulated entities*.

VADE is an acronym for:

- **V**oluntary *compliance*, or behaviours
- **A**ssisted *compliance*, or behaviours
- **D**irected *compliance*, or behaviours
- **E**nforced *compliance*, or behaviours

For example, the *VADE Model* reflects *regulated entites* who are:

- complying **V**oluntarily, without any additional assistance from the *regulator*;
- complying after they have received some form of additional **A**ssistance from the *regulator*;
- complying after they have been **D**irected to do so by the *regulator*; or
- only complying because they have been **E**nforced to do so by the *regulator* (or other body, e.g., a *court*).

The *VADE Model* is commonly used by *regulatory agencies* in New Zealand.

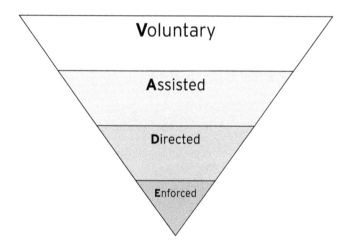

Working Together

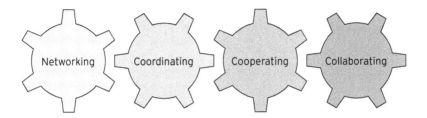

Working together is something that *regulators* are increasingly doing, and not only with other *regulators* but also with non-regulatory, enforcement, policing, military, and intelligence agencies.

Working together is multi-faceted and can occur in numerous situations. Including:

- involving individuals, teams, and groups within an agency;
- involving agencies within and across portfolios, and at a whole of government level;
- within and across disciplines (e.g., licensing, *audit, inspection, investigation*, and *prosecution*); and
- within and across professions (e.g., legal, scientific, and technical).

From a *regulator's* perspective, *working together* can take various forms,[200] including:

- networking – exchanging of mutually beneficial *information*;
- co-ordinating – exchanging *information* and altering activities for a common purpose;
- co-operating – exchanging *information*, altering activities, and sharing resources for a common purpose; and/or
- collaborating – exchanging *information*, altering activities, sharing resources for a common purpose, and enhancing capacity of other partners.

Regulatory Language

Regulatory language is a reference to the professional language used by staff working within and across the *regulatory profession*.

Regulatory language is a common and shared language which enables *regulators* to communicate with each other around the core or foundational issues of *regulation* and *regulatory delivery* – irrespective of the *regulatory domain* in which they operate and/or the specific industries, sectors, or commodities they regulate.

However, at present, *regulators* operate **without** a fully common and shared language. Their current language:

- produces limited and sub-optimal cross commodity, industry, jurisdictional, and sectoral liaison, and
- can lead to or result in regulatory confusion, duplication, and failure.

Establishing a distinguishable *regulatory language* forms a critical pathway to establishing an identifiable *regulatory profession*, which in turn is required to advance the concept of *regulatory professionalism*.

CONCLUDING COMMENTS

Restating – the aims of the book

I had two groups in mind when I decided to write this book, namely:
- people who work within and across *regulatory agencies*; and
- the *regulatory profession* itself.

For the first group. This book aims to assist *regulatory practitioners, regulatory managers, regulatory executives,* and *regulatory agencies.* Especially, practically in their day-to-day regulatory roles and in their interactions with:
- regulatory staff;
- non-regulatory staff;
- *regulated entities;*
- *stakeholders;*
- members of the *wider community;* and
- anyone willing to engage in a discussion on regulatory matters.

For the second group. This book aims to assist and advance the capability, capacity, credibility, and competence of those operating in the regulatory field, in what is an emerging *regulatory profession.*

As mentioned in the Preface, I felt strongly and was committed to the title accurately reflecting the nature, contents, and usefulness of the book. And again, I hope it meets the self-imposed brief!

The overall aim of this book is to assist *regulators, regulatory practitioners, regulatory managers, regulatory executives,* and *regulatory agencies* – to achieve greater clarity, a shared understanding, and an increased ability to work together, for mutual benefit.

Respecting – healthy and appropriate differences

The diversity of backgrounds and professions that readers will be coming from, coupled with their different and changing operating contexts, means that from time to time there will be differences.

Often these differences are healthy and appropriate differences, arising from different perspectives. What is important is that these differences result in deliberate and focussed discussions, and that these discussions clarify or narrow the issues. Noting that generally, it is more acceptable that there is variation on specific aspects as opposed to generic aspects – variation on the former tend to relate to specialisation whereas the latter tend to reflect a personal preference – which at extremes can lead to work-arounds and un-sustainable practices.

And of course, sometimes it can just be a matter of perspective!

Remembering – the importance of regulatory literacy

Basic *regulatory literacy* and regulatory communications matter. They matter because they help to improve:

- *regulatory capability*;
- *regulatory capacity*;
- *regulatory culture*;
- *regulator performance*;
- *regulatory posture*; and
- achieving or advancing *regulatory outcomes*.

Developing, maintaining, and advancing *regulatory literacy* is a key aspect of:

- establishing the *regulatory profession* as a profession in its own right; and
- the need for ever increasing professionalism in relation to *regulatory practice* and *regulatory delivery*.

Reminder – about the book's note of caution and practical tip

In Part 1 there was a 'note of caution' and a 'practical tip'.

The 'note of caution' advised of the specialist reference materials and resources available that cover the issues touched upon in this book to a greater level of detail. Especially so where those issue are specific to:

- a legal, *operational*, scientific, or technical matter/issue; and
- a *jurisdiction*, industry, sector, or *regulated commodity*.

The 'practical tip' suggested that readers may find it is useful to either manually check hard copy documents or use the word search function on their computer to check electronic documents. The important thing is to check relevant *regulatory* documents to see how these words, terms, and concepts:

- are used;
- relate to other corresponding/adjacent words; and
- provide additional information or insights which influence general and specific usage in your regulatory and enforcement context.

Realising – the benefits of regulatory literacy

The benefits of *regulatory literacy* include, but are not limited to, helping to improve:

- *regulatory capability*;
- *regulatory capacity*;
- *regulatory competence*; and
- *regulatory culture*.

Finally, it is hoped that this book can be a resource for collating, clarifying, and creating information – and act as a repository that will facilitate increased and greater consistency in terms of *regulatory language*.

Regulatory language, like all languages, will continue to evolve. It will evolve as individuals, teams, and organisations interact and engage with one another. The more frequent and more focussed that these interactions are – the more that *regulatory language* will be clarified and honed.

As a reader and user of this book you are on a regulatory journey or in a regulatory transition with fellow travellers. Sometimes you will be in front of your fellow travellers and sometimes you will be behind them. For maximum sharing, learning, and benefit to occur you will ideally be alongside them.

I hope this book helps you as you navigate your regulatory journey.

NOTES AND IN-TEXT REFERENCES

1 *Gray's Anatomy* was published in 1858. The most current, 42nd edition was published in 2020. This reflects over 160 years of continuous publication and unequivocally reinforces that Gray's Anatomy remains the definitive and comprehensive reference for the medical profession, about anatomy which informs all aspects of clinical practice.

2 The four central shaded phases are drawn and adapted from the Productivity Commission (2014, pp. 18–25) and the two additional (first and last) phases have been added by Grant Pink. Combined, the six phases form the *Extended Regulatory Spectrum (ERS)*. The ERS reflects the operational and non-operational aspects of an entire regulatory spectrum.

3 Noting here that remedy, response, and sanction are used somewhat interchangeably. This is consistent with the fact that the *regulatory language* used around how regulation is carried out remains unsettled, with examples including 'tools', 'methods', 'instruments', 'measures', and 'interventions'. For further information see Freiberg (2010, p.107).

4 See Freiberg (2017, pp. 401–17) for a comprehensive coverage and analysis of *administrative sanctions*.

5 In some *jurisdictions infringement notices* may fall under civil or criminal sanctions, so it is important that *regulators* fully understand and have mapped what *sanctions* they have access to within administrative, civil, and criminal realms. See Freiberg (2010, p. 86) for a representative list of *sanction* options across administrative, civil, and criminal realms.

6 See Freiberg (2017, pp. 401–17) for a comprehensive coverage and analysis of *administrative sanctions*.

7 See Armstrong, Gorst, & Rae (2019, p. 21).

8 See Attorney General's Department (AGD) (2011, p. 5).

9 See AGD (2011, p. 12).

10 See Freiberg (2017, pp 303–4) for examples of the main types of *authorisations*: *licence, permit, registration*, certificate, and *accreditation*.

11   See Moore (1995 & 2013). The concept of *authorising environment* is part of Professor Mark Moore's broader work that describes how public sector organisations seek to deliver what is described as *public value*.

12   See Mumford (2011, pp. 36–37) for more on *regulatory regimes* as experiments and the fact that *regulators* (often) do not know in advance precisely how *regulation* will play out and work in practice.

13   See OECD (2014c) for a comprehensive overview of *behavioural economics* in terms of *regulatory policy*, regulatory design, and *regulatory delivery*.

14   See van der Heijden (2019a) which includes an international literature review on *behavioural insights* and *regulatory practice*.

15   See NZPC (2014, p. 132) which considers issues, options, and benefits of investing in intellectual leadership roles as part of advancing *regulatory practice*.

16   Noting here that remedy, response, and sanction are used somewhat interchangeably. This is consistent with the fact that the *regulatory language* used around how regulation is carried out remains unsettled, with examples including 'tools', 'methods', 'instruments', 'measures', and 'interventions'. For further information see Freiberg (2010, p. 107).

17   See Freiberg (2017, pp. 417–23) for a comprehensive coverage and analysis of *civil sanctions*.

18   However, there are some *regulated entities* who seem to prefer CAC *regulation*. This is because they do not have to expend effort and resources interpreting the requirements, instead they simply need to comply.

19   See Wenger (1998) and Wenger, McDermott & Snyder (2002) which are seminal works in the field on *Communities of Practice* and related matters.

20   The MARPOL Convention is the International Convention for the Prevention of Pollution from Ships, established in 1973.

21   The Ramsar Convention is the International Convention covering Wetlands of International Importance, established in 1971.

22   See OECD (2010, p. 3). In this instance the target audience were environmental enforcement authorities. The findings are considered relevant and applicable to all *regulatory* and *enforcement agencies*.

23   See OECD (2010, p. 8) The subject area of the study was *regulation* of pollution prevention and control.

24   See OECD (2010, pp. 16–17) for additional information and examples of the four categories.

25   See SEPA (2010, p. 9) diagram adapted from the 'Compliance and Engagement Spectrum'.

26 See Lumsden (n.d., p. 1).

27 See Lumsden (n.d., p. 2).

28 See Lumsden (n.d., p. 2).

29 Including through the *Commercial Television Industry Code of Practice* and the *Commercial Radio Australia Code of Practice*.

30 Including through the *Harbour Marine Safety Code*.

31 Noting here that remedy, response, and sanction are used somewhat interchangeably. This is consistent with the fact that the *regulatory language* used around how regulation is carried out remains unsettled, with examples including 'tools', 'methods', 'instruments', 'measures', and 'interventions'. For further information see Freiberg (2010, p.107).

32 See Freiberg (2017, pp. 423–39) for a comprehensive coverage and analysis of *criminal sanctions*.

33 See Sparrow (2000, pp. 62–64) for additional information surrounding the relationships between *regulators* and *regulated entities*.

34 See Wauchop & Manch (2017, p. 11) who consider whether *regulated parties* are *customers*, and what impact a customer-focus lens has on *regulatory activities*.

35 See Manch (2017) for additional insights into *decision-making* associated with *regulatory activities*.

36 See Hodges & Steinholtz (2017, pp. 26–43) who have dedicated an entire chapter to the role of *deterrence* and the traditional way laws have been enforced. Their book more broadly offers a comprehensive coverage, analysis, and alternative viewpoint of *deterrence*, especially in reference to the concept of *ethical business regulation*.

37 See Freiberg (2017, pp. 395–99) for a comprehensive coverage and analysis of *regulation, enforcement,* and *discretion*.

38 See Farmer (2007, pp. 15–17) for additional information on enforceable (and unenforceable) regulation.

39 See Freiberg (2017, pp. 295–99) for a comprehensive coverage and analysis of *enforceable undertakings*.

40 See Department of Environment and Science (2019).

41 See Commerce Commission New Zealand (2018).

42 Depending on the *regulator's* preference, and/or *regulatory posture*, the order of the first two E's may change. For example, *educate, engage,* and *enforce* involves: *educating* broadly across *regulated entities*; then *engaging* in a more focussed or targeted manner with specific *regulated entities*; and then *enforcing* as necessary. Whereas *engage, educate,* and *enforce* involves:

engaging broadly across *regulated entities*; then *educating* in a more focussed or targeted manner with specific entities; and then *enforcing* as necessary.

43   See Hodges & Steinholtz (2017, p. xxiii) for a more detailed overview and application of *EBP*.

44   See Hodges & Steinholtz (2017, p. xxiii) for a more detailed overview and application of *EBR*.

45   As mentioned in the 'Note of Caution' in Part 1, there are legal aspects which go beyond the scope of this book. For example, and relevant to giving *evidence*, the Hearsay Rule is one such matter. The Hearsay Rule and its exceptions can be complex and worth discussing with the relevant *prosecuting authority* and/or inhouse legal counsel.

46   The Australian Federal Police represent and operate at the national and international level of policing in Australia.

47   State and Territory police agencies represent and operate at their respective subnational (or provincial) levels in Australia.

48   Meaning Australia's national level Customs and Border agency.

49   Meaning Australia's national level Quarantine and Biosecurity agency.

50   See Sparrow (2020, pp. 11–30) for a comprehensive coverage and analysis of the *Expert Model* and its overlapping relationship with the *Legal Model, of regulation*.

51   See Pink (2018, slide 14).

52   See AGD (n.d.) for further information concerning the differences between the *fault elements*.

53   As permitted by the Convention on International Trade in Endangered Species of Wild Fauna and Flora (CITES).

54   See de Bruijn, ten Heuvelhof, & Koopmans (2007) for a comprehensive coverage of 'the game(s) between inspectors and inspectees'.

55   See Hampton (2005, p. 7).

56   See Sparrow (2008) where the author notes that in 'harm-reduction endeavours; they also reflect a rather deliberate focus on the reduction of *bads* as opposed to the construction of *goods*' (p. 5); and that '[f]or many regulatory agencies, organizing around specific *bads* turns out to be a substantial departure from business as usual' (p. 7).

57   The distinction of undue influence here relates to there being no influence or pressure exerted as the *regulator* makes individual (day-to-day) *operational* regulatory decisions. As opposed to the appropriate issuance of a *statement of expectations* on the broader behaviours and conduct of the *regulatory agency*.

58 See OECD (2014b & 2016) for a comprehensive coverage and analysis of regulatory *independence*/independent regulators.

59 See UNODC (2000, p. 5) where a serious *crime* is defined as meaning 'conduct constituting an offence punishable by a maximum deprivation of liberty of at least four years or a more serious penalty' under the United Nations Convention against Transnational Organized Crime (UNTOC).

60 See OECD (2014a, p. 9).

61 See OECD (2018, p. 3).

62 See OECD (2010, pp. 16–17) The other three categories of *compliance assurance indicators* are: 'final outcomes'; 'intermediate outcomes'; and 'inputs'.

63 See Ratcliffe (2004, p. 6).

64 See Quarmby & Young (2020, p. 12).

65 See AGD (2011, p. 1).

66 See AGD (2011, pp 9–12).

67 For example, in circumstances where the necessary or requisite *criteria* and evidentiary standards have been satisfied or met.

68 The *RPF* was produced by the Australian Government 's Department of Prime Minister and Cabinet (PM&C) in 2014, and on 1 July 2021 was replaced by the *Regulator Performance Guide*.

69 See Department of Prime Minister and Cabinet (PM&C) (2014a, p. 1) Regulator Performance Framework.

70 See Freiberg (2017, p. 484).

71 Several examples of specialist enforcement agencies from the United States of America would include the Bureau of Alcohol Tobacco, Firearms, and Explosives (ATF); Drug Enforcement Administration (DEA); and Federal Bureau of Investigation (FBI).

72 AAOs formally allocate executive responsibility among ministers, ministries, portfolios, and agencies.

73 See Sparrow (2020, pp. 11–30) for a comprehensive coverage and analysis of the *Legal Model* and its overlapping relationship with the *Expert Model* of regulation.

74 An EPIRB (or Emergency Position Indicating Radio Beacon) is used to alert search and rescue services in the event of an emergency.

75 See Macrory (2006, pp. 29–31) for a full description and explanation of the six principles.

76   See Macrory (2006, pp. 32–33) for a full description and explanation of the seven characteristics.

77   See Office of Parliamentary Counsel (2017).

78   See Birchall & Colwill (1996 pp. 124–25).

79   See Faure, De Smedt & Stas (2015) and Pink & Bartel (2015) for examples of how this translates to environmental enforcement.

80   See Pink (2015a, 2015b); Pink & Bartel (2015).

81   See White (2011a & 2011b); Pink (2011); Pink & Lehane (2011).

82   See Caldero & Crank (2011) for additional information and insights into *noble cause corruption* in policing and mainstream *law enforcement*.

83   See Australian Refrigeration Council (n.d.).

84   See Shepherd & Griffiths (2021) for a comprehensive coverage and analysis of investigative interviewing including the history and development of the *PEACE Model*.

85   See Freiberg (2017, pp. 235–39) for a comprehensive coverage and analysis of *performance-based regulation*.

86   Stages adapted from Farmer. See Farmer (2007, pp. 68–71) for additional information on the interaction between the *permit cycle* and *permit process*.

87   See Freiberg (2017, pp. 239–46) for a comprehensive coverage and analysis of *principles-based regulation*.

88   See Better Regulation Task Force (2003, p. 1).

89   See Freiberg (2017, pp. 434–35) for additional information on *probation orders*.

90   See Judicial College of Victoria (n.d. Section 29.4.6) for additional information and context.

91   See Sparrow (2000, p. xvi) for more information on the *problem-solving* approach which is attributed to and is central to the overarching concept of the *regulatory craft*.

92   See Sparrow (2008, pp. 157–60) for further information on the stages of the protocol.

93   See Commonwealth Department of Prosecution (CDPP) (n.d.) for further information relating to each of the steps in a *prosecution*.

94   See Freiberg (2010, pp. 186–89) for additional information on *quasi-orders*.

95   See Baldwin & Black (2008) for additional information on *really responsive regulation*.

96 As part of taking a more sophisticated approach, 2021 saw the Australian Government establish a regulator performance function within a central government agency to 'increase accountability, promote best practice, build the professionalism of regulators and support cultural change' (PM&C, n.d.(a)).

97 See PM&C (2020, p. 10).

98 See Black (2002), as cited in (NZPC, 2014, p. 16).

99 See OECD (1997, p. 6).

100 See OECD (1993, p. 73).

101 Bullet points adapted from OECD (2016).

102 See OECD (2016) which has produced an entire report dedicated to the issue of being an independent regulator; (OECD 2017) for a companion piece to the OECD (2016) report, which provides practical guidance for *regulators* against undue influence; and NZPC (2014, pp. 215–57) which comprehensively considers issues relating to *regulator independence* and institutional form.

103 See PM&C (2014a, p. 1).

104 The *RPF* was produced by the Australian Government's Department of Prime Minister and Cabinet in 2014, and in 2021 was replaced by the *Regulator Performance Guide.*

105 The *RPG* was produced by the Australian Government's Department of Prime Minister and Cabinet in 2021.

106 See PM&C (2021, p. 4).

107 See OECD (2010) for additional information on the use of *compliance assurance indicators* in environmental regulation.

108 The *RPF* was produced by the Australian Government's Department of Prime Minister and Cabinet in 2014, and in 2021 was replaced by the *Regulator Performance Guide.*

109 See National Audit Office (2016).

110 See National Audit Office (2016, p. 7) and HM Treasury & others (2001).

111 See Better Regulation Delivery Office (2014).

112 See Kirkman & Sanderson (2019, pp. 78–84) for a more detailed overview of the *Regulators' Code* in terms of how it shapes the behaviour of *regulators.*

113 See Better Regulation Delivery Office (2014, p. 7).

114 See Du Rées (2009).

115 See OECD (2014b) for additional information on the factors that shape regulatory institutions.

116 See NZ Transport Agency (Waka Kotahi) (n.d.).

117 See Clean Energy Regulator (2019).

118 See Consumer Affairs Victoria (n.d.).

119 See Makkai & Braithwaite (1992) for more on the 'revolving door' or *regulatory capture*, which involves – *regulated entities* from industries going in the door to become a *regulator* of the industry they came from – and *regulators* going out the revolving door to take up a job in the industry that they previously regulated.

120 See Sparrow (2000). The *regulatory craft* is attributed to Sparrow who authored a book by the same name *The Regulatory Craft: Controlling Risks, Solving Problems, and Managing Compliance*.

121 See NZPC (2014 pp. 77–110) for a comprehensive consideration of *regulatory culture* and leadership.

122 See Schein (2010, p. 24) for more on artefacts, espoused beliefs and values, and basic underlying assumptions.

123 See Farmer (2007 pp. 8–11).

124 See Freiberg (2010, pp. 79–80) for more on *regulatory cycles*.

125 See Russell & Hodges (2019) who have compiled an entire book on the topic with the title *Regulatory Delivery*.

126 See CCCP (2011) which is a comprehensive and practical guide, intended to support *regulatory agencies* to improve their *regulatory delivery*, with a focus on capturing and sharing information with *co-* and *peer- regulators*.

127 See Coglianese (2017, pp. 10–11) for additional information and examples of TAO.

128 See Coglianese (2017) who has compiled an entire book on the topic with the title *Achieving Regulatory Excellence*.

129 See Finkel (2017, p. 170).

130 See Freiberg (2017, pp. 486–92) where these factors are drawn from and for additional information concerning *regulatory failure*.

131 See NZPC (2014, p. 17) where the functions listed here are expanded upon.

132 See OECD (2020a), for guidance and a summary of key elements to include in a RIA framework.

133 See Quarmby (2018, p. vi).

134 See Quarmby (2018) who has compiled an entire book on the topic with the title *Intelligence in Regulation*.

135 See UK Cabinet Office (2017, p. 13).

136 See van der Heijden (2020b, p. 9).

137 See Education Alberta (n.d.)

138 See UNESCO (2013, p. 2).

139 See van der Heijden (2021, p. 704) for further information on how increasing *regulatory literacy* assists public servants to understand how regulatory theory translates into practice, and then how nuanced practice is approached in different regulatory *authorising environments*.

140 See Freiberg (2017, pp. 198–202) for a comprehensive coverage and analysis of *regulatory methods* and the similarity and overlap with *regulatory tools*.

141 See NSW Department of Finance, Services and Innovation (2016, p. 8) Section 2.1 for further information.

142 See OECD (n.d.).

143 See OECD (2000) which considers how to reduce the risk of policy failure, with a particular focus on the challenges for *regulatory compliance*.

144 See OECD (2012, pp. 6–7) for additional information on what should be included in a *regulatory policy* and how governments might go about advancing or achieving them.

145 See PM&C (2020).

146 See PM&C (n.d.(b)).

147 See PM&C (2021).

148 For Australian Government agencies, the *Regulatory Powers (Standard Provisions) Act 2014*, provides an example of an *Act* that details and harmonises the standard provisions for *monitoring, investigation*, and *enforcement* powers that can be used by *regulatory agencies*. Other *Acts* in that *jurisdiction*, which require *regulatory powers*, simply draw down on these standard provisions without the need to duplicate them.

149 See Fantham *et al* (2020) which considers aspects associated with professionalising *regulatory practice*.

150 See Russell & Hodges (2019) who have compiled an entire book on the topic with the title *Regulatory Delivery*.

151 See Australian National Audit Office (2014, p. 7) for a more comprehensive coverage of the key principles supporting *regulatory practice*.

152 See van der Heijden (2019c) which includes an international literature review on aspects associated with *regulatory practice*.

153 See Office of the Conservation Regulator (2021) which identified the following risk areas for 2020–21: illegal campfires; illegal take of firewood; illegal vehicle use on public land; regulating native timber harvesting; regulating the use, keeping, trade, treatment and control of wildlife.

154 See Liquor and Gaming NSW (2019).

155 See Australian Securities & Investments Commission (n.d.).

156 See van der Heijden (2020b) which includes an international literature review on aspects associated with efforts to establish a *regulatory profession*.

157 See Manch, Mumford, Raj, & Wauchop (2017) for their observations and commentary on the birth of the *regulatory profession* in New Zealand.

158 See OECD (2014, pp. 63–64) which has Professionalism as Principle 11.

159 See OECD (1997, p. 6).

160 See Winson (2017) for additional information on *regulatory stewardship*.

161 See Freiberg (2017, pp. 198–202) for a comprehensive coverage and analysis of *regulatory methods* and the similarity and overlap with *regulatory tools*.

162 See Freiberg (2017, pp. 443–54) for a comprehensive coverage and analysis of *responsive regulation*.

163 See van der Heijden (2020a) which includes an international literature review on aspects associated with *responsive regulation* in practice.

164 See Zehr (2002, p.21).

165 See Professional Standards Authority (2015, pp. 6–7) for more information on *right-touch regulation*.

166 See International Organization for Standardization (2018, section 3.1).

167 See Standards Australia & Standards New Zealand (2004, p. 3).

168 See Department of Finance (2014, p. 20).

169 See Russell & Kirkman (2019, pp. 267–83) for a comprehensive coverage and analysis in their chapter named and dedicated to *risk-based prioritisation*.

170 See Freiberg (2017, pp. 458–65) for a comprehensive coverage and analysis of *risk-based regulation*, including its limitations.

171 See Freiberg (2017, pp. 454–57) for a comprehensive coverage and analysis of *risk-based regulation*, including *operational* examples.

172 See Productivity Commission (2013, pp. 274–75), for additional information and examples of incorporating and implementing risk-based regulatory approaches.

173 See van der Heijden (2019b) which includes an international literature review on aspects associated with *risk-based regulation*.

174 See Black (2008, slide 4).

175 See Sparrow (2008, p. 12, and pp. 38–39) for additional insights into *risk communication*.

176 See Sparrow (2008, p. 12).

177 See Russell & Kirkman (2019, pp. 275–77) for more detail on *risk ratings* and *regulatory risk* frameworks.

178 See Freiberg (2017, pp. 206–10) for additional information and examples of the various forms of *rules*.

179 See CDPP (2018, pp. 28–29) and Freiberg (2010, p. 210) for additional information, but a non-exhaustive list of factors that inform *sentencing* submissions and sentences.

180 See Freiberg (2017, pp. 466–70) for a comprehensive coverage and analysis of *smart regulation*.

181 See Freiberg (2017, pp. 211–15) for a comprehensive coverage and analysis of the various forms of *standards*.

182 See NSW Government (n.d.) for numerous examples of *statements of regulatory intent*.

183 Noting that here a *statutory authority* is taken to mean one that is established by law, rather than by administrative arrangements.

184 See OECD (2020b).

185 See UNODC (2000, p. 5) where a serious *crime* is defined as meaning 'conduct constituting an offence punishable by a maximum deprivation of liberty of at least four years or a more serious penalty' under the United Nations Convention against Transnational Organized Crime (UNTOC).

186 See the *Surveillance Devices Act (2004)* as an example from Australia.

187 See Freiberg (2017, pp. 405–06) for a comprehensive coverage and analysis of *suspension notices* and similar related notices.

188 See *Environment Protection Act 2017*, (No. 51 of 2017), s309(1); 2(a–b); s313(2)(a–c) from the State of Victoria in Australia.

189 See Scholz (1984) which is the seminal work regarding *tit-for-tat* and which outlines additional information on *tit-for-tat*.

190 What constitutes generalist or specialist *training* depends on several key factors including the agency itself, the *jurisdiction* it operates in, and the sectors and industries it regulates.

191 See OECD (2016, pp. 40–41).

192 See de Rosa & Malyshev (2008, p. 11) for further analysis and explanation of independence across a spectrum, where institutions are classified according to their increasing *independence* from *The Executive*.

193 See NZ Transport Agency (Waka Kotahi) (n.d.).

194 See Clean Energy Regulator (2019).

195 See Consumer Affairs Victoria (n.d.).

196 See Pink & White (2016) which considers how regulatory (environ-mental), enforcement (border and customs); and policing (local, state/provincial, and international) agencies come together and work together, in the field of transnational environmental *crime*.

197 See Pink & White (2016) for various examples and forms of regulators collaborating.

198 See de Bruijn, ten Heuvelhof, & Koopmans (2007, pp. 97–108) who dedicate a chapter of their book to *zero tolerance*.

199 The four central shaded phases are drawn and adapted from the Productivity Commission (2014, pp. 18–25) and the two additional (first and last) phases have been added by Grant Pink. Combined, the six phases form the *Extended Regulatory Spectrum (ERS)*. The ERS reflects the operational and non-operational aspects of an entire regulatory spectrum.

200 See Pink & White (2016) for various examples and forms of regulators collaborating within and between: regulatory and enforcement *networks*; international coordination and capacity building institutions; consultants and courts; and academic and research institutions.

REFERENCES

Note: *all website hyperlinks correct and operating as at date of publication.*

Armstrong, H., Gorst, C., & Rae, J. (2019). *Renewing Regulation: Anticipatory regulation in an age of disruption.* London: NESTA.

Attorney-General's Department (AGD). (n.d.). *Division 5 Fault elements, Commonwealth Criminal Code: Guide for practitioners.* Retrieved from: <https://www.ag.gov.au/crime/publications/commonwealth-criminal-code-guide-practitioners-draft/part-22-elements-offence/division-5-fault-elements>

Attorney-General's Department (AGD). (2011). *Australian Government Investigations Standards.* Canberra: AGD.

Australian National Audit Office (ANAO). (2014). *Administering Regulation: Achieving the right balance – better practice guide.* Canberra: ANAO.

Australian Refrigeration Council (ARC) (n.d.). *About the ARC.* Retrieved from: <https://www.arctick.org/information/about-arc/>

Australian Securities & Investments Commission. (n.d.). *Changes to regulatory work and priorities in response to COVID-19.* Canberra: ASIC. Retrieved from: <https://asic.gov.au/regulatory-resources/find-a-document/regulatory-document-updates/changes-to-regulatory-work-and-priorities-in-response-to-covid-19/>

Baldwin, R., & Black, J. (2008). Really Responsive Regulation. *The Modern Law Review, 71*(1), 59–94.

Better Regulation Delivery Office (2014). *Regulators' Code.* Birmingham: Better Regulation Delivery Office.

Better Regulation Task Force (BRTF). (2003). *Principles of Good Regulation.* London: Whitehall.

Birchall, G., & Colwill, J. (1996). *Working Relationships: Managing effective working relationships.* Melbourne, Australia: Longman Australia.

Black, J. (2002). *Critical reflections on regulation.* CARR Discussion Papers, DP 4. Centre for Analysis of Risk and Regulation. London, United Kingdom: London School of Economics and Political Science.

Black, J. (2008). *Risk Based Regulation*. Presentation to OECD, 1st December 2008. Retrieved from: <https://www.oecd.org/gov/regulatory-policy/44800375.pdf>

Caldero, M., & Crank, J. (2011). *Police Ethics: The Corruption of Noble Cause* (3rd edn.). Burlington, MA: Anderson Publishing.

Clean Energy Regulator. (2019). *Compliance policy for education, monitoring and enforcement activities*. Canberra: CER. Retrieved from: <http://www.cleanenergyregulator.gov.au/About/Policies-and-publications/Compliance-policy-for-education-monitoring-and-enforcement-activities#3>

Coglianese, C. (Ed.). (2017). *Achieving Regulatory Excellence*. Washington DC: The Brookings Institution.

Commerce Commission New Zealand. (2018). *Enforcement criteria*. Retrieved from: <https://comcom.govt.nz/about-us/our-policies-and-guidelines/investigations-and-enforcement/enforcement-criteria>

Commonwealth Director of Public Prosecution (CDPP). (2018). *Sentencing of Federal Offenders in Australia: a guide for practitioners*. Canberra: CDPP.

Compliance Common Capability Programme (CCCP). (2011). *Achieving Compliance: a guide for compliance agencies in New Zealand*. Wellington: CCCP.

Consumer Affairs Victoria. (n.d.). *Our regulatory approach*. Retrieved from <https://www.consumer.vic.gov.au/about-us/regulatory-approach-and-compliance-policy/our-regulatory-approach>

de Bruijn, H., ten Heuvelhof, E., & Koopmans, M. (2007). *Law Enforcement: The Game Between Inspectors and Inspectees*. Florida: Universal Publishers.

de Rosa, D., & Malyshev, N. (2008). *Regulatory Institutions: A Blueprint for the Russian Federation*, OECD Working Papers on Public Governance, No. 10. Paris: OECD Publishing.

Department of Environment and Science (DES). (2019). *Department of Environment and Science Enforcement Guidelines*. Brisbane: Qld DES. Retrieved from: <https://environment.des.qld.gov.au/__data/assets/pdf_file/0030/86619/enforcement-guidelines.pdf>

Department of Finance (DoF). (2014). *Commonwealth Risk Management Policy*. Canberra: DoF.

Department of Prime Minister and Cabinet (PM&C). (n.d.(a)). *Regulator best practice and performance*. Canberra: PM&C. Retrieved from: <https://deregulation.pmc.gov.au/priorities/regulator-best-practice-and-performance>

Department of Prime Minister and Cabinet (PM&C). (n.d.(b)). *Commonwealth Regulator Burden Measure*. Canberra: PM&C. Retrieved from: <https://rbm.obpr.gov.au>

Department of Prime Minister and Cabinet (PM&C). (2014a). *Regulator Performance Framework*. Canberra: PM&C.

Department of Prime Minister and Cabinet (PM&C). (2014b). *The Australian Government Guide to Regulation*. Canberra: PM&C.

Department of Prime Minister and Cabinet (PM&C). (2020). *The Australian Government Guide to Regulatory Impact Analysis*. Canberra: PM&C.

Department of Prime Minister and Cabinet (PM&C). (2021). *Regulator Performance Guide*. Canberra: PM&C.

Du Rées, H. (2009). Can criminal law protect the environment? In R. White (Ed.), *Environmental Crime: a reader* (pp. 638–655). Devon: Willan Publishing.

Education Alberta. (n.d.). *What is literacy?* Canada: Government of Alberta. Retrieved from: <https://education.alberta.ca/literacy-and-numeracy/literacy/everyone/what-is-literacy/>

Fantham, P., Kale, W., Manch, K., McGirr, N., Mumford, P., Raj, S., & van der Heijden, J. (2020). *Professionalising regulatory practice: Lessons from the New Zealand G-REG Initiative. State of the Art in Regulatory Governance Research Paper – 2020.05*. Wellington: Victoria University of Wellington/Government Regulatory Practice Initiative.

Farmer, A. (2007). *Handbook of Environmental Protection & Enforcement: Principles and Practice*. London: Earthscan.

Faure, M., De Smedt, P., & Stas, A. (Eds.). (2015). *Environmental Enforcement Networks: Concepts, Implementation and Effectiveness*. Cheltenham UK/Northampton MA: Edward Elgar.

Finkel, A.M. (2017). Beyond Best-in-Class. In C. Coglianese (Ed.), *Achieving Regulatory Excellence* (pp. 166–187). Washington DC: Brookings Institution Press.

Freiberg, A. (2010). *The Tools of Regulation*. Leichhardt: The Federation Press.

Freiberg, A. (2017). *Regulation in Australia*. Leichhardt: The Federation Press.

Hampton, P. (2005). *Reducing administrative burdens: effective inspection and enforcement*. London: HM Treasury.

HM Treasury, Cabinet Office, National Audit Office, Audit Commission & Office for National Statistics. (2001). *Choosing the Right FABRIC: A Framework for Performance Information*. London: HM Treasury. Retrieved from: <https://webarchive.nationalarchives.gov.uk/ukgwa/20170207052351/https://www.nao.org.uk/wp-content/uploads/2013/02/fabric.pdf>

Hodges, C., & Steinholtz, R. (2017). *Ethical Business Practice and Regulation: A Behavioural and Values-Based Approach to Compliance and Enforcement.* Oxford: Hart Publishing.

International Organization for Standardization (ISO). (2018). *Risk management – Guidelines (ISO: 31000:2018).* Geneva Switzerland: ISO. Retrieved from: <https://www.iso.org/obp/ui/#iso:std:iso:31000:ed-2:v1:en>

Judicial College of Victoria. (2017). Probation, *Children's Court Bench Book.* Melbourne: Judicial College of Victoria. Retrieved from: <https://www.judicialcollege.vic.edu.au/eManuals/CHCBB/60898.htm>

Kirkman, H., & Sanderson, P. (2019). Code-based Approaches, the Use of Codes to Change the Behaviour of Regulators in the UK. In G. Russell & C. Hodges (Eds.), *Regulatory Delivery,* (pp. 73–86). Oxford: Hart Publishing.

Liquor and Gaming NSW. (2019). *Strategic Plan 2017–2019.* Sydney: Liquor and Gaming NSW. Retrieved from: <https://www.liquorandgaming.nsw.gov.au/__data/assets/pdf_file/0006/858975/lgnsw-strategic-plan-2017-2019.pdf>

Lumsden, A. (n.d.) *Continuing Professional Development Requirements.* CPD Requirements. Sydney: Professional Standards Council. Retrieved from: <https://www.psc.gov.au/sites/default/files/CPD%20Requirements_0.pdf>

Macrory, R.B. (2006). *Regulatory Justice: Making Sanctions Effective – Final Report, November 2006.* London: Cabinet Office.

Makkai, T., & Braithwaite, J. (1992). In and Out of the Revolving Door: Making Sense of Regulatory Capture. *Journal of Public Policy, 12*(1), 61–78.

Manch, K. (2017). What Does Good Regulatory Decision Making Look Like? *Policy Quarterly, 13*(2), 72–81.

Manch, K., Mumford, P., Raj, S., & Wauchop, B. (2015). Watching the birth of the regulatory profession *Policy Quarterly, 11*(4), 71–76.

Moore, M.H. (1995). *Creating Public Value: Strategic Management in Government.* Massachusetts: Harvard University Press.

Moore, M.H. (2013). *Recognizing Public Value.* Massachusetts: Harvard University Press.

Mumford, P.J. (2011). Best practice regulation: setting targets and detecting vulnerabilities. *Policy Quarterly, 7*(3), 36–42.

National Audit Office. (2016). *Good practice guide: Performance measurement by regulators.* London: National Audit Office.

New Zealand Productivity Commission (NZPC). (2014). *Regulatory institutions and practices.* Wellington: NZPC.

NSW Department of Finance, Services and Innovation. (2016). *Guidance for regulators to implement outcomes and risk-based regulation.* Sydney: NSW DoF.

NSW Government. (n.d.). *Statements of regulatory intent.* Sydney: NSW Fair Trading. Retrieved from: <https://www.fairtrading.nsw.gov.au/about-fair-trading/legislation-and-publications/statements-of-regulatory-intent>

NZ Transport Agency (Waka Kotahi). (n.d.). *NZTA reviewing regulatory compliance and getting tough on enforcement.* Retrieved from: <https://vehicleinspection.nzta.govt.nz/news/nzta-reviewing-regulatory-compliance-and-getting-tough-on-enforcement>

Office of the Conservation Regulator. (2021). *Regulatory Priorities 2020-2021.* Retrieved from: <https://www.vic.gov.au/publications-conservation-regulator>

Office of Parliamentary Counsel (OPC). (2017). *Legal Services Directions 2017, Appendix B – The Commonwealth's obligation to act as a model litigant.* Canberra: OPC. Retrieved from: <https://www.legislation.gov.au/Details/F2017L00369>

Organisation for Economic Co-operation and Development (OECD). (n.d.). *Regulatory Policy.* Retrieved from: <https://www.oecd.org/gov/regulatory-policy/#d.en.194409>

Organisation for Economic Co-operation and Development (OECD). (1993). *Glossary of Industrial Organisation Economics and Competition Law.* Paris: OECD.

Organisation for Economic Co-operation and Development (OECD). (1997). *The OECD Report on Regulatory Reform: Synthesis.* Paris: OECD.

Organisation for Economic Co-operation and Development (OECD). (2000). *Reducing the risk of policy failure: Challenges for regulatory compliance.* Paris: OECD. Retrieved from: <https://www.oecd.org/gov/regulatory-policy/1910833.pdf>

Organisation for Economic Co-operation and Development (OECD). (2010). *Outcome Performance Measures of Environmental Compliance Assurance: Current Practices, Constraints and Ways Forward.* Paris: OECD Publishing.

Organisation for Economic Co-operation and Development (OECD). (2012). *Recommendation of the Council on Regulatory Policy and Governance.* Paris: OECD Publishing.

Organisation for Economic Co-operation and Development (OECD). (2014a). *Regulatory Enforcement and Inspections, OECD Best Practice Principles for Regulatory Policy.* Paris: OECD Publishing.

Organisation for Economic Co-operation and Development (OECD). (2014b). *The Governance of Regulators, OECD Best Practice Principles for Regulatory Policy*. Paris: OECD Publishing.

Organisation for Economic Co-operation and Development (OECD). (2014c). *Regulatory Policy and Behavioural Economics*. Paris: OECD Publishing.

Organisation for Economic Co-operation and Development (OECD). (2016). *Being and Independent Regulator, The Governance of Regulators*. Paris: OECD Publishing.

Organisation for Economic Co-operation and Development (OECD). (2017). *Creating a Culture of Independence: Practical Guidance Against Undue Influence, The Governance of Regulators. OECD Best Practice Principles for Regulatory Policy*. Paris: OECD Publishing.

Organisation for Economic Co-operation and Development (OECD). (2018). *OECD Regulatory Enforcement and Inspections Toolkit*. Paris: OECD Publishing.

Organisation for Economic Co-operation and Development (OECD). (2020a). *Regulatory Impact Assessment, OECD Best Practice Principles for Regulatory Policy*. Paris: OECD Publishing.

Organisation for Economic Co-operation and Development (OECD). (2020b). *Reviewing the Stock of Regulation, OECD Best Practice Principles for Regulatory Policy*. Paris: OECD Publishing.

Pink, G. (2011). Assessing the Utility of Environmental Enforcement Networks: In an Attempt to Maximise Benefits to Members. In *INECE 9th International Conference on Environmental Compliance and Enforcement, 20–24 June 2011 Whistler, British Columbia, Canada, Proceedings* (pp. 797–804). Washington, DC: INECE.

Pink, G. (2015a). Environmental enforcement networks: Theory, practice and potential. In M. Faure, P. De Smedt & A. Stas (Eds.), *Environmental Enforcement Networks: Concepts, Implementation and Effectiveness* (pp. 13–36). Cheltenham UK/Northampton MA: Edward Elgar.

Pink, G. (2015b). Environmental enforcement networks: their 'value proposition' during times of reducing resources and budgets. In M. Faure, P. De Smedt & A. Stas (Eds.), *Environmental Enforcement Networks: Concepts, Implementation and Effectiveness* (pp. 153–171). Cheltenham UK/Northampton MA: Edward Elgar.

Pink, G. (2018). *Regulatory Professionals, do they exist? How would we know? Why should we care?*, presentation to inaugural National Regulators Community of Practice (NRCoP) event. Perth. Retrieved from: <https://www.anzsog. edu.au/preview-documents/publications-and-brochures/5224-regulatory-professionals-do-they-exist-how-would-we-know-why-should-we-care/file>

Pink, G., & Bartel, R. (2015). Regulator Networks: Collaborative Agency Approaches to the Implementation and Enforcement of Environmental Law. In P. Martin and A. Kennedy (Eds.), *Implementation of Environmental Law* (pp. 308-337). Cheltenham UK/Northampton MA: Edward Elgar.

Pink, G., & Lehane, J. (2011). Environmental Enforcement Networks: Development of a Network Evaluation Matrix. In *INECE 9th International Conference on Environmental Compliance and Enforcement, 20–24 June 2011 Whistler, British Columbia, Canada, Proceedings* (pp. 805–21). Washington, DC: INECE.

Pink, G., & White, R. (2016). Collaboration in combating environmental crime: Making it matter. In G. Pink & R. White (Eds.), *Environmental Crime and Collaborative State Intervention* (pp 3–19). Basingstoke Hampshire: Palgrave Macmillan.

Productivity Commission (PC). (2013). *Regulator Engagement with Small Business, Research Report*. Canberra: PC.

Productivity Commission (PC). (2014). *Regulator Audit Framework*. Canberra: PC.

Professional Standards Authority for Health and Social Care (PSA). (2015). *Right-touch regulation*. London: PSA. Retrieved from: <https://www. professionalstandards.org.uk/docs/default-source/publications/thought-paper/right-touch-regulation-2015.pdf?sfvrsn=eaf77f20_20>

Quarmby, N. (2018). *Intelligence in Regulation*. Leichhardt: The Federation Press.

Quarmby, N., & Young, L. (2010). *Managing Intelligence: The art of influence*. Leichhardt: The Federation Press.

Ratcliffe, J. (2004). The structure of strategic thinking. In. J. Ratcliffe (Ed.), *Strategic Thinking in Criminal Intelligence* (pp. 1–10). Sydney: The Federation Press.

Russell, G., & Hodges, C. (2019). *Regulatory Delivery*. Oxford: Hart Publishing.

Russell, G., & Kirkman, H. (2019). Risk-based Prioritisation. In G. Russell & C. Hodges (Eds.), *Regulatory Delivery*, (pp. 267–83). Oxford: Hart Publishing.

Schein, E.H. (2010). *Organisational culture and leadership, 4th edition*. San Francisco, CA, United States: John Wiley and Sons.

Scholz, J. T. (1984). Voluntary Compliance and Regulatory Enforcement, *Law & Policy*, 6(4), 385–404.

Scottish Environment Protection Agency (SEPA). (2010). *Better Environmental Regulation: SEPA's Change Proposals*. SEPA. Retrieved from: <https://www.sepa.org.uk/media/117142/better-environmental-regulation-consultation-document.pdf>

Shepherd, E., & Griffiths, A. (2021). *Investigative Interviewing: The Conversation Management Approach* (3rd edn.). Oxford: Oxford University Press.

Sparrow, M. (2000). *The Regulatory Craft: Controlling Risks, Solving Problems, and Managing Compliance*. Washington DC: Brookings Institute Press.

Sparrow, M. (2008). *The character of harms: operational challenges in control*. Cambridge: Cambridge University Press.

Sparrow, M. (2020). *Fundamentals of Regulatory Design*. Malcolm K. Sparrow.

Standards Australia & Standards New Zealand. (2004). *Handbook – Risk Management Guidelines Companion to AS/NZS 4360:2004*. Sydney: Standards Australia.

UK Cabinet Office. (2017) *Regulatory Futures Review*. London: Cabinet Office.

United Nations Educational, Scientific and Cultural Organization (UNESCO). (2013). *Education Sector Technical Notes: Literacy and Non-Formal Education*. France: UNESCO. Retrieved from: <https://unesdoc.unesco.org/ark:/48223/pf0000222125>

United Nations Office of Drugs and Crime. (2000). *United Nations Convention against Transnational Organized Crime And The Protocols Thereto*. Vienna: UNODC.

van der Heijden, J. (2019a). *Behavioural insights and regulatory practice: A review of the international academic literature. State of the Art in Regulatory Governance Research Paper – 2019.01*. Wellington: Victoria University of Wellington/Government Regulatory Practice Initiative.

van der Heijden, J. (2019b). *Risk governance and risk-based regulation: A review of the international academic literature. State of the Art in Regulatory Governance Research Paper – 2019.02*. Wellington: Victoria University of Wellington/Government Regulatory Practice Initiative.

van der Heijden, J. (2019c). *Regulatory philosophy, theory and practice: Ka mua, ka muri. State of the Art in Regulatory Governance Research Paper – 2019.03*. Wellington: Victoria University of Wellington/Government Regulatory Practice Initiative.

van der Heijden, J. (2020a). *Responsive regulation in practice: A review of the international academic literature. State of the Art in Regulatory Governance Research Paper – 2020.06*. Wellington: Victoria University of Wellington/ Government Regulatory Practice Initiative.

van der Heijden, J. (2020b). *Towards a profession of public regulation: Lessons from the New Zealand G-REG Initiative. State of the art in Regulatory Governance Research Paper – 2020.07*. Wellington: Victoria University of Wellington/ Government Regulatory Practice Initiative.

van der Heijden, J. (2021). Regulation As Public Service, Public Servants As Regulators. In H. Sullivan, H. Dickson, & H. Henderson (Eds.), *Palgrave Handbook of the Public Servant* (pp. 703–720). New York: Palgrave Macmillan.

Wauchop, B., & Manch, K. (2017). Are Regulated Parties Customers? *Policy Quarterly, 13*(4), 10–12.

Wenger, E. (1998). *Communities of Practice: Learning, Meaning, and Identity*. Cambridge: Cambridge University Press.

Wenger, E., McDermott, R.A., & Snyder, W. (2002). *Cultivating Communities of Practice: A Guide to Managing Knowledge*. Boston USA: Harvard Business School Publishing.

White, R. (2011a). *Transnational Environmental Crime: Toward and Eco-Global Criminology*. Abingdon: Routledge.

White, R. (2011b). Environmental Law Enforcement: The Importance of Global Networks and Collaborative Practices. *Australasian Policing: A Journal of Professional Practice and Research, 3*(1), 16–22.

Winson, S. (2017). Regulatory Stewardship: Voice of the Regulator, *Policy Quarterly, 13*(4), 3–9.

Zehr, H. (2002). *The Little Book of Restorative Justice*. Intercourse USA: Good Books.

STAYING IN TOUCH

Regulatory language, like all languages, will continue to evolve.

This book will also need to evolve and be updated to ensure that it remains fit for purpose.

Please email me direct (grant@recapconsultants.com.au) with suggestions for future editions if you believe there are:

- additional listings for regulatory and enforcement matters (i.e. words, terms and concepts) that should be included in this book; or
- changes required to existing listings because the interpretation has changed over time.

ABOUT THE AUTHOR

Dr Grant Pink is a **'regulatory praca-demic'**, meaning his work and research activities span practitioner and academic worlds.

Grant has 30 years' experience: in regulatory, enforcement, and policing agencies; across practitioner, leadership, senior management, academic, and consultant roles; at subnational, national, and international levels.

Grant is a recognised expert: in regulatory and enforcement networks; and building capability and capacity within and across regulatory and enforcement agencies.

Grant has delivered: keynotes, presentations, seminars, and workshops at international conferences in Africa, Asia, Europe, Oceania, and North America.

Grant has written more than thirty publications.

Grant's views are drawn from six (6) very different, but mutually reinforcing perspectives. Perspectives including those of a:

- *regulatory practitioner* – having been an *authorised officer, inspector, ranger,* and *warden* engaged in **regulatory practice** under dozens of *acts* and pieces of *legislation*;
- *regulatory manager* – managing regulatory staff and teams engaged in **regulatory delivery**;
- *regulatory executive* – leading regulatory teams to deliver **regulatory outcomes**;
- regulatory scholar – completing research at both Master and Doctorate level on networking and interoperability between regulatory, enforcement, and policing agencies; and building regulatory capability and capacity in regulatory and enforcement

agencies respectively. And then translating and transferring this research into writings and teachings on the **regulatory profession** and **regulatory professionalism;**

- regulatory consultant – advising numerous regulatory, enforcement, and policing agencies, at all levels of government, both domestically and internationally, on issues relating to **regulatory capability**; **regulatory capacity**; **regulatory culture**; and **regulator performance**; and

- regulatory coach and mentor – assisting individuals, as they perform in and/or transition between regulatory: practitioner; manager; executive; or regulatory board/committee roles, as they engage in **regulatory leadership**; and **regulatory management**;

Splitting his time between consulting, pracademic, and research activities, Grant is:

- the founder and Managing Director of RECAP Consultants Pty Ltd (RECAP). RECAP provides specialist regulatory advisory services globally;

- the Pracademic Advisor to the Australian and New Zealand School of Government (ANZSOG) National Regulators Community of Practice (NRCoP); and

- is an Adjunct Professor (Regulation and Enforcement) at the University of Tasmania.

Grant's combined experiences have him ideally placed and has led him to be your translator – on this part of your regulatory journey – through this *Navigating Regulatory Language* book.